MW01058346

" Our lives are
mapped by books "

The smile as an
invitation to happiness
The smile as an equal
road to happiness.

Thanks 4 2020
Covid

HELEN TAYLOR

Why WOMEN Read FICTION

The Stories of Our Lives

OXFORD

UNIVERSITY PRESS

OXFORD

UNIVERSITY PRESS

Great Clarendon Street, Oxford, OX2 6DP,
United Kingdom

Oxford University Press is a department of the University of Oxford.
It furthers the University's objective of excellence in research, scholarship,
and education by publishing worldwide. Oxford is a registered trade mark of
Oxford University Press in the UK and in certain other countries

The moral rights of the author have been asserted

First Edition published in 2019
Impression: 1

Published in the United States of America by Oxford University Press
198 Madison Avenue, New York, NY 10016, United States of America

British Library Cataloguing in Publication Data
Data available

Library of Congress Control Number: 2019949804

ISBN 978–0–19–882768–9

Printed and bound in Great Britain by
Clays Ltd, Elcograf S.p.A.

Dedicated to all those women who love fiction and who generously shared with me life stories, anecdotes, reflections on and comments about their reading.

P.1 Marilyn reading *Ulysses*

Eve Arnold/Magnum Photos

Preface: 'A Friend, a Bible, a Perfume'

*I have a book with me at ALL times—the thought of being stuck anywhere,
or worse still on a motorway with nothing to do and all that 'free reading
time' lost is a complete fear.*

*A good memory for me is sitting in a car at the seaside even on bitter cold,
windy days, looking out to sea and reading. I used to spend a lot of time as a
child with my aunt (who reads back-to-back romance novels even today) and
uncle who loved fishing. Stormy weather was good for the mackerel at Seaford
and my aunt and I would stay in the warm in the car facing the sea front
talking, reading and dozing. I no longer live near enough to the sea to do this
regularly but I have on occasions made a trip out to the coast on my own and
sat in the car with a view out to sea reading, for a lazy day-out, whatever the
weather.*

Marie B

*My reading life has always been a joy. A way of connecting with the world at
your own pace, lighting the imagination and creating characters and places
within it, challenging and supporting your own views. It's an ongoing romance.*

Esther W

Such are the pleasures of a lifetime's reading. Reading as escape; a
joyous connection with the world beyond the self; a challenge to the
imagination and intellect; a solitary luxury; an activity in special
shared times and places with people close to us; a life-enhancer and
lifesaver in many situations. I've spent my life reading, teaching
English in universities, writing and speaking about literary culture,
organizing, chairing events at and directing literature festivals. I've
seen how much the act of reading—especially fiction—means to
people and how deeply literary works can affect readers' lives, helping
free us temporarily from the burdens of daily life, to see, explain, and
transform our worlds through a literary lens. I've also become increasingly intrigued by the fact that the large majority of fiction purchasers,
library users, and readers, are women.

If I look back at my own life, in childhood magical worlds were
illuminated for me through fiction and poetry; in my teenage years,

the mysteries of adult life, especially sexuality, were fleshed out through novel reading in ways that both heightened and also rendered somewhat disappointing real-life experiences. I went to fiction to fantasize, find out how to aspire to be a grown-up individual, creative citizen, companion, friend, and lover. Emulating my reading, I scribbled in exercise books little stories about girls in boarding schools with ponies, and even recreated (to miserable effect) a midnight feast for my best friend in my bedroom. The stories novels told narrated my own secret lives, richer and more colourful than life in a Birmingham suburb. Some years later, while studying and teaching in Louisiana, I discovered American literature by men and women of all races and especially African American novelists, which deeply affected my politics. As an adult reader, my preoccupations with the meaning of life, death, the body, ageing, and bereavement have found voice and shape in fiction. Through fiction I've expanded my limited perspectives by empathizing with characters of different lived experience, racial and ethnic identity, class position and sexual orientation. All my reading has enriched and helped shape my life.

When a child, I enjoyed a visceral, sensual relationship with novels. I loved their smell and touch. I would sit in bed gazing at, sniffing, and fondling them, placing them lovingly on my little bookshelf or bedside table and feeling enlarged by their ownership. Having them in my hands made me feel happy, mature, and serious; I knew they were powerful talismans. So my first intense love affair was with novels as objects. Like Patti Smith, I felt 'Oh, to be reborn within the pages of a book.'[1] When I began researching women's reading, I hadn't realized just how common those feelings are—and why the book is winning the war against the tablet.

My family bought very few books, usually as Christmas presents, but my mother, brothers, and I went weekly to the Selly Oak Library, a modest space redolent of old paper, bookbinders' glue and the librarian's talcum powder (a mélange of sweet smells I can still recall). I once looked round the shelves and thought that here was all knowledge. How quickly I would read my way through it and then know everything. And I was not alone. Julian Barnes describes the 'book-shop' (a fancy-goods and stationery store with books) in his childhood home town, Northwood, Middlesex: 'Part of me assumed that these were all the books that there were.'[2]

Becoming curious about others' reading histories, in the mid-1990s I interviewed my bookish mother Ida. Her story is not untypical. Born in 1916 into a working-class Lancashire family, forced to leave school at fourteen and go to work to pay her sister's medical bills in a pre-NHS society, she nevertheless read voraciously. Discovering libraries when young—astonished to be told she could borrow *any* book there—she borrowed for the rest of her life. She never bought books since purchasing books was 'extravagant' and 'they only harbour dust'. Like many another, she chose from librarians' recommendations and the piles of recently returned books on library trolleys, while in later life—until macular degeneration set in—pursued writers mentioned or adapted on radio and TV.

She recalled to me the solitary, secretive nature of her childhood reading punctuated by trips to the library unknown to her parents or sister. Like many women of her generation, she was encouraged at school to read aloud and learn by heart, and found pleasure in the sounds of language. On Bolton tram journeys to work at a tannery in her teenage years, she read constantly, and when married with children she looked in the library for writers whose names aroused her curiosity: Rumer Godden, Ruth Prawer Jhabvala, Iris Murdoch.

Also in common with most other women (as my later research discovered), she gravitated more to fiction than poetry, naturalist than fantasy writing, women writers rather than men. The 'broad-brow' books she most loved include Mary Webb's *Precious Bane*, Jessamine West's *The Massacre at Fall Creek*, and novels by Margaret Drabble, Alex Haley, James Michener, and Jean Plaidy. And at difficult times of life, stories were a lifeline. When my father was slowly dying and she was caring for a demanding patient, she reread *Gone With the Wind*: 'Scarlett O'Hara pulled me through,' she said: 'It was her attitude, she just wouldn't give in; she does give people courage. She did me.'

Until her death, my mother's prize possession was a small, much-thumbed quotation book I gave her when I first left home. She took to it immediately, writing phrases, lines, and paragraphs she valued in her miscellaneous reading. When talking about it, she used that term so often in play in relation to women's reading, 'a friend': 'Every one of these quotations is a friend . . . In a way this is my Bible. This is a sort of perfume of what I've read in life.'

A friend, a Bible, a perfume . . . the memory traces of a lifetime that suggest how intertwined reading memories are with other forms of remembrance. So it is with many other women. Readers choose books randomly or from recommendation, and can track their life narratives through fragments of books read, half-recalled, or recreated in the imagination. These are shared with family and friends, at literary festivals and bookshop writers' events, and on literature and creative writing courses.

One of the books my mother passed to me was that copy of *Gone With the Wind* (1936), inscribed by my father 'in memory of our best holiday ever, May 1939'. In the 1980s, when I was writing about American Southern literature, I began to ask friends, colleagues, and passing acquaintances what they felt about this work. I quickly found myself part of a community of readers who couldn't wait to tell me about their special relationship with this book; their experiences of reading and avid re-reading; and sharing book and film with mothers, sisters, daughters and friends. (Men had often seen the film but rarely read the book). I sent out letters and questionnaires by snail mail—no email then—and received hundreds of replies, on which I drew for my book, *Scarlett's Women: Gone with the Wind and its Female Fans* (1989).

Women told me how proud they felt to have read and shared with others such a long book (almost one thousand pages); how they had read the novel many times over, returning to passages they loved and re-reading the ending—hoping this time heroine Scarlett would get back departing hero Rhett Butler. Since the novel (1936) and then film (1939) came out around the start of the Second World War (when families were torn apart, homes and lives destroyed), women of a certain age found it comforting and inspirational, particularly following periods of bereavement and divorce, as well as the hazardous birth of children. They said they had learned from this book (and later the film) about love, loss, and courage. Younger women saw Scarlett as a feisty feminist, loving her defiant resilience but questioning the work's reactionary racial agendas. All of them claimed *Gone With the Wind* had given them fresh female role models, and new ways of thinking about masculinity and romantic love, even when they rejected its rosy picture of American slavery and the Civil War.

The intensity of this reading passion intrigued me, and as time passed, I wanted to ask more questions about how women value and relate to fiction. I wondered if it was a secret obsession, an activity shared with others or only in solitude. Did women (like my mother) regard reading fiction in the morning as decadent, and reading at bedtime absolutely vital? How do women—the keenest book buyers, reading group members, and literature festivalgoers—think about and relate to writers, libraries, and bookshops? How has reading fiction transformed or disturbed women's social, political, and emotional understandings? These are huge questions that would challenge even the most rigorous social scientist. As a lone literary scholar, I decided to explore these issues in my own way. Over many years, I discussed their reading with dozens of individuals (including some men). I conducted lengthy interviews with selected women writers and professionals in publishing and the media. I sent out an informal email questionnaire (see Appendix) to women I knew, had worked with, met at literary festivals and events, in book groups and bookshop events; many of them forwarded it to their families, friends, and colleagues. I make no claims for scientific objectivity (my 428 respondents aren't a representative sample). Nevertheless, their varied and detailed responses have enriched my understanding of women's reading. *Why Women Read Fiction* draws on more than 500 conversations and email responses.

These have all revealed that reading isn't just another 'hobby'. It's a lifeline, a passion, 'my best friend', 'the love of my life', an occupation that both gives meaning to and also disturbs daily lives and the narratives we tell ourselves. One woman told me it was 'fractionally less important than breathing, but only just!' Another said she would 'wither and die without it', and a couple of women wrote of feeling 'bereft' if they had no novel to read. From the earliest days when we lucky ones were read to by (usually) mothers, associating the written word with the comfort of a parent voicing a story, in a bed which set a pattern for night-time reading, women learned that the world could metaphorically open wide. School reading sometimes felt more disappointing (especially if a girl's reading age was higher than the rest of the class so she became bored) but—often from inspired, usually female, English teachers—introduced her to novels and poems she still remembers, along with the much-read kids' books borrowed from the library or bought by her parents and grandparents. The child who enjoyed being read to became the girl who read long into the night and sought out her own books—and who then, in adolescence and adulthood, found ways of squeezing reading into a complex life.

As she became busier, with job, home, partner, children, and all the other activities and distractions of adult life, reading had to be fitted into daily routines, work, and family responsibilities. She often felt the resentment of those closest to her if she 'disappeared into' a book, and learned strategies to circumvent this. One woman used to say she was going downstairs to sort laundry, stealing ten minutes of reading time before returning to the family fray. Several readers have told me that football on TV is a blessing, since they can leave absorbed male partners to watch while curling up guiltlessly with a book. As women get older, sometimes widowed or living alone, they feel the urgency of 'so many books, so little time', and thus become more selective, abandoning the difficult or dreary, and instead rereading old favourites.

Publishing is an inexact science, and if everyone knew the secret of the bestseller, they would all adopt it. Lee Child joked that every great novel needs just two things; unfortunately, no one knows what they are. If you ask writers to describe their readers, they laugh and say they haven't a clue. Industry statistics, emails, letters, Facebook and Twitter posts give feedback, but the exact nature, quality, and preferences of readers are too complex to pin down. And since this is an impossible task, all I can provide here is a snapshot of British women's fiction reading in recent years, and—after a lifetime's experience of teaching and talking about literature—an insight into and celebration of those women readers who keep the fiction market buoyant.

The book moves between questionnaire responses, anecdotes, and observations from personal and professional interviews, media (including social media) accounts, and academic research. I quote respondents to my questionnaire by using a first name and initial (e.g. Helen T) to protect identities. I've excluded discussions of magazine and journal fiction, which is a wholly different story, and focus on printed, online, and digital novels and short stories.[3] The question I'm hoping to answer is, 'What does fiction reading mean to women?'

*   *   *

This book is divided into four parts, interspersed with personal accounts by individual women readers. Part I, 'How, Where, and

Why Women Read Fiction', traces the ways female readers—as I've pointed out, the majority of fiction buyers and borrowers—select their reading and include it in the patterns of daily life. I discuss secret and guilty, solitary and group reading, fiction consumption as 'straw-berries and cream', reading on tablets, the representation of women reading in Western culture, and the snobberies around reading. I describe 'upstairs and downstairs' books, and the sheer variety of fiction women consume. The fate of beloved bookshops and libraries is of concern to avid readers, and I allude to the way we read, reread, or abandon particular books. I also uncover the passion women have for women writers, and the bond between the two. Finally, the way women turn to fiction for therapy and empathy is crucial in terms of the ways we create our own life narratives and identities, and share those with others.

In Part II, 'What Women Read', women's reading histories feature, beginning with our reading as children and the manner in which we acquire the habit of reading from a young age. I then zero in on the two novels most cited by my correspondents and interviewees as favourites—Jane Austen's *Pride and Prejudice* and Charlotte Brontë's *Jane Eyre*. And I examine the genres of romance and erotica, written mainly by women for women, followed by crime, sci-fi, and fantasy—not usually associated with female readers but increasingly popular.

In Part III, 'Writers and Readers', I look first at the public, festive, and gregarious aspects of writing and reading, beginning with the way women writers see themselves as readers and gendered (or not) writers—including a glance at the influential Women's Prize. This is followed by an examination of the phenomenon of (largely women-only) book groups, the boom in literary festivals, at which women form the majority of audiences, and the phenomenon of literary tourism. In Part IV I explain why I believe fiction gives women readers inspiration and tools to tell our own stories and create unique life narratives.

Acknowledgements

In the course of many years' research for this book, I've been grateful for conversations, emails, and phone calls with a large number of women (and men), friends and family, too numerous to name.

Thanks to the hundreds of women who completed questionnaires, sharing with me so generously their memories and thoughts about reading fiction. I had far more wonderful material than I could use, so forgive me if your words don't appear in the book. However, they have all been crucial to the way I've developed my ideas.

I am indebted to The Leverhulme Trust for the Emeritus Fellowship I was awarded in order to carry out invaluable research and travel.

I am particularly grateful to the following individuals: Rosie Bailey, Janet Beer, Liz Bird, Jo Jane Borek, Anthea Callen, Sarah Duncan, Debbie Eddolls, Anne Finlay-Baird, Lynn Forth, Victoria Fox, Jo Gill, David Glover, Ali Griffiths, Mary Grover and Sheffield Reading, Lynne Hapgood, Lynne Hatwell, Tania Herschmann, Rosie Jackson, Kate Johnson, Zainab Juma, Cora Kaplan, Sarah Mitchell, Jill Morgan, Lesley Murphy, Debra Myhill, Sian Norris, Susan O'Connor, Kevin Parker, Guy Pringle, Janet Reibstein, Kim Reynolds, Francesca Rolle, Libby Shaw, Zoe Steadman-Milne, Geoffrey Taylor, my mother (the late) Ida Taylor, Shelley Trower, Lucy Tunstall, Sarah Turvey, Liz Willis, Ann and David Willmore, and colleagues at the University of Exeter. From all over Europe, Richard Dyer sent me a stream of wonderful postcards of women reading.

Special thanks to The Wedmore Book Circle; Fiona Philipp and 'Friends for Life' women's reading group, Southmead Library, Bristol (including Carol Wainwright); Catherine Filmer and Avonmouth/ Shirehampton and Sea Mills Library Group (Jac Blacker, Shirley Flanagan, Dianne Frances, Judith Hadley, Jane Manley Jackson, Eileen Jarrett, Carole Jenkins, Val Jenkins, Pat Maule, Julie Morgan, Gill Slee, Janet Thayer, and Janet Thomas); Jill Morgan and 'Love Reading Fiction Group', Henleaze Library, Bristol; Shulah Palmer-Jones, Library Supervisor, J3 Library and Learning Centre and St Paul's Library, Bristol; Cheryl Warner and Wick Road Library Parents' Book Club, Brislington, Bristol; Karen Weatherly and Bramley Reading Group; Chapter Severn Reading Group.

The following writers kindly agreed to interviews and conversations: Sara Barnard, Sally Beauman, Bidisha, Louise Doughty, Sarah Dunant, Bernadette Evaristo, Katie Fforde, Harriet Gilbert, Lennie Goodings, Veronica Henry, Anne Karpf, Sarah LeFanu, Alison Light, Hilary Mantel, Bel Mooney, Kate Mosse, Elaine Showalter, Ali Smith, and Kit de Waal. The late Helen Dunmore was a great friend and inspiration. The Poetry Group she established in the last years of her life was a magical literary forum.

I'm grateful to friends who advised on questionnaires and commented on draft chapters—especially Anthea Bruges, Margaret Kirkham, Emily Murdoch, Pauline Trudell, and Avril Horner (who critiqued an early draft). Zoe Bulaitis was a terrific research assistant, accessing for me wonderful, often obscure materials, and helping with complex email communications.

My anonymous reader gave shrewd and helpful advice, Aimee Wright worked wonders with illustrations and practical matters, and my editor Jacqueline Norton has been a great support, as well as an enthusiastic and careful reader.

As ever, my greatest debt is to Derrick Price. His eclectic reading, love of language, and analytic mind have saved me frequently from my soggier thoughts. He is the finest companion and greatest cook, and his wit and wicked sense of humour have always kept me going.

Contents

List of Illustrations   xxi

Part I How, Where, and Why Women Read Fiction

Introduction   3
1. 'Cheap Sweet Vacations'—Reading as a Woman   25
   What Their Books Yield or, Why I Am Not Buying a Kindle
   Rosie Jackson   51

Part II What Women Read

2. Reading as a Girl   55
   The Poet on her Childhood Reading
   U. A. Fanthorpe   77
3. *Pride and Prejudice* and *Jane Eyre*, the Novels Women Love Best   79
4. Romance and Erotica—Fiction by Women for Women   105
5. Women, Crime, Sci-Fi, and Fantasy   127
   The Literary Blogger
   dovegreyreader   145

Part III Writers and Readers

6. Women Writers on their Reading and Readers   151
7. Book Clubs in Women's Life Stories   175
8. Festivals, Literary Tourism, and Pilgrimage   197
   Fiction in Lives, Lives in Fiction   219

Part IV The Stories of our Lives

9. Conclusion   225

Appendix: Questionnaire about Women's Fiction Reading   235
Notes   239
Select Bibliography   255
Index   259

List of Illustrations

P.1 Marilyn reading *Ulysses* vii
Eve Arnold/ Magnum Photos

0.1 'The Sisters', 1900, Ralph Peacock 5
© Tate, London 2019

0.2 A Good Book (birthday card, detail) 13
Lucy Howard

0.3 'The Reader', 1760, Pierre-Antoine Baudouin
The Picture Art Collection / Alamy Stock Photo 19

1.1 'The Convalescent', 1923–4, Gwen John 27
© The Fitzwilliam Museum, Cambridge

1.2 Persephone bookshop, London 36
Photo by Lydia Fellgett. By permission of Persephone Books

1.3 'Amaryllis and Henrietta', 1952, Vanessa Bell
© Estate of Vanessa Bell, courtesy Henrietta Garnett / Bridgeman Images 40

Int.1 Rosie Jackson at desk, surrounded by books 52
Gordon McKerrow

2.1 Mother and daughter sit on sofa in lounge reading book together 56
MBI / Alamy Stock Photo

2.2 Meg Young and two librarians, Sheffield Library, 1956 65
Photographer unknown

2.3 Louisa Alcott's Little Women and their mother (n.d.) 69
Chronicle / Alamy Stock Photo

3.1 Characters on the Jane Austen Parade in Bath, September 2014 85
TimLarge / Alamy Stock Photo

3.2 The Jane Austen Society South West, Exeter, June 2017 86
Photo by Helen Taylor

3.3 *Rebecca*, 1940, Laurence Olivier and Joan Fontaine 100
Photo 12 / Alamy Stock Photo

3.4 Haworth Parsonage, Yorkshire 103
Ken Biggs / Alamy Stock Photo

4.1 Barbara Cartland at home 108
Stephen Shepherd / Alamy Stock Photo

4.2 Women campaigning against domestic abuse demonstrate
at premiere of film *Fifty Shades of Grey*, Leicester Square,
London, 12 February 2015   120
     ZUMA Press, Inc. / Alamy Stock Photo

5.1 Val McDermid signing books, Liverpool Literary Festival,
October 2018   131
     Photo by Helen Taylor

5.2 Naomi Alderman with her book *The Power*, winner of
Baileys Women's Prize for Fiction 2017   142
     WENN Rights Ltd / Alamy Stock Photo

Int.2 dovegreyreader's tent, Port Eliot Festival   146
     Photo by Tommy Hatwell

6.1 Helen Dunmore   154
     Photo by Charlie Forgham-Bailey

6.2 From *A Secret Garden* by Katie Fforde, published by Century,
David O'Driscoll   159
     Reproduced by permission of The Random House Group Ltd. © 2017

6.3 Hilary Mantel   162
     Photo by Els Zweerink

6.4 Bernardine Evaristo   167
     Martin Beddall/ Alamy Stock Photo

7.1 The Wedmore Book Circle, May 2018   181
     Photo by Helen Taylor

7.2 A reading group at Hay Festival, 2018   193
     Photo by Helen Taylor

8.1 Jackie Kay signing books at Cheltenham Literature Festival,
October 2017   206
     Photo by Helen Taylor

8.2 The bookstall at Bradford Literature Festival, July 2017   211
     Photo by Helen Taylor

8.3 Lyme Park House, Disley, Cheshire (Mr Darcy's Pemberley
in BBC *Pride and Prejudice*, 1995)   214
     Andrew Turner / Alamy Stock Photo

8.4 Greenway Boat House at Agatha Christie's South Devon home   216
     John R Elliott / Alamy Stock Photo

9.1 'Like a Woman' pop-up bookshop, Shoreditch, London,
March 2018   232
     Photo by Helen Taylor

9.2 The Second Shelf bookshop, 14 Smiths Court, London   233
     Photo by Helen Taylor

PART I

How, Where, and Why Women Read Fiction

Introduction

When I've gone through times of not being able to read fiction, I feel fundamentally at odds with the world. It's as if fiction offers me a doorway into another dimension, and if I can't live in it regularly a bit of me dies off.

Shelley H

My reason for reading is . . . to live more lives than one . . . [Novels] take me to a world I've never been before—from a small house on a street with people I've never met, all the way to another time, another country, another set of values, a strife I've never experienced, a war I've never known, a love or a grief or a problem I've never encountered.

Emylia H

Some years ago, novelist Ian McEwan conducted an (admittedly unscientific) experiment. He and his son went into a London park at lunchtime and began handing out free books; within a few minutes, they had given away thirty. Nearly all the takers were women who, he claimed, were 'eager and grateful' while men 'frowned in suspicion, or distaste'. McEwan's comment was: 'When women stop reading, the novel will be dead.'[1] In surveys of UK, US, and Canadian fiction markets, women account for 80 per cent of sales. Editor-in-chief of Bloomsbury Publishing Alexandra Pringle wrote: '[T]he nest of fiction is kept feathered by the efforts of women: the women who write fiction, the women who publish it, the women who buy and read it and discuss it in their book groups.'[2]

Statistics for the gender balance of fiction reading can be measured in different ways according to purchases, library borrowings, shared books, and so on.[3] However, the trends are fairly clear. Nielsen Book Research, the Bible of sales figures, provided me with statistics for 2017, confirming that—in all categories of fiction (physical and digital) except for fantasy, science fiction, and horror/ghost stories—women purchasers outnumber men.[4] Overall sales for fiction books and e-books are 63 per cent female to 37 per cent male. Women outnumber men in the following categories, with e-books showing an even larger discrepancy:

General fiction	74 female to 26 male (e-books 80 to 19)
Crime, thriller, adventure	58 to 42 (e 63 to 37)
Classic fiction	52 to 48 (e 53 to 47)
Historical fiction	57 to 43 (e 57 to 43)
Erotic fiction	71 to 29 (e 70 to 30)
Romance	92 to 8 (e 93 to 7)
Saga	94 to 6 (e 96 to 4)
Young adult fiction	67 to 33 (e 79 to 21)
Mills & Boon	87 to 13 (e 89 to 11).

Male preferences are for fantasy (53 male to 47 female), horror (54 to 46), and science fiction (75 to 25), and although audiobooks are read more evenly by both men and women, there is a clear pattern of gendered reading I'll explore throughout this book. In terms of ethnicity, well over 90 per cent of UK purchasers in every category (except classics and Young Adult) are white.[5]

The woman reader provides the glue for an informed and literate society. We are the main readers of fiction, the largest market for novels and short stories—for ourselves and our children—and the main buyers and borrowers of fiction. Women constitute the majority of library and book club (including online) members, literary bloggers, audio book readers, members of literary societies and literature evening classes, literary site tourists, audiences at literature festivals, and bookshop readings. Women are usually the parents and grandparents who read to children at bedtime, teach children to read in school as well as home, and take them along to libraries, bookshops, and supermarkets, where we also borrow and buy books for ourselves. Through the ages, literacy has been allowed or encouraged in women in order to provide children with reading skills and some rudimentary education. We share fiction with mothers, daughters, sisters, and friends, and chivvy along male partners to readings and festivals. The reading group movement and literary blogging have been led and dominated by women. Women disseminate and

Figure 0.1 'The Sisters', 1900, Ralph Peacock
© Tate, London 2019

promote fiction as teachers, librarians, festival directors, radio and
TV producers, and publishing house editors and publicists. We are
the gender most likely to go to websites such as BookBub, Goodreads,
W. H. Smith's Richard and Judy, Zoella and Zoe Ball Book Clubs, to
get ideas for our next read. And yet, when did you last see a woman
character in a play, film, or TV drama absorbed in reading or sharing
a book *with real pleasure*, not because she was a sad and lonely figure
(Figure 0.1)?

The publishing industry is a business, and like all businesses it
creates markets, moulds consumers, and dictates tastes. The female
reader is a commercial and critical force to be reckoned with, and a
powerful voice in literary culture. Publishers, writers, and reviewers
alike know that, for most fiction to succeed, it must attract female
readers, and they keep a vigilant eye on this market. But, even with all
the marketing surveys and statistics used to target readerships, no one

really knows who is reading a book, how and where it is read, or who or what persuaded them to buy, borrow, or steal it. Journalists and commentators often talk of 'the reader' as if s/he were a single figure, whose relationship to a book is straightforward and has no history or context. But each reader has her own story—of class, race, sexuality, generation, education, personal and family experience. Reading fiction, then, isn't a simple, passive process. It demands a certain degree of literacy. It requires access to books, thus financial and other resources, time, energy, and active imaginative engagement—as well as encouragement. Besides, each woman reads differently, creating a unique story in her head in relation to her chosen book. There are bewildered, resisting, struggling, or skipping readers, and whenever we share a reading experience with others, we often find a startling variety of interpretations. How many times have you found that you and a friend have contrasting perspectives on a central character, key scene, or even an ending? Book clubs thrive on such differences.

Reading fiction can both transform and disrupt a life. It can be a source of guilt and anxiety. What if a powerful novel or story has insinuated ideas through characters that challenge my own life choices or fragile daily existence? How do I know which writers to choose to suit me? Should I be 'just' reading a story when there are other jobs to do? Why haven't I read the great novels that other people seem to know back to front? Why can't I remember the names of any of the characters in a book I've just finished? Why are much-hyped novels published in hardback when I can't afford them?

These questions are asked by the many readers with whom I've shared ideas about fiction. Although there have been histories of women's reading, and many research projects examining reading practice, no one to my knowledge has tried to describe how fiction matters to contemporary women of different ages, classes, and ethnic groups, and how we use it in our lives to create and sustain life narratives. I don't pretend to speak for everyone or indeed to answer all those questions. Instead, as I indicated in the Preface, my book draws on questionnaires and interviews to capture the memories and thoughts of selected women readers and writers, discussing their reading histories from earliest memories, cherished books, regular patterns of reading, and periods of inability or refusal to read. Some women are in reading groups; others share reading with female (and occasionally male) friends and partners. Others read alone, enjoying the solitary pleasures of a good book on a rainy afternoon or listening to an audiobook while driving or doing housework. Many of us find fiction to be a companionable and reliable friend through the chapters of life—sometimes of emotional, psychological, and political importance, at other times for pure escapism and pleasure. In Emily Dickinson's words: 'There is no Frigate like a Book / To take us Lands away.'

Life stories are defined in a literary way. We identify with fictional figures and sometimes see the passage from childhood through adolescence to work, marriage, motherhood, and old age in terms of 'chapters'. A treasured childhood classic or contemporary novel can be central to defining who we are. As writer Bel Mooney puts it, 'I am surely shaped by everything I have read since childhood, and certainly see my life in general as an enthralling literary work-in-progress!'[6]

Of course I'm aware that men too enjoy reading fiction (though in smaller numbers), and the differences between male and female readers are determined by many factors other than gender, such as class, education, sexual orientation, race and ethnicity, and personal choice. One of my older correspondents, Penny S-L, expressed a view that reflects the mindset of earlier generations:

> Boys are not encouraged to live in a make believe world. When I was a child, boys were steered towards the practical—Physics, Chemistry, woodwork etc; girls could be creative. Boys were outdoor creatures, girls indoor. I don't think this has changed. Books for males are informative and boys' books used to mould the future man. Men 'do', women are introspective.

Even though this may seem a dangerous generalization, there's plenty of anecdotal evidence that men and women connect with and share fiction in different ways, and I've become convinced there's a special tale to tell about women readers. Countless correspondents tell me their male family members either avoid or actively despise fiction, preferring to choose biography, history, and other non-fiction. By contrast, a passion for reading fiction seems to facilitate women's imaginations and engage us with others, so that we make productive connections between those stories and other people, as well as the way we live.

The great pleasures of reading have always been hedged around with social and cultural expectations and constraints. Any generalization about women's fiction reading is bound to oversimplify this activity that is both central to and complicated by our diverse society. Of course there are women who cannot read and those who have never been encouraged or allowed to read fiction, and much of my evidence and material in this book emanates from correspondence and conversations with literate, reasonably educated readers. That said, I'm well aware that two-thirds of the world's illiterate are women—a point brought home by the heroic stand taken by Pakistani schoolgirl and Nobel Prize laureate Malala Yousafzai. When her Malala's Fund was established, she was quoted as saying: 'Extremists have shown what frightens them most: a girl with a book.'[7] As Azar Nafisi reminds us in *Reading Lolita in Tehran*, many women are forbidden novels and thus cannot search for what she calls 'not so much reality but the epiphany of truth'.[8] Over the centuries and across the globe, women have had to fight for the right to read and write.

In many different cultures, there are examples of women reading secretly, defiantly, discovering life and finding their identities within the pages of both religious and secular books, but mainly fiction. Reading has long been of paramount importance to the educational and employment progress of the second sex. Belinda Jack relates that élite women from classical to modern times—independently-wealthy, tradeswomen and nuns, for instance—read widely and deeply; indeed, nunnery libraries contained books donated by women with tracts calling for female literacy.[9] Of course there were barriers to non-élite women, and until recently advanced literacy in the developed as well as developing worlds has been a privilege denied to economically inactive or impoverished women, especially from minority ethnic backgrounds. Vietnamese-American poet Ocean Vuong's family were illiterate, and regarded his passionate reading as 'an act of sorcery'. One day, looking at Ocean's book, his mother asked what he got out of it: 'It just looks like a bunch of dead ants,' she said.[10]

Issues of Class and Race

This 'act of sorcery' is both liberating and threatening, since reading offers people intellectual and social opportunities that enable them to challenge and escape the constraints of their family and class backgrounds. Women have variable access to reading, whether at home or in school and work. But my questionnaires and interviews produced a plethora of stories by women from different class, race, and ethnic backgrounds, seeking out new reading experiences and improving their life chances and social mobility as a result of reading fiction. As Jeanette Winterson put it: 'Reading is a life-long collision with minds not like your own.'[11] An empowering practice indeed.

And yet, readers have a right to expect to see their own experience reflected in that fiction. In November 2017, BBC Radio 4 broadcast 'Where Are All the Working Class Writers?' introduced by novelist Kit de Waal, daughter of an Irish mother and Caribbean father.[12] Earlier that year, she had contributed to an essay collection, *Know Your Place*, in which she wrote about being a working-class reader-writer. Quoting a saying, 'Literature is a record of the middle classes for the middle classes,' she argues that the canon rarely includes productions of the working class or underclass: 'street literature, songs, hymns, spoken word, dialect and oral storytelling'. Fellow essay contributor Durre Shahwar claims that for her, a working-class BAME (black, Asian, minority ethnic) writer, figures such as Zadie Smith, Monica Ali, and Hanif Kureishi who wrote about working class and BAME experience, have been 'my source of affirmation ... in the face of mainstream, "high class" dominantly white narratives'.[13] It is now recognized that UK publishing has failed to do justice to a diverse range of voices, and working class and BAME writers struggle to be heard within an overwhelmingly white middle-class publishing world. As a result, in recent years—not before time—diversity initiatives have made waves: individuals such as Nikesh Shukla (editor of *The Good Immigrant* and co-founder of The Good Literary Agency backing non-mainstream writers); major publishers like Hachette (the diversity and inclusion programme, 'Changing the Story'); and small independents such as Jacaranda (planning to publish twenty black British writers in 2020), supported by crowd-funding, progressive sponsors, and agencies.

Time will tell whether these developments dramatically increase the range of writers and produce fresh kinds of fiction for a broad readership. Meanwhile, assumptions are still made about readers that can seem to simplify or erase their life experiences. Here's a comment by Sian Norris, writer and director of Bristol Festival of Women's Literature, who as a woman in her thirties felt uneasy about the critical description of Sally Rooney's acclaimed first two novels, *Conversations With Friends* (2017) and *Normal People* (2018), as 'the voice of a generation':

> Is Sally Rooney the voice of a generation? And if generation, whose? Millennials—generally defined as being born between 1980 and 1995, although dates differ wildly? Or Generation Z, who came after? And how can you even define the voice of a generation, when within any such grouping there'll be wildly different experiences, backgrounds, intersecting oppressions and privileges?
>
> Rooney's novels engage with issues that are associated with young people or the younger generation. There's the internet, which is almost its own character in *Conversations With Friends*, and university life, moving on from school to the big city, friendship, good sex and messy sex and confused sex. Rooney writes with a piercing insight about young people's relationships—sexual and not—and her honesty about the complexities of love and friendship is refreshing. Sex is a big feature in Rooney's novels, and her incisive portrayal of a young woman's ambivalence towards sex and her own sexuality in *Normal People* is, again, really refreshing ... This, and the internet, is why I think Rooney has been tagged with this 'voice of a generation' label.
>
> Rooney has never asked to be the voice of a generation, so the following criticism is not a fault of hers. She wrote the novel she wanted to write ... But the comings and goings of a group of white, privileged students in a university city is a tiny sliver of life. There's nothing wrong in writing a novel about those kinds of characters, especially when you write as well as Rooney. It's just sometimes I found myself wondering if so many critics see her as the voice of their generation, because like her characters they too went to university in a big city and could afford cool stylish clothes, and went to parties or drank champagne in posh villas. That's not what life is like for most people. Then there's Marianne in *Normal People*, and the girls in *Conversations with Friends*—characters who are cool, beautiful, a bit messed up, spending money on vintage clothes and drinking champagne in foreign villas out of antique flutes. I feel like we are expected to find this relatable. And it's not. They're all so *thin*.
>
> While everyone was praising a novel for being such a clever portrayal of a generation, for accurately bringing to life the concerns of young people today, I found myself wondering *which young people*.

While Norris voices unease about a popular novelist's class issues, the problems of racial representation raised by Nikesh Shukla, Kit de Waal, and Durre Shahwar are finally being addressed. In an influential 2015 report, journalist Danuta Kean criticized the lack of diversity in the UK publishing industry (both staff and output) and argued that by 2045 the average British reader would be an educated young woman of mixed heritage, who would wish to find her experience and interests reflected in her reading. Responding to such criticism, in 2018 the conglomerate Penguin Random House announced that, by 2025, its authors and staff would reflect the diversity of UK society. This move caused a media storm when novelist Lionel Shriver mocked the policy, claiming: 'From now until 2025, literary excellence will be secondary to ticking all those ethnicity, gender, disability, sexual preference and crap-education boxes.'[14] Hostile responses to Shriver highlighted her (and others') myopic disregard of those silences and absences within literary culture that have excluded a whole body of under-represented writers *and* readers.

There are interesting parallels here with the spirited debates in the late twentieth century about class and gender, with Marxist and feminist critics arguing that the canon was created and sustained by 'Dead (and Living) White Men' who reified 'literary excellence', unaware of their own privileged position and thus blinkered judgements. These challenges to hitherto-revered critics played out largely in universities and polytechnics, focused on the English literature curriculum, resulting in new publications and courses that challenged orthodox literary history. In recent years, with the rise of post-colonial studies and international movements such as Black Lives Matter, the 'culture wars', and identity politics, disputes about the importance of diversity within literature have become more impassioned, spreading widely across the media and the publishing industry as well as the academy. In the turbulent days of the twenty-first century, Lionel Shriver's elitist aestheticism seems tired and tetchy indeed.

'The Reader as Human Being'

These days, the subject of reading has considerable fascination for commentators in high-literacy Western society. Book programmes, magazine questionnaires, bibliomemoirs, blogs, university research centres, and newspaper profiles all focus on the literary tastes of established writers, celebrities, and general readers. In 2014, there was a clutch of books outlining writers' reading and its effect on their life choices. For instance, Andy Miller wrote a book with the apocalyptic title *The Year of Reading Dangerously: How Fifty Great Books Saved My Life*. As Leon Robson claimed: 'Reading has the best PR team in the business . . . [claiming] reading will make you healthier, stronger, kinder'.[15] But in his review of four new books about reading, he described those by *women* writers—Wendy Lesser's *Why I Read* and Rebecca Mead's *The Road to Middlemarch*—with terms like 'warmer', '[an] unhermetic vision of engagement with literature', 'shimmying perspective—the reader as human being'. This male critic recognized that women don't see themselves as reading 'hermits'—sealed away from the 'human'.

The history of women's very human engagement with reading has been traced by scholars such as Jacqueline Pearson, Kate Flint, and Belinda Jack,[16] and many of the most engaging and personal books about the process and quality of reading in a lifetime have been by *women*: Azar Nafisi's *Reading Lolita in Tehran*, Bee Rowlatt and May Witwit's *Talking About Jane Austen in Baghdad: The Story of an Unlikely Friendship* (2010), Penelope Lively's *Ammonites and Leaping Fish: A Life in Time* (2013), Samantha Ellis' *How to be a Heroine; Or, What I've Learned from Reading too Much* (2014), Phyllis Rose's *The Shelf, from LEQ to LES: Adventures in Extreme Reading* (2014), and Lucy Mangan's *Bookworm: A Memoir of Childhood Reading* (2018). They may not claim reading makes them 'healthier, stronger, kinder', but they do see reading as essential to their identity. All of them describe their reading histories through personal anecdotes and accounts of real and virtual intellectual and emotional journeys and friendships. As one of my correspondents Kathy J wrote to me: 'Reading has seen me through good times and bad. It has taken me to places I longed to go and some I did not want to go. At times, it has challenged, at times comforted.' Women often name their daughters (or cats and dogs) after strong female fictional characters: Emma, Tess, Scarlett, Lyndall, and—in the case of Vera Brittain, mother of politician Shirley Williams—Charlotte Brontë's 'gallant little cavalier in her novel of that name, a champion of social justice'.[17]

The Reading Woman

For my last birthday, I received a card picturing a casually dressed woman with her feet up on a sofa, a pile of books on the floor and one in her hand (we presume fiction!), while the other gently strokes a cat asleep on the carpet. Slumped in a familiar chair, surrounded by favourite pictures and knick-knacks, she has placed within easy reach a cup of tea and large piece of cake (Figure 0.2). This woman occupies a private space to indulge herself, evade the demands of other people and duties, cuddle her cat, and free her imagination to

Figure 0.2 A Good Book (birthday card, detail)
Lucy Howard

enter worlds different from and sometimes challenging her own. She is
doing what so many women value in fiction: escaping from daily life to
go somewhere else in her head.

The figure of a reading woman in Western culture has a long
pedigree.[18] The dominant image of the female reader (painted repeatedly by male artists) is of the Virgin Mary with a book, often at the
scene of the Annunciation. A favourite Christmas present for mothers
and sisters-in-law is the Pomegranate calendar, 'The Reading
Woman', with reproductions for every month of famous painters'
portraits of solitary women sitting with book in hand. This series of
calendars includes works by painters such as Edgar Degas, Pierre-
Auguste Renoir, Laura Coombs Hill, and Mary Stevenson Cassatt.
All show a woman, usually seated elegantly and looking down or
dreamily into space, with an accessory book in her hand or lap.
Some of the most reproduced images we have—from Johannes
Vermeer to Gwen John—are of a woman 'lost' in a book. While
male portrait subjects are also represented reading, they are usually
clerics, scholars, and saints standing proudly with formal documents
such as the Bible or a significant letter, but rarely with a text that
allows escape and reverie.

The Amazon website describes the 'Reading Woman' calendars in
these words: 'She is absorbed, content, perhaps quietly thrilled.
She might be seizing a precious moment to take comfort in a book,
or she might be searching its pages for a means to transform her life.'
These words—designed to sell a product—gesture to an important
truth about the act of reading for women. Absorption, contentment,
thrill, precious moments, and a search for life transformation . . . what
better reasons could a woman have for making reading a central and
constant part of her life?

In 2017, a monthly subscription service was launched by two
businesswomen. 'Reading in Heels' is a digital book club for 'intelligent, stylish modern women, letting you discover the latest in modern
literary fiction alongside our Expert Edit of beauty and lifestyle treats.'
Aimed at busy professional women in their twenties or thirties who
want to spend less time with their phones in order to enjoy 'me-time',
reading a good book while in the bath, curled up on the sofa, and
drinking tea, for a monthly fee 'Reading in Heels' sends out a fancy
box. It contains their chosen book of the month together with three or

four goodies—upmarket chocolate with goji berries and cacao nibs, lipstick, a powder compact, some wildflower seeds for your window box. Its target is an aspirational audience that chooses 'literary' fiction, promising its members 'no chick lit or trashy crime', and selecting paperbacks rather than hardbacks, 'not too heavy for your handbag'. A great combination—heels, handbags, hot baths, and the hottest of contemporary fiction. This venture signals a confidence by millennial marketing businesswomen that publishers and gift companies will back female literature consumers.

Belinda Jack's study of the woman reader suggests that our calendar image of lone woman with head bowed is what appeals to us. She reminds us that no one outside the reader knows what is going on in her mind or indeed body; lone reading is 'an inherently antisocial activity . . . the onus on women has been, and often remains, to be sociable and to facilitate easy human relations. Reading is intensely private and literally self-centred.'[19] In contemporary times, this is echoed in the 'me-time' for which websites like readinginheels.com are catering.

And yet, this is only part of the truth. In her collection, *Public Library and Other Stories*, Ali Smith offers a symbolic anecdote about a woman who, sitting in a Toronto public library, sees her own mother walk in, stretch out on a sunny window seat, and go to sleep. A female library assistant tries to wake her, then steps back and leaves her sleeping.[20] Three women readers, familiar with and comfortable in a library, leave one another alone because they share a quiet pleasure around books, and tacitly acknowledge that—for women—libraries are a rare public space in which they feel at home. And, as Belinda Jack reminds us, communal reading and reading aloud to groups were common practice until the Middle Ages, when private reading for the silent, solitary study of scripture was encouraged, to develop a unique personal relationship with God.[21] In the eighteenth and nineteenth centuries, with the rise of the novel, group reading (often aloud) again became common in bourgeois households. In our digital age, Twitter is alive with female fictional chat, and young women post on literary fandom websites 'reader selfies' in hyperfeminine clothing, presenting photographic self-portraits together with a reading-related quote from a famous author.[22]

From my own experience, I know that the bowed head of the solitary woman reader devoid of any wider context by no means tells the full story. For many women—in various aspects of our lives drawn to collaborate rather than compete—the act of reading is a collective activity, something we do in family and friendship gatherings, school and college groups, festivals and reading groups, in casual conversations with those close to us, colleagues and strangers. Students taking English courses in school, college, and university—where literature is discussed in group seminars and tutorials—are overwhelmingly female. We bring to many books the assumptions and preferences of those who recommended them to us and whose judgement we trust. One of my correspondents, Wendy S, captured the female reading culture that she and others inhabit:

> I recently bought *The Unlikely Pilgrimage of Harold Fry* for a friend because I wanted her to read it. I often text or email friends if I enjoy a book and I discuss books with female friends and a male ex-colleague. I read *Eat Pray Love* because my niece recommended it. My daughter then read it because I liked it. My elder daughter introduced me to all the Susan Hill detective books.

Literary Opium, Main Courses, and Puddings

A general preoccupation with the topic of women and fiction has grown since at least the seventeenth century when reading for pleasure by bourgeois women became an acceptable practice. The reading of novels by girls and women was the subject of many religious and political discourses, with warnings given from the eighteenth century onwards about the possibility of excitement, indulgence, the problem of women neglecting their duties, and fiction as corruption or 'literary opium'.[23] Admittedly, reading a great deal by either gender can be seen as an excessive form of consumption—'voracious reading', 'being a bookworm', or 'swallowing a dictionary'. But women seem to have a special gustatory relationship to reading. Writing in 1576 of the Holy Scriptures, Queen Elizabeth 1 walked into their 'pleasant fields . . . where I pluck up the good green herbs of sentences, eat them by reading, chew them up by musing, and lay them up at length in the high seat of memory . . . so I may the less perceive the bitterness of this miserable life'.[24] Women's relationship to fiction has often been characterized as eating or drinking too much of the wrong thing. Samuel Johnson urged Frances Sheridan to let her daughter loose into the library: '[I]f she is well inclined, she will choose only nutritious food.'[25] William Thackeray, editing *The Cornhill Magazine*, referred to fiction as 'sweets' which everyone loves, but he recommended 'roast' (non-fiction) for a balanced diet.[26] Matilda Pullan echoed Thackeray, warning her daughters that in one's appetite for fiction no pastry should be a substitute for a 'solid joint', while in *Home Education*, Charlotte Mason warned that to read (the novel) *The Newcomes* to yourself 'is like sitting down to a solitary feast of strawberries and cream'.[27]

The association of masculinity with the solid main course and femininity with puddings and sweets recurs, reminding us of the perennial warnings against women's sensual indulgence of any kind.[28] God forbid that a woman should relish her reading! In her study of a year of reading from home, novelist Susan Hill repeatedly equates this with eating, comparing 'ice-cream reading' of superficial books with 'literary' works that nourish. Advocating 'slow reading' (by analogy with slow food), she recommends Michael Mayne's rich books that 'need to be treated like fruit cake, taken a small, dense slice at a time'.[29] Consuming fiction is often compared with the sweet and sugary by women readers themselves. And when you reflect on the fact that we usually associate nurturing (especially in terms of feeding—from the sweetness of breast milk onwards) with mothers, and that it is most often mothers or other female adults who introduce women to reading, is it surprising that women equate their gobbling down of fiction with sweet and delicious food treats? Hilary D described herself as 'a glutton, omnivore, snatching and grabbing and cramming in the delectable goodies like the sweet-greedy (but sweet-deprived) child that I was'. Erotica novelist Victoria Fox told me her best compliment came from a 60-year-old woman who said her novels were 'spicy fruitcake as compared with bland vanilla sponge'.[30]

But it's not merely sweet treats. For women there may be a *general* visceral pleasure in reading. Food for thought, nutrition for the imagination and the heart, and a source of erotic and sensual pleasure. Dorothy D talked of her 'print tooth'. Linda Grant describes a personal library as 'a full larder for the soul'.[31] This deliberately domestic metaphor of the larder claims reading for the female gender as a reliable, well-stocked source of intellectual and spiritual nourishment in our own space. And healing, too. In 2018, journalist Laura Freeman published *The Reading Cure: How Books Restored my Appetite*. After a decade of anorexia (from age 14) she began to read descriptions of food in writers from Siegfried Sassoon to Nancy Mitford, and claims this restored her pleasure in eating (Christmas pudding after Dickens, dairy after *Tess of the d'Urbervilles*), and thus her physical and emotional health.

Guilty and Solitary Reading

As if we didn't feel guilty enough about indulging in sweets, there's another cause for readerly anxiety. For a woman to be contentedly alone, and worse to be *reading alone*, has long been a subject of suspicion, since a woman or girl might dream, fantasize, go elsewhere in her head (or indeed body) out of parental and male control—as, of course, she does! From the late eighteenth century, when family group reading was considered safe and acceptable, these anxieties were about 'the seduction narrative' and female sexuality, with reading euphemistically described in Matthew Lewis' 1796 novel *The Monk* as awakening 'sleepy passions... [inculcating] the first rudiments of vice'.[32] A graphic painting (*c*.1760) by Pierre-Antoine Baudoin, 'The Reader', shows a woman apparently masturbating while perusing a novel (Figure 0.3), and a century later, in 'The Reading Girl' (1886–7), Théodore Roussel depicts a languidly naked model absorbed in her book. This concern embraced all classes, since working-class female readers might get ideas above their station, and middle-class readers become dissatisfied with their circumscribed lot. Both could act dangerously if allowed too much autonomy.

Like moral panics today about young women eating too much, or too little, drinking and taking drugs to excess (and then accused of inviting rape or sexual harassment), by the end of the eighteenth century clerics and writers fretted about women's reading as a bug or disease, or—in Jane Carlyle's words about borrowing books—'like having an illicit affair'.[33] In Sheridan's famous play *The Rivals* (1775), the character of Lydia Languish is condemned by Sir Anthony Absolute for her reading ('the black art') confusing 'sense and sentiment, fantasy and reality, licit and illicit texts'.[34] A common plot motif in the early nineteenth century was a heroine misled by—usually solitary—

Figure 0.3 'The Reader', 1760, Pierre-Antoine Baudouin
The Picture Art Collection / Alamy Stock Photo

novel reading, and the words 'poison' and 'soften' recurred to suggest wider erosion of social and economic order.[35] From the nineteenth century onwards, family reading was encouraged and women urged to join reading circles, reading rooms, and ladies' rooms in libraries.

The British Museum Reading Room was popular with women but men objected to their rustling dresses and giggling.[36] Solitary reading may be threatening, but even more is a joyous community of relaxed female readers who appear to challenge patriarchal control.

So it's a dangerous business, giving stories to girls and women, likely to corrupt or excite, leading them into sexual and other dangers. Women in earlier centuries were to be protected from excessive indulgence and books (notably fiction) that might prove dangerous to their moral and emotional welfare. Eighteenth-century novelist Fanny Burney's very literary family insisted on sewing in the morning, reading only in the afternoon. Dorothy Wordsworth was made to sew an old shirt when she really wanted to read *The Iliad*, and many other women readers (and writers) of eighteenth- and nineteenth-century literary families shared Burney's morning sewing, were locked out of their fathers' libraries, and—even if allowed to read—put away their book when a man was present or were anxious not to be seen to be reading alone, away from the family group.[37] Hermione Lee describes two kinds of reading—'vertical' and 'horizontal': 'the first regulated, supervised, orderly, canonical and productive, the second unlicensed, private, leisurely, disreputable, promiscuous and anarchic'.[38] The negative associations with the latter are all too frequently assigned to female readers.

And while reading has been recognized since the nineteenth century as a key element in educating women—and thus their children—there's no doubt that women have internalized a guilt about reading alone, too much, and too much of the wrong thing. Sometimes this is exacerbated by others, notably parents or male partners, but it's certainly true of many of the women who wrote and spoke to me. Pleasurable reading is a guilty treat—hence all those references to sweets and cakes we know we shouldn't eat. One of my correspondents, Dawn R-W, wrote: 'Having an affair is dangerous, masturbation requires solitude and privacy. Reading a book offers both without anyone noticing . . . I can live a different life through books, especially fiction.' That 'different life' can seem both exhilarating and also threatening, a reminder of the power of fiction to excite and disturb.

Women are socialized to feel we can't indulge ourselves until our other duties are done. Among my interviewees, the majority rarely if ever read fiction in the morning or (apart from a few pages over lunch) during the day, similar to that common taboo on enjoying daytime television. Both suggest a slippery slope into idle self-indulgence upon which others might frown. Of course, women within and outside the home often have little space, but it seems that—whether a busy working mother or retired singleton—housework, routine chores, exercise, and other dutiful activity must take precedence in the daylight hours. Retired Library Development Manager Karen W admitted reading was 'a pleasure I can only do when I've done everything else (washing, Hoovering etc.)', and another academic said her mother was a devoted reader all her life but apologetic about it: ' "It's just escapism," she'd say, rather as if confessing to being a secret drinker.' A retired teacher, Rosie B, described 'sneaking' off to read but was often 'caught' by her mother who needed her to help. 'This, I think, initiated my life-long slight feeling of guilt about reading.' College lecturer Anne K has a sense of urgency: 'I often take my lunch into my car as I have a book I want to read instead of joining workmates in the staff room. I sometimes think I could be turning anti-social but there are so many books and so little time.' This emphasis on being anti-social recurs. Twenty-six-year-old Jemma K's parents always told her off for reading in the car or when company was present. 'I feel guilty if I read around my partner so I enjoy the times when he's absent and I can just read a book.' And Lisa W, a 34-year-old chartered accountant, has on her bedside table Dr Nick Bayliss' *A Rough Guide to Happiness* which, she told me, describes 'voraciously reading novels'—along with over-work, over-exercise, and wall-to-wall activity—as 'some of the more disguised methods of avoidance'. She writes: 'Perhaps he is right. A reminder to cycle, sew, run, swim, bake or crossword sometimes instead.' She doesn't sound convinced.

As with women in earlier centuries, many of my correspondents and interviewees recognize the fact that reading alone can seem subversive. Novelist Emylia H told me: 'There's always something deliciously secret about reading—no one can ever know quite where you are or what you're doing when you're reading a book,' and another told me that reading 'is solitary and internal and not compatible with a social self, which is perhaps why so many people find a bookwormish child quite threatening'. Some relate parental—almost always maternal—disapproval of the practice of reading for pleasure. Seventy-year-old Claire D told me a familiar story—her mother didn't approve of reading during the day: 'To this day I cannot read with comfort until the evening.' Several shared my own experience of mothers telling them to 'get their nose out of that book' on a sunny day, and go out of the house instead. Anxiety would be expressed about eyesight being ruined, or lack of fresh air, but often mothers seem to have worried their daughters might turn into 'bookworms'—a code for unmarriageable bluestockings. Many girls and women tell me they have always made lists of the novels they've read (sometimes, as with the adolescent Margaret Forster, with mini-reviews). Perhaps this reflects a need to confirm reading as a serious, self-improving occupation to justify it to themselves and others.

Being accepted as a good reader has offered women one of the few ways to achieve greater social status and class mobility. I remember with embarrassment that as a teenager I would carry a book with me, ensuring others could read the title and thus see me as the deep thinker I aspired to be. Other women have shared my aspirational affectation or cultural naïveté. Mavis, the socially isolated daughter of a colliery weigh station manager, won a scholarship to her school and was invited to interview at Leeds University. For the train journey, she bought a *Reader's Digest* (the only thing her mother read). When asked in her interview what she had been reading, she explained that her mother wasn't a reader but did enjoy the *Reader's Digest* and furthermore 'I had never been on a train before and I was on a stopping train as the most suitable one and I didn't want to get into a book because after Leeds the train didn't stop until it reached Scotland.' After that, she was aware 'there were things you didn't own up to'.[39] Tracey P, a working-class woman who became an academic, was the eldest of four, expected to look after her siblings and contribute to the running of the house, which contained only half a dozen books (the Hamlyn Children's Bible, some Enid Blyton, *Black Beauty*, and *Treasure Island*). Her encouragement to read came from school teachers and she studied for her 'O' level exams secretly in the public library. At eighteen, she got a job with the restaurant chain Little Chef, and recalls

> cultivating an intellectual (on reflection, insufferably pretentious) air, reading Sartre's *Nausea* and *Brideshead Revisited* in my breaks... Looking back, it was clear I was desperate to distinguish myself from my fellow workmates and to align myself with the students

who worked there every summer...My early adult taste was pretty
snobbish and pompous.

On the other hand, reading is now something everyone does all the
time—on phones, tablets, and computers. You never know whether
your teenage daughter or son is Googling some historical fact or
contacting a stranger on Tinder, let alone reading a book or blog of
which you might not approve. But to a certain extent this has freed
women—we can look busy with work or domestic arrangements but
can also be reading a novel on a device. Fifty-four per cent of e-books
are now read on mobile phones, and women over forty-five (who can
enlarge the font on tablets to suit middle-aged or failing eyesight) are
75 per cent of the most active e-readers: 'the engine that powers the
industry'.[40] Increasingly popular audiobooks can be listened to, without the scrutiny of others, while we are cooking, cleaning, and doing
the school run.

E-readers have freed readers from the shame of being seen with
'unsuitable' books, but there's no doubt women have internalized
taboos on the consumption of certain kinds of fiction. In 1961, when
she was 12, Sarah L went to a convent boarding school where all
books taken had to be signed by a parent. Recently she opened a copy
of Graham Greene's *The Burnt-Out Case* to find her father's signature
and also 'MMA' (Mother Mary A—) with, in parenthesis, '*not* general', meaning no other girl was allowed to read it. In the mid-1960s,
Colm Tóibín found three forbidden books on top of his mother's
wardrobe, all banned by the Irish Censorship Board: John McGahern's
The Dark, Edna O'Brien's *The Country Girls*, and John Updike's *Couples*.
He writes that he can imagine his mother and her friends, 'Catholic
women in a provincial town who desperately sought a window
onto the wider world, swapping them, discussing them and hiding
them from the children.'[41] Judie N read the Bible at school, and
passed round the 'dirty bits' [Potiphar's wife and Onan]. Refreshingly,
Shelley H says she no longer apologises for reading books like *Scruples*
and *Princess Daisy* that, for a child after lights out, were regarded as
'naughty' and 'low-brow'.

That notion of naughtiness recurs in women's accounts. Veronica
C remembers reading Georgette Heyer in secret and 'passing the
books round like illegal drugs'. Sue W calls herself a 'great closet

fan' of romance novels, Lindsey B read hundreds of donated Mills & Boon novels gathered in her house for the church bookstall, and Marilyn H read her brother's copy of *Lady Chatterley's Lover* hiding under a schoolfriend's bed. Jilly Cooper is a frequently cited 'guilty pleasure', and there's a whole body of lesbian and queer fiction from Radclyffe Hall to Sarah Waters that has given a voice to those yearning for validation of their sexuality. For some girls, accessing forbidden books in secret places was an early act of rebellious action and thought, a tentative move into independent life. Since the eighteenth century, girls' and women's ability to choose our own fictions has freed us to question and sometimes flout the values and guidance of parents and teachers, providing some precious control over our own destinies.

1

'Cheap Sweet Vacations'—Reading as a Woman

A book is one of the few things that can absorb you totally, allow you to relax and completely take you away from real life for a period of time . . . Following a complicated knitting pattern also gives you that total concentration, but it doesn't permit you to relax like reading does.

Tilly W

So how, when, and where do female readers indulge the fiction habit? How do we choose books, and why do we care about them so much? Is reading changing with e-books, and how important are women readers to writers?

Gloria Steinem quotes Stephen King's mother describing paperback mystery novels as '"cheap sweet vacations"'—so he continues to write them for her.[1] In those three words, she sums up the desire for self-indulgent escape that reading so well satisfies. The link between the idea of a good book and a holiday persists (think of the sub-genre of 'airport books'). And vacations—a break in routine and normal life and duties—are a space which many women look forward to filling with reading fiction. One Facebook blog features a 'reader selfie' showing a young woman sitting on a window seat in her pyjamas, reading. The text reads, 'Real life? Can't. I'm booked.'[2]

As a second best to vacations, a favourite relaxation space is bed. As I've already noted, many of us first heard stories read to us as children in bed, so bedtime reading remains a habit. In the eighteenth century, such reading was associated with sloth, seduction, and possible conflagration from candles.[3] The latter was involved in Germaine Greer's secret bedtime reading, since she used pinched candle ends from the parish church: 'My front hair still stands up in a crinkly quiff from being regularly singed.'[4] Now it is more acceptable, just. 'It's nice to spend a little bit of time in a fictional space before going to sleep,' says Sarah R, and Helen M says her brain won't switch off at bedtime 'unless I stare at some words'. It is also seen as 'time for myself' away from partners, children, domestic labour, and general stress. A large number of my correspondents admit their bedtime reading is of short duration, mainly because of fatigue and what Amy W calls the 'no-need-to-engage-brain variety', and Sharon F has learned not to read hardback books in bed as they hurt when dropped on your sleeping face. Some (usually retired) women describe the luxury of reading fiction in bed in the morning. One woman said she'd love to do this 'but dog and husband demand otherwise'. Frances T echoes others when she says: 'In marriage, reading in bed has had to be—shall we say—negotiated.'

And negotiating for time and space in which to indulge their reading habit is a frequent refrain in my correspondence. Finding a real or virtual room of one's own is an uphill struggle for many women. Because only a minority are 'professional' readers (teachers, academics, journalists) most must select and devour books in the cracks of working and domestic lives. But keen readers find opportunities everywhere. Sue T sets aside forty-five to sixty minutes around 5 p.m. daily to read on the sofa, her cat beside her. When she's on holiday she finds a coffee shop and a hot chocolate where she reads happily. My correspondents read when eating, cooking, travelling by train or bus, on the loo, in the car (in one case while her husband fills up with petrol). Kate I, in her early twenties with young children, propped Lawrence Durrell's *Alexandria Quartet* on the Aga while she cooked (recalling Emily Brontë's reading while kneading bread). Others neglect domestic duties in order to read. Sue W describes her romance novel reading as a 'guilty pleasure' on which she spends much time, 'often to the detriment of chores'. Sandra J, however, asked angrily why women feel guilty about sitting down with a cup of coffee and a book, while 'men spend hours sitting on a riverbank with a rod in hand, doing absolutely nothing, without a twinge of guilt'.

One woman has 'Upstairs' and 'Downstairs' books, and (unusually among my correspondents) for her the Upstairs fiction needs more concentration than the Downstairs non-fiction. Pamela M compares reading with Indian classical music, saying there are certain ragas for

Figure 1.1 'The Convalescent', 1923–4, Gwen John
© The Fitzwilliam Museum, Cambridge

morning, and others for afternoons and evenings. Bev B says her husband cannot understand why she has different piles of books in different places around the house—one 'good book for first reading', a classic or two, an early twentieth-century detective novel, and a fantasy work for re-reading. Sue T says she reads voraciously for weeks or months, and then weeks go by with very little reading except for *The History Magazine* and the *Times Literary Supplement*. At times of sorrow and stress, reading helps but 'anything too harrowing, mournful or sentimental has the potential to make me worse'.

One of the times women describe reading as essential is hospital stays or periods of illness (Figure 1.1). The intense experience of reading imaginative literature when at your most vulnerable gives a special flavour to chosen books. If tired or ill, women return to familiar novels. Jane S says that when under the weather she goes to bed with

Georgette Heyer. Linda B is disabled and in great pain, but says that when reading fiction she becomes so engrossed that she feels less pain and forgets her troubles. When Crysse M has flu, she rereads *'Pride and Prejudice, A Passage to India* and *The Code of the Woosters*. If it's really bad, *House at Pooh Corner'*. Polina M was hospitalized for four days and got through long days and nights with *Jane Eyre*: 'I must have read the marriage proposal scene a hundred times!' Shelley H remembers being sent to hospital with her baby son when he came down with chicken pox at a tender age: 'I rang my husband to have him bring some necessities for me—a toothbrush and [Sarah Waters'] *Fingersmith* being top of the list. In between feeding the baby and talking to the doctors I'd escape into Victorian London. It kept me sane.' The Sarah Waters a woman reads by her son's hospital bedside will hold very different meanings from those of a reader who takes it on holiday for a relaxing beach read. Each work of fiction takes a different shape in the hands of its specific reader, and satisfies our need for escape, comfort, solace, or inspiration in different circumstances. Over the years, scholars have debated the question of whether a novel exists in the writer's words on the page or only in particular readers' imaginations. As different testimonies show, fiction engages hearts and minds at many levels, allowing us to draw on those narratives to create or enhance our own stories.

But there are times when reading is impossible—a reminder of the power of story to disturb and unsettle. Humorist Maureen Lipman wrote that when her husband Jack Rosenthal died, she stopped reading fiction: 'My imagination died with him. I was always such a reader . . . *She's always got her nose in a book*, my mother repeated, as though it was an affliction she had to bear . . . Only now I had my nose in a box of tissues, and real life was stranger than any fiction.'[5] My correspondent Marie B stopped reading after her divorce and mother's death, while Sarah H found she couldn't cope with complex books when her father was very ill and her grandmother dying. On these occasions, she read *Sweet Valley High* and *Alice in Wonderland*. Helen G found reading too difficult in her mother's last days in hospital and after the death: 'Books were something we always shared and it was just too painful to read.' A good friend of mine, never without a book, sat at her husband's hospital bedside following his stroke, for weeks on end miserably unable to read a word. Depression calls for no reading or particular writers (Patrick O'Brien helped Olivia R through a bad patch). By contrast, some women say they don't read much when things are going well or they're in celebratory mood; reading is perhaps associated with quiet reflection, times of problem or crisis. Rosie J, who used to be a voracious reader, now finds she is far more selective: 'The big moments have happened without books.'

How Do Women Select Fiction and What's On Your Bedside Table?

So how does a woman, of whatever age, class, sexual, racial, or ethnic identity, choose her fiction? Does she buy books from bookshops, supermarkets, or online companies like Amazon? Does she use libraries, and how would she feel if her local library closed down (as so many have already done)? And does she read fast or slowly, re-read precious books, and sneak a look at the ending before starting out?

These questions must be seen within the context of those publishing, distribution, marketing, and reviewing industries that create and support readerships. The rise of the novel is also a history of publishing houses, bookshops, private and public libraries, publicity and PR, school and college set reading, book prizes, literary journals, newspaper reviews, and more. Readers select fiction mainly according to availability, price, and the critical and commercial profile of particular books and writers, though there are still ways in which enterprising readers discover new or forgotten fiction without prompting. Through my research, I gained insights into where twenty-first-century women go for literary inspiration. Generations differ. Young women read Young Adult fiction or a certain amount of romance and crime, while in their twenties and thirties women seem to choose more 'literary' novels; from their forties onwards there's a tendency for short fiction and old favourites, as well as non-fiction and some poetry.

Women select fiction from a wide range of sources. What most of my readers are looking for is a strong narrative, memorable and believable characters, and a strong sense of place—including vivid descriptions of landscape, cityscape, exotic locations, and domestic interiors. Apart from word of mouth, they follow media recommendations (radio interviews, TV profiles, magazine and newspaper reviews), and a few women read more specialist literary journals such as the *Times Literary Supplement, London Review of Books, Nudge Books*, and so on. Heather Wright said she 'garnered from eclectic sources including Radio 4, TLS, friends' recommendations, TV adaptations, reviews, cinema, bibliographies'. We know that any screen or TV version of a novel—be it the Poldark series or *Girl with a Pearl Earring*—instantly bumps up book sales and library borrowings, and increasingly writers and their publishers have an eye to lucrative media tie-ins. There are numerous online bloggers, sites, and magazines to help you choose—theliteraryaddict, BookBub, The Book People, The Happy Reader, Mslexia, For Books' Sake, Booktube, The Killer Women Crime Club, bookshop and publishers' email recommendations, and fan sites.

In recent years, with the rising influence of social media and individual blogspots, a democratization (some would call dumbing-down) of literary criticism has meant there's a bewildering variety of views about fiction available to very large audiences. Readers exchange ideas on Twitter, Facebook, and Mumsnet. Book prizes have a huge influence (sales increasing as soon as a book hits the shortlist), and the book clubs run by Oprah Winfrey in the US and Richard and Judy in the UK have made a great impact. There is an informal canon of writers and novels that are popular with and circulated around reading groups, often encouraged by librarians and booksellers (Julian Barnes, Helen Dunmore, Victoria Hislop, Ian McEwan, Zadie Smith, *Captain Corelli's Mandolin, Trumpet*, and so on). Book covers are important, and Penelope K details her own criteria: 'spine, title, cover design, then details on the back and reading of small sections inside'. Annie D goes by recommended lists on Amazon or in newspapers, especially Books of the Year each Christmas, as well as book exchanges on holiday.

In order to get a picture of women's current reading, I asked which books or other publications are on their bedside or coffee tables. And although most claim to read fiction more than anything, they describe an impressive variety of texts lying around their homes (usually in bedrooms), in their handbags, on tablets, or in other nooks and crannies. The Bible and other religious or spiritual works, seed catalogues, cookery books, women's magazines, political journals, biographies, and travel guides jostle together with poetry collections,

Sunday supplements, *Private Eye*, and much more. Here are some examples:

> Linda E: Currently reading Hilary Mantel's *Wolf Hall* and slowly making my way through *Clarissa*. I have the most recent issue of *Tatler* on the go, too.

> Amy W: Ian M. Banks (in my handbag), Rutherford, *London* (beside bed), Star Trek fan fiction (iPad), Cool Knits for Kids (living room).

> Stef B: A couple of Scandinavian detective novels, *The Complete Works of D. H. Lawrence*, Barbara Castle's memoir, Andrew Marr's *The Making of Modern Britain*, and a book of Somerset walks.

> Lynda R: P. D. James, *Death Comes to Pemberley* and Anne Tyler's *Beginner's Goodbye* (our next book circle reads). Don Paterson's edition of Shakespeare's *Sonnets* and various yoga magazines and quarterly bulletins. A biography of Rupert Brooke.

> Laura R: Mervyn Peake's *Titus Groan*, Joan Didion, *The Year of Magical Thinking*, Mikey Walsh, *Gypsy Boy on the Run*, George R. R. Martin, *A Game of Thrones*, Pat Barker, *Regeneration*, and a *BBC Wildlife* magazine.

> Claire M: *Gravity's Rainbow* (started and put aside), a Lee Child, *Eat, Pray, Love*, Codeword Magazine. On landing windowsill *Tipping the Velvet* 'casually re-reading while appearing not', on coffee table cookery books and 1959 Federation of Women's Institutes 'Home-made wines, syrups and cordials'.

> Jean P: *Alex's Adventures in Numberland* by Alex Bellos, *A Rival Creation* by Marika Cobbold, and *Step by Step Veg Patch* by Lucy Hassall. The latest issue of *English Bridge* and an old issue of *Gardener's World* magazine.

> Jennifer L: [on my Kindle] lots of Sarah Waters, George Orwell, Oscar Wilde, Stella Duffy, Victorian true crime/detection and books on programming and vet science.

These very different lists—some fairly highbrow, others a mixture of comfort reading and practical information—are typical of the variety of women's reading. A mixture of fiction and non-fiction, muddled up with other kinds of publication, testifies to different routes to eclectic knowledge. Often my correspondents describe following the lead of fiction into historical and political fields. Sian N (like many others) explored Tudor history after devouring the novels of Philippa Gregory and Hilary Mantel, and Lucy H researched the Biafran wars as a result of reading *Half of a Yellow Sun*. Following her reading group's discussion of the plight of Palestinian refugees in Susan Abulhawa's *Mornings in Jenin*, they investigated and then sponsored education work in the area.

You may wonder why I am confining my discussions to fiction, when many women have a poetry book near to hand. And it's true that some women read poetry with the enthusiasm they have for fiction. However, sadly, many women told me that school classes put them off poetry, and/or they find it too difficult and rather frightening. Poet and broadcaster Michael Rosen confirmed this when he said people experience poetry in education as 'a series of mild humiliations'.[6] We know that—despite the high profile of recent Poet Laureates Andrew Motion and Carol Ann Duffy, and the rise of younger performance poets—poetry sales are small and poets struggle to make a living. It seems that the fear of not being able to understand a poem is much greater than that of misinterpreting or losing the plot of a novel or short story. And yet, ironically, one of the key elements in women's passion for fiction is an appreciation of poetic language within that genre, and a love of imagery and symbolism in writers (often both poets and novelists) from Emily Brontë to Chimamanda Ngozi Adichie, D. H. Lawrence to Michael Ondaatje.

In those bedside table descriptions, I was struck by the gender balance of choices. Women read and admire male novelists, and few make distinctions between the two. Their coffee tables and bedrooms abound with novels by both genders. However, I recall a series of *Guardian* accounts of their favourite and most revered books by eighteen key published writers, most of whom cited a majority of novels by men. Salman Rushdie was a blatant masculinist example, with a depressingly familiar list: naming twelve male writers who had influenced him, he responded to the question 'The book I couldn't finish' by naming a book by a woman, George Eliot's *Middlemarch*: 'I know, I know. I'll try again.'[7]

Ironically, that novel is one of the most cited by my correspondents, the central female character resonating through many lives. Marion

G made her partner read *Middlemarch* as a way of getting to know her. Like Rushdie, he couldn't finish it, but she wanted him to understand how important this novel was to her. I believe Marion speaks for many other women in seeing herself in the character of Dorothea, 'idealistic, wanting to help, to make a difference, but not knowing how in her small world, also very stubborn of course and other wrong-headed things'. For Trudi L, the novel contains 'a whole world, insight into what it is to be human, plus political and social comment'. And in Lesley M's words, the novel expresses 'the depth of human dilemmas and themes of hope, ideals often unfulfilled, misguided passion for people or cause, disappointment, despair. Poor Dorothea!' Even though George Eliot portrays a whole society through many complex male and female characters, it is Dorothea who is most referenced by my correspondents. As with plain Jane Eyre, women are drawn to this flawed and undistinguished character who seems to give voice to our dreams while embodying our human weaknesses.

Disappearing Bookshops and Libraries

So where do women buy or borrow books? Annie D, whom I quoted earlier, follows Amazon and media recommendations, and at times claims to 'go to a section in a bookshop, close my eyes and put my hand on a book (always seems to work)'.

But closing eyes in a bookshop looks set to become an increasingly rare experience. Outside major cities, most people don't live near a good bookshop, and must rely on the limited middle-brow range of W. H. Smith and the supermarkets. Although there remain some outstanding independent and second-hand shops in large cities, small towns such as Penarth, and book towns Hay on Wye and Wigtown (with a small increase in 2018), the direction of bookselling is towards larger national and international groups. Indeed, despite some signs of resurgence in recent years, the decline of the small and independent village or town shop is a source of considerable anguish among my correspondents. Claire H regretted that Amazon's 'Other Books you might Enjoy' didn't compare to 'a bookseller chatting to you'. Ann and David Willmore, the owners of a small bookshop in Fowey, Cornwall, told me that women enjoyed consulting them on what to read, and took advice on writers, asking which were *their* favourite books; men hastened in, headed for (usually) the non-fiction section and didn't chat. Marion W deplored the closure of her local bookshops: 'I enjoy selecting real books from real shelves and the experience of "browsing" . . . and in second-hand bookshops the experience of coming across the undiscovered or the long forgotten.' Independent shops are compared with places of worship ('the calm, the quiet, the slightly musty smell'). But while some offer refreshments and comfortable sofas, the pleasure of sweet treats and reading—a connection I've already shown to be important in our lives—is better catered for in those larger stores such as Waterstones where you can linger around books in a designated café and buy discounted books that independents (alas) can't afford to offer.

It's not uncommon to hear women say they browse bookshops or displays at literature festivals, then—to save money—order from the library or Amazon. Some women frequent online shops such as AbeBooks, ReaditSwapit and Green Metropolis. Owning book collections is often a matter of pride, and the objects themselves give great pleasure. Jeannie F told me she preferred to buy books because she makes notes in margins, underlines things and turns back pages to remind her to return to passages:

> I know some people will cringe at this, but if you genuinely see books as friends that are to be referred to again and again, then you need to have a conversation with those friends and, for me, that means leaving notes and reminders about what you thought the last time you 'talked'. I think an unmarked book is sterile—and I love it when I find a book that someone else has annotated, because then the conversation becomes three-way, and I can see how the other person has thought about the book.

The cost of books is something to which many women are sensitive, and helps explain the popularity of charity shops and car-boot sales, especially for crime and other genre fiction which tends to be in good supply. Some of these—like the Amnesty bookshops in various cities—have taken over many of the roles of the (closed) libraries, with kids' areas, community meetings, and people popping in daily to check out new stock. Everyone is aware of the fragility of the independent book sector and—in an ominous sign that bookshops are entering the territories of nostalgia and museum—there is a plethora of films and novels dedicated to them, from Helene Hanff's *84, Charing Cross Road* (1970, film 1987) and Penelope Fitzgerald's *The Bookshop* (1978, film 2017) to Asne Seierstand's *The Bookseller of Kabul* (2002), Nina George's *The Little Paris Bookshop* (2015), and Susan Orlean's *The Library Book* (2018).

Small women's bookshops flourished at different periods—in London alone, the Virago shop, Silver Moon, and Persephone. While the first two have gone the way of other independents, a new feminist and rare book store opened in Soho in 2018.[8] And in Lamb's Conduit Street, London, the elegant Persephone Bookshop (also a publishing house) thrives and is even a tourist destination. Championing what its owner Nicola Beauman calls 'neglected classics', Persephone reprints fiction and non-fiction by mid-twentieth-century (mostly) women writers such as their first bestseller, Winifred Watson's *Miss Pettigrew Lives for a Day* (1938), or Dorothy Whipple's *Someone at a Distance* (1953) and E. M. Delafield's *Diary of a Provincial Lady* (1930). Most of the 125 books (listed by number, 'as in a Chinese restaurant menu', as Beauman says) are jacketed in elegant timeless grey—with an additional twelve 'Persephone Classics' bearing colourful illustrated covers. All their gorgeous books have endpapers drawn from fabric designs, and are printed in Germany with 'dispersion binding'—a form of book production ensuring you can open the book fully so it can be read while eating, cooking, or holding a toddler in your arms. The majority of their books are sold via mail order, with a biannual newsletter and catalogue, and Christmas gift packages. Their target reader is 'a woman who comes home tired from work, and there is a book waiting for her, and . . . she knows she will enjoy it' (a description echoed by online club Reading in Heels). The Bloomsbury shop embodies the emphasis of all their books on the idea of 'home', creating a jumbled and artfully untidy middle-class feminine space with fabrics, pot pourri, soft lamps, posters, and vases of flowers. On one table is a swatch of fabric for sale, with a label suggesting: 'To be used as a scarf or a napkin or a muslin for a baby to be sick on' (Figure 1.2). When I visited, a customer asked if she could pull up her tights in the shop (she could).[9]

The scarcity of good independent bookshops is one thing. But the importance of *libraries* was stressed by almost every woman who shared her reading memories with me. Geraldine N wrote:

Figure 1.2 Persephone bookshop, London
Photo by Lydia Fellgett. By permission of Persephone Books

> Without siblings and few children in our street, books became my
> friends very early on . . . I was allowed to join the library and visited
> every Saturday morning. Receiving a postcard on the morning of my
> wedding day saying a reserved book was now ready for collection,
> I walked into the town centre to collect it because I was reluctant to
> leave it there while on honeymoon, and was still only fashionably five
> minutes late for my wedding at 11 o'clock!

Virginia Woolf's coruscating critique of women's exclusion from
'Oxbridge' lawns and libraries underlines the importance of our
access to books and thus knowledge. She remains the writer who has
expressed most eloquently women's vital relationship with fiction, as
well as celebrating many neglected women writers in her essays. In *A
Room of One's Own* (1928), she provided what novelist Kate Mosse
summarized as the twentieth century's 'most significant statements
on the question of women and writing', with 'its brilliant interweaving
of personal experience, imaginative musing and political clarity'. Like
other feminist critics, Mosse notes that while Woolf exhorts women
writers not to allow anger to distort the integrity of their work, 'the
essay itself bristles with anger' at the way women are discriminated

against and patronized.[10] Woolf writes as both woman writer and woman reader—because to forbid a woman a room of her own, and to exclude women readers from the library, is also to restrict women writers' access to the research material, knowledge, and dignity they need as artists. Anuradha Roy describes the qualities many of us treasure about libraries:

> [F]or their scent of old pages, for the shared solitude, for the alleys between racks where we wander from physics to geography and lose ourselves in fiction . . . if we never needed libraries because nobody read any more, we would still mourn their loss as we mourned stone Buddhas in an Afghan desert, forgotten until they were destroyed.[11]

Woolf's anger and Roy's encomium speak for countless female reader-writers about these special places. I'll return to libraries in Chapter 2.

The Habits of Reading

So how do the practices and habits of reading function in women's lives? To my surprise, not many women claimed to be (as I am) slow readers—perhaps because this sounds like readerly failure. But many did admit to not finishing novels, and re-reading—for comfort—novels that had pleased them in the past. Even though many have a certain conscientiousness about books and loyalty to the writer, dozens of women justified abandoning books that bored or failed to engage them: 'Life's too short,' they said, 'too many books and not enough time', although it seemed to be older women who were most willing to let go. 'When younger, I felt I owed the book and author an obligation to read to the end,' said Marion W, who in her seventies no longer felt guilty about giving up. Many women struggle through twenty to thirty pages before deciding whether to carry on, though Julie P perseveres until the point she wants to throw the book across the room. Books abandoned include Thomas Pynchon's novels, A. S. Byatt's *Possession*, 'the odd Martin Amis through irritation', and David C. Mitchell's *Cloud Atlas* (the latter abandoned by *all* of one reading group).

And women feel free to move around a book rather than reading from beginning to final page, demonstrating an active engagement with the work. They take a fairly cavalier approach to novels and sneak peeks at endings for many reasons. Although one woman echoed my own feeling that such peeking 'is like opening a Christmas present before Christmas Day', another confessed she turns to the final page because she's increasingly unable to handle nasty things happening to characters with whom she identifies ('but I recognize this as immature and wimpish'). Rebecca K reads the last couple of pages of a crime novel to see which characters make it to the end: 'My friend says it's because I find it difficult to commit to a character who is going to die. I just think I'm impatient.' Rosie O flicks to them 'often just to reassure myself that the good guy is still there at the end!'

The question of e-book versus real book remains a live issue. Julian Barnes claimed the e-reader would never completely supplant the physical book since each book you read feels and looks different, while Kindle download feels and looks exactly the same. He suggests, however, that the e-reader may one day 'contain a "smell" function, which you will click to make your electronic Dickens novel suddenly reek of damp paper, fox-marks and nicotine'.[12] Statistically, as I write, tablet downloading has flat-lined, while purchase of fiction books has increased (though, as I've pointed out, e-books are widely read on phones and this will certainly increase among younger readers). My correspondents, across generations, are pragmatic; they value the Kindle as a 'portable treasure chest' (Martha v.d.L) and take Kindles to hospital appointments or on holiday because of luggage space and weight restrictions. One woman who works cruise ships noticed how common they were on board. Kindles and iPads, with their flexible fonts, are carried when commuting to work or college, and are handy when reading erotic and other books women don't wish others to know about. Sharon F said: 'If people can't see the cover, it makes me more prepared to read things like Mills & Boon.' Women compare e-readers with functional emails as opposed to personal letters, and downloaded music compared with collectable vinyl records; and they are aware how much of their lives are already lived in front of screens.

However, responding to my question, 'Would it matter if books disappeared and we all read on Kindles?', a large number of women—of all ages—became emotional about their attachment to the book, expressing alarm at the idea of books disappearing in favour of digital readers. They comment (despite Julian Barnes' predictions!) that the feel, smell, and substance of a book can't be replicated, and that e-readers don't allow you to flip to and fro, use a pencil in margins, or employ a bookmark. As Claire M put it, 'Batteries die, readers freeze. Spill coffee on a book and it will dry out, spill on a Kindle and that's £80 gone.' Many women complain that e-reading— lacking a book cover, blurb, pages to flick through quickly—often leads them to forget the name of the book itself, the characters and the story. Hilary D (57) said I might well ask whether it would matter if real food were replaced by nutritionally balanced milkshakes: 'But just as NBMs have their place for the sick, the very young or the very old, Kindles have a place in the reading world. On [a] crowded train to Waterloo, principally.' The response of Lisa W (34) was more robust:

> It would matter terribly. No one would put away a box of treasured books in the hope their children would one day love them too. No one would have the thrill of turning the pages of the same book as their mother, father, grand- parent. No one would collect first editions. No one would press the first flowers or letters sent by their lover between the pages of a Kindle. No one would scribble in their Kindle. No bus, train or plane passenger would strike up a conversation with a stranger based on what they are reading . . . No old soldier would tell the story of how the Kindle in their pocket stopped the bullet, blade or piece of shrapnel that would have killed them.

Next I asked how many resort to re-reading cherished books. Not surprisingly, answers related very much to women's comfort zones. A large number have re-read childhood and middlebrow favorites— Enid Blyton, Charles Dickens, Thomas Hardy, The Moomins, *Wind in the Willows*, *Wuthering Heights*, *The Great Gatsby*, *Jamaica Inn*, *Diary of a Nobody*, Dorothy Whipple, Margaret Drabble, M. R. James, Rumer Godden (whose *The Greengage Summer* was described by broadcaster Harriet Gilbert as 'the most erotic book ever').[13] Janice J named Maeve Binchy and Agatha Christie 'for post-flu type days' and another respondent said: 'At the beginning of my bereavement I went back to "safe" books which I knew would not challenge or upset me: Ellis Peter's Cadfael books, Georgette Heyer, Elizabeth Goudge, Alexander McCall Smith.' Terms like 'old friends' and 'comfort food'—those signifiers of early female friendships and mother's cooking—recur to

Figure 1.3 'Amaryllis and Henrietta', 1952, Vanessa Bell
© Estate of Vanessa Bell, courtesy Henrietta Garnett / Bridgeman Images

remind us how valuable books can be in the stories of our lives when things get too much and we feel at our most vulnerable (Figure 1.3).

'Woman Writer—Man Writer'

I've already noted the catholic tastes of women readers—from heterogeneous lists of book group choices to novels named in my questionnaires. They read male and female fiction alike, and are often startled when I ask whether they choose or prefer books according to a writer's gender. Women claim to read fiction by men just as much as by women, though if you scratch the surface, or go through reading groups' lists, you find there's often a preponderance of titles by women. Indeed, in 2014, a survey of 40,000 readers found that most readers read fiction by writers of their own gender.[14] And there are certain novels that have become cult favourites among women, passed on and often ensuring bestseller status for their authors: Barbara Kingsolver's *The Poisonwood Bible*, Alice Walker's *The Color Purple*, and all the works of Kate Atkinson and JoJo Moyes.

Certainly, the publishing and marketing industries make very clear distinctions. You only have to look wearily at the persistence of the term 'woman writer', while the normative, universal 'man writer' seems a comical notion. Lennie Goodings, now chair of Virago Press, has said that while 'poetess' and 'authoress' have disappeared, 'woman writer' is still very much with us. (Though there are still exceptions to that; a recent plaque on a house in Bristol's Windsor Terrace celebrates the residence there of 'authoress' Hannah More). Whole genres of writing by women have been named with female readers in mind, from the romantic novel to the Aga Saga, 'Mummy porn', 'chick-' or 'hen-lit', 'clit-lit', 'chick noir', 'Up-Lit' (feel-good novels by women, exemplified in *Eleanor Oliphant is Completely Fine*, 2017) and 'YA' (Young Adult, increasingly signifying writing for adolescent girls). As Goodings has pointed out, male genre writing—crime, adventure, SAS, sci-fi—is never called 'men's writing'—and I can think of no diminutives referring to these.

Paradoxically, while read avidly by women readers, *women's writing* has always been reviewed, acclaimed, and discussed far less than that of men. Danuta Kean's 2019 report, 'Are You Serious? The Emelia Report into the Gender Gap for Authors',[15] demonstrated that male writers received 12 per cent more reviews than women, and that women's ages and domestic circumstances were referenced far more than men's. Feminist critics and journalists frequently comment on the casual disregard shown to the world's finest women writers within many genres. For example, critic Rachel Cooke complained about the 'relative obscurity' of novelist Tessa Hadley, suggesting 'she is likely just another victim of a literary culture that tends to prize the male over the female, the grandly thematic over the so-called domestic.'[16] This is not simply a British phenomenon. In an angry diatribe, American novelist Meg Wolitzer railed against the bias towards male fiction by reviewers, prize awards, male readers, and distributors like Amazon—all lumping together women's fiction as if it were a single genre: '[T]he top tier of literary fiction—where the air is rich and the view is great and where a book enters the public imagination and the current conversation—tends to feel peculiarly, disproportionately male.'[17] Nonetheless, she also acknowledged the popularity of women's writing in reading groups, and the envy by some male writers of the 'attentive and passionate . . . femaleness' of the novel-reading and -buying community. Fortuitously, a male novelist joined in. Perhaps mindful of V. S. Naipaul's view that no woman writer could be considered his equal, John Boyne claimed that—in his view (one that would get him kicked out of the 'Fraternity of Underappreciated Male Authors (FUMA)'—women are better writers than men, but overlooked by male readers and badly under-valued.[18] In Joyce Carol Oates' words, 'the woman who writes is a writer by her own definition, but a "woman writer" by others' definitions.'[19]

Although there are many disadvantages to this ongoing discrimination, for female *readers* there is a big plus. Women can enjoy sharing those designated-female genres, and claim women writers as our own, identify with them, and most of all buy their books, read them and pass on the word. *A Room of One's Own* has iconic status among women writers and readers partly because of a witty, informal style that makes women feel we are being addressed in a language and tone that include and embrace, rather than intimidate and exclude. The Orange (now Women's) Prize was established as a way of addressing the literary establishment's indifference to women's writing, as was actress Emma Watson's online feminist book club, Our Shared Shelf. Together with feminist presses, women's writing magazines and webzines such as Mslexia and For Books' Sake, The Women's Prize is a way of cocking a snook at the Beadle who forbade Woolf's 'Mary Beton/Seton/Carmichael' and all other women from walking on the college turf and into the university library.

'Avalanche Love'

Women readers keep the flame burning. For those in their forties upwards, there is a group of favourite women writers from childhood and adolescence, beginning with figures such as Louisa M. Alcott, Susan Coolidge, Daphne du Maurier, Georgette Heyer, and Jilly Cooper. There are then the adult choices of Jane Austen, Charlotte and Emily Brontë, George Eliot, Kate Chopin, Virginia Woolf, and Doris Lessing (whose *The Golden Notebook* remains one of the most resonant novels for many a reader). In contemporary times and among younger readers, novels by women popular with reading groups and passed around female friendship circles include Jeanette Winterson's *Oranges Are Not the Only Fruit* (1985), Toni Morrison's

Beloved (1987), Gillian Flynn's *Gone Girl* (2012), and the four volumes of Elena Ferrante's Neapolitan novels (2012–15). That huge female readerly mentorship, from grandmothers, mothers, and sisters to female booksellers, librarians, and English teachers, have shared reading passions with younger women because they know how precious fiction by women is to female identity and self-confidence. That said, as we've seen since the eighteenth century, such guidance has also operated as a form of censorship, keeping girls away from what their guardians and teachers defined as unsuitable or morally dubious texts (usually of a sexual nature).

In *How to be a Heroine*, Samantha Ellis sees reading as a life-saver in a patriarchal world. Fiction reading has been crucial in her formation of self, choice of career, lovers, hair colour, and much else. For her, the heroines created by predominantly female novelists save her from feeling 'undefined, formless, [with] no narrative arc, no quest, no journey'. Novels such as Lucy Maud Montgomery's *Anne of Green Gables* (1908) and Shirley Conran's *Lace* (1982) showed her the importance of *work* and gave her permission to be a writer, and Emily Brontë's *Wuthering Heights* encouraged her to settle for nothing less than 'intensity . . . avalanche love'. Her main conclusion is that this heroinical reading taught her 'I wanted to write my own life.'[20] In his comic novel, *The Uncommon Reader*, Alan Bennett imagines the Queen of England transformed into a passionate reader and then deciding to abdicate in favour of being a writer, observing as she does, '"You don't put your life into your books. You find it there."'[21] Of course, for some men reading undoubtedly has that power, but it's rare to find them expressing as strongly as women the ways fiction reading has impacted on their emotional, spiritual, and sexual lives.

Lennie Goodings told me she 'wonders if men are not curious about women or if it's that they are anxious about connecting to fiction by women'—a wise nuanced view suggesting male insecurity about, rather than indifference or hostility to, women's writing. Novelist Sarah Dunant argues that men don't wish to exercise their emotional imaginations as much as women, and that fiction allows women an all-important emotional imaginative space. John Boyne agrees, arguing that women's historically subservient role has 'made them understand human nature more clearly' and 'have a better grasp of human complexity' including having a 'pretty good idea of what's going on in men's heads most of the time [while men] haven't got a clue what's going on in women's'.[22] His point is about women *writers*, but the same can apply to readers. As Dawn R-W put it, 'Reading fiction is like people-watching.'

This link between human understanding and communication is recognized by The Reading Agency, a nationwide organization with the motto 'Because everything changes when we read'; its aim to inspire people of all ages and backgrounds to read 'for pleasure and empowerment'. Offering a range of programmes—'Reading Ahead', 'Reading Friends', and so on—it supports the annual World Book Night on 23 April, when books are given to non-readers to help them get started. This agency, based on a belief in the power of reading to help with confidence, tackle the symptoms of dementia, and boost mood, operates largely in libraries with volunteers who run small reading groups with specially selected material. Another organization, The Reader, has pioneered the idea of 'shared reading' to 'improve well-being, reduce social isolation and build resilience in diverse communities across the UK and beyond'. Led by volunteers, reading groups are set up in libraries, hospitals, prisons, and schools, where the best literature is read aloud in an uncompetitive environment. The success of this method—making reading part of ordinary life—has led to commissions from NHS trusts and other organizations wanting humane and rehabilitative therapy. Although both The Reading Agency and The Reader work hard to involve both genders, the majority of volunteers and participants are women. This isn't surprising, given women are the main 'joiners' in our society, but it's also a measure of how much women recognize the emotional value of reading stories.

With similar aims, self-styled 'bibliotherapists' Ella Berthoud and Susan Elderkin, who believe in the restorative power of reading fiction, published a book clearly targeted at women readers offering 'fictional plasters and poultices' to transform and comfort lives at particular times. Following Victorian publications offering conduct guides, and the self-help books of our own times, *The Novel Cure: An A–Z of Literary Remedies* offers witty therapeutic advice to readers such as (among many others) 'Brontë to re-boot your Broken Heart... Austen to curb your Arrogance ... an injection of du Maurier for your low Self-Esteem'.[23] Bookseller Jean Perdu, in Nina George's *The Little*

Paris Bookshop, acts as a 'literary apothecary' to soothe his customers' troubled breasts. And in recent years, psychologists David Comer Kidd and Emanuele Castano of the New School for Social Research, New York, claim to have proved by scientific tests that reading literary fiction (defined as having aesthetic qualities and character development rather than plot-led genre or pulp fiction) enhances people's ability to understand and empathize with others. In novelist Barbara Kingsolver's memorable words, 'literature sucks you into another psyche'.[24]

'Attentive Love'

Exercising our emotional imaginations means women share wide-ranging reading tastes—from the critically celebrated Jane Austen, constantly topping polls for people's favourite novelist and novel with *Pride and Prejudice* (1813), to E. L. James, the critically damned but commercially bestselling author of the erotic trilogy *Fifty Shades of Grey* (2011–12) and later sequels, that has hit a nerve with millions of contemporary women readers. Even though they have male admirers, both Austen and James are especially dear to women readers, and both writers are aware of the importance, and potential dangers, of reading for women. In *Northanger Abbey* Austen famously satirized the Gothic novel and its impact on immature girls, and with her reference to Fordyce's Sermons in *Pride and Prejudice*, mocked conduct books aimed at young women. E. L. James uses Thomas Hardy's *Tess of the d'Urbervilles* as both a warning sign and romantic link between Anastasia Steele and Christian Grey. And, like poor Catherine Morland (also sounding suspiciously like Gustave Flaubert's Madame Bovary), first-person narrator Ana Steele reflects: 'Sometimes I wonder if there's something wrong with me. Perhaps I've spent too long in the company of my literary romantic heroes, and consequently my ideals and expectations are far too high.'[25] On the other hand, a remarkable number of novels by women feature the reading by girls or women as an inspirational or subversive power. In the works of Ann Radcliffe, Susan Warner, and George Eliot, reading well and sharing ideas derived from that solitary practice are a measure of female maturity and good sense, and honourable men respond accordingly. *Pride and Prejudice*'s Mr Darcy gave Samantha Ellis the delightful message that 'real men liked bookish girls'.[26] In Anna Bush's 2018 Man Booker Prizewinning *Milkman*, however, we see how threatening a modern reading woman can be; the protagonist's habit of 'reading-while-walking' (nineteenth-century novels only) marks her out to her community as both weird and potentially seditious.

But increasingly women are bold and demanding readers. Not content with one helping of a favourite dish, we demand and gobble down numerous second helpings, as devotees of sequels, rewritings, companion novels, fanfic, and parodies of all the Jane Austen canon, *Great Expectations, Gone With the Wind,* and *Rebecca*. The desire to wrap ourselves in a particular writer's imaginative world that will go on and on (something children also adore) explains women's enthusiasm for more servings of a literary dish. This may explain the successful trend for self-publishing, which hit a nerve with young adult and mature readers alike, taking aback the whole publishing industry (as with *Fifty Shades*—see Chapter 4).

The Bond between Women Readers and Women Writers

As I've said, women don't simply read fiction by women—indeed, as Ian McEwan has pointed out, where would male novelists be without us? But there is a special bond, a mutual loyalty, between women writers and readers. Popular novelist Marian Keyes expressed a view many women have shared with me. Claiming she reads books almost exclusively by women, she said: 'I read to find out how other humans think and feel, and it's no trouble to discover the male take on life—their voices and opinions dominate our media.'[27] Feminist presses such as Persephone which publish a majority of books by women have responded to a felt need. Since 1978, the Virago Modern Classics series has provided hungry women readers with a diet of neglected and out of print texts that have helped reshape women's understanding of themselves and our literary heritage. Lennie Goodings claims there is a close and passionate relationship between Virago's writers and readers, with women feeling they 'own' the publishing house. She is told everywhere she goes how much Virago changed women's lives, even rescuing some from terrible isolation and unhappiness simply by giving them a wide range of women's voices. 'I think we get far more response from readers than other publishers, because people know women run it and that we're representing and publishing women's hidden voices . . . We take women seriously [and] Virago has a big fan base.'[28] This was also the case with other small feminist presses in the 1970s, and many women described to me the treasures on their bookshelves: yellowing and much-thumbed novels from Pandora, Onlywomen Press, Sheba, and The Women's Press, as well as American presses such as Herbooks, Shameless Hussy, and Kitchen Table: Women of Color. These feminist publishers were largely responsible for introducing British readers to diverse minority voices from around the world—relatively unknown, non-white, lesbian, and working-class writers such as Zora Neale Hurston, Maxine Hong Kingston, and Louise Erdrich from the US, Ama Ata Aidoo from Ghana, and Suniti Namjoshi from India. The rise of women's studies courses in adult and higher education created new readers—women teachers and academics—who went on to transform the curricula in schools and colleges, opening students' eyes to hitherto neglected or out of print writers. Larger publishers were quick to jump on the bandwagon, and the demise of feminist presses testifies both to changing financial pressures in publishing but also to their success in moving women's writing into the mainstream.

When I asked Judy Finnigan, of the Richard and Judy Book Club, about all the loving allusions to women writers in her first novel, *Eloise*, she compared her choices with female friendship:

> I find the books I love the most are written by women. I think women and men want very different things from fiction. Richard and I do our Book Club and we have to agree on books to include, but there are always some books I feel more impressed by and passionate about, and others Richard will, and they're not usually the same, though we can both recognize very good writing. I think that—similar to female friendship—in a good, well-written woman's book you can recognize the universal experience.

Judy later told me she believes women read more fiction than men because 'women lead such strong emotional inner lives . . . Women are profoundly reflective and emotional about their children and relationships and I think they gain much satisfaction from reading about the inner lives of other women.'[29] It is presumably no coincidence that, on a gender count of books recommended between 2004 and

2017 by the Richard and Judy Book Club, I found at least two-thirds of the authors were female. In recent years, the number of women writers has increased dramatically—perhaps an indication of Judy's greater influence or the Club's confidence in the popularity of women writers with its base of loyal women readers.

Female friendship is also a theme in Hilary Mantel's relationship with readers. Since the huge success of her Thomas Cromwell novels (*Wolf Hall, Bring Up the Bodies*), she is admired by both genders, and yet more female than male readers contact her about her writing (partly because of her memoir, *Giving Up the Ghost*, tracing the history of her endometriosis):

> What's remarkable is the freedom and informality of women's letters because they sit down and write to you as if you were a friend with whom they've slightly lost contact for a year or two. Men tell you their life stories as well but it's usually triggered by something in the book— something in their family or historical connections. But with women who write to me, the starting point is Thomas Cromwell, but then they write to me about their lives and insides.[30]

As the American writer Roxane Gay shrewdly argued: 'Male writers get treated as intellectuals, women writers get treated as friends.'[31] It may exasperate some women writers that they are seen as chums rather than cerebral creatures, but they also recognize that fiction plays an important emotional and therapeutic role in women's lives.

Wished-For Lives

The psychotherapist Adam Phillips suggests that we all learn to live 'somewhere between the lives we have and the lives we would like', and this seems a helpful way to describe women's responses to fiction. For Phillips, the story of our lives 'becomes the story of the lives we were prevented from living', and more important to us than our 'so-called lived lives' are the lives we live in fantasy, the more transgressive 'wished-for lives'.[32] Throughout history, the material constraints of women's lives have been countered by our imaginations, fed and nurtured in recent centuries by fiction. For many generations, women have taken their reading seriously and recorded it as part of their life story—keeping reading diaries, journals, meticulous notes on and quotations from works they've read. Singer-songwriter Tracey Thorn, suffering from flu over New Year, 2017–18, started a fresh page of her reading diary with 'notes and quotes. Some get a full page, others just a word of approval or otherwise...a great reminder of everything I read in 2017.' Penelope Lively describes the personal library a woman has on her shelves but also the 'virtual library in the head—the floating assemblage of fragments and images and impressions and information half-remembered that forms the climate of the mind, the distillation of reading experiences that makes each of us what we are'.[33]

More than ever before, diverse Western women have access to 'wished-for lives' through rooms of our own—literature classes in school and university open to girls and women as well as men, book groups where we can share wine and reading with our friends, literature festivals where we can indulge in a cream tea in a tent after buying signed copies from writers we've watched reading their work, and libraries, bookshops, and supermarkets where we can select reading for ourselves. And now there are virtual rooms of our own where we can chat online, share literary blogs, try out self-publishing, check writers' websites to find frequently asked questions, and thus feel part of a broad community of writers and readers.

What Their Books Yield or, Why I Am Not Buying a Kindle

Rosie Jackson

The carnation: a wedding buttonhole
pressed into sepia, wafer-thin,
between the pages of Gibbon's Decline and Fall.

Frayed edges of birthday cards, bus tickets,
black and white photos, torn Rizla, notes,
quotes copied out in his copperplate script.

A ribbon marking her favourite sonnet,
an oil stain where, impatient to know who did it,
he forgot to wash the grease from his hands.

This folded-over corner because here it was
her soul first quickened to poetry,
the hurried turning her hunger for the light.

That squiggle in the margin in *The End of the Affair*,
the asterisk, the tide mark where they walked on water,
the fervent pencilled full capitals *YES*!

So many pages opening like French windows
onto unexpected afternoons:
he reading out loud to himself,

she to the stranger just out of sight.
Their love of words, their cherished lines,
the imprint of their touch, their sleepless nights.

Rosie Jackson, from *The Light Box*
(Cultured Llama, 2016).

Int.1 Rosie Jackson at desk, surrounded by books
Gordon McKerrow

PART II

What Women Read

2

Reading as a Girl

*I cannot remember NOT being able to read. I believe it was aged four at
primary school. Taught by Miss Frisby, spinster of this parish, who always
wore long tweedy skirts. Was tall, dark blonde hair in a bun, very pale skin
with the longest fingers and coldest hands. (Years on, I was reminded of her
on seeing photos of Virginia Woolf.)*

Anonymous questionnaire

*When I was a child there was a large rambling bookshop in a beautiful
15th century building in the nearest town. When my Mum had to take us
shopping on the bus, she would leave me in this bookshop when she needed to
go to the bank or other errands. I was so happy to be able to wander the
children's section until she came back for me. The bookshop was over several
floors. In my mind it had bean bags for small readers and a cat that slept in
front of the empty fireplace. I think in heaven I might be back in my childhood,
in Ancient House free to browse a world of books yet to be discovered before it
closed and reopened as a branch of Lakeland Plastics!*

Lisa W

Of all the periods of our reading lives, childhood is undoubtedly the
most intense and vivid. If you're lucky enough to be a child who is
taught to read, introduced to books, has access to and falls in love with
them, you'll know how unique that experience is, and how invaluable
for the rest of your life. Reading as a child is special. In later life, rarely
do you completely forget where you are or what you should be doing,
while absorbed in a book. Never again do those images conjured up
by bedtime storytelling seem so overwhelming. How simple our reading seemed once, and how all-engrossing. Alas, in adulthood you
usually notice the world around you and are conscious you should
be chopping vegetables or checking your emails.

Figure 2.1 Mother and daughter sit on sofa in lounge reading book together
MBI / Alamy Stock Photo

We know that children acquire language and learn to read in different ways—not simply from words on the page read by parents or teachers. Children learn from food labels, street signs, TV and phone text, the McDonald's M sign. Carol Ann Duffy has said she taught herself to read by decoding *Alice in Wonderland* word by word. But children also weave together fragments from picture books, fairy stories, folk tales, Greek and Roman myths, readings from sacred books, and their own life experience, to imbue themselves with a knowledge and love of language, and to tell their own stories. Since the 1960s, the explosion of sophisticated illustrated children's books that tell stories through pictures (and often very few words) has given young readers new ways into the rules and delights of narrative.[1]

I've already argued that most women were taught to read by other women—grandmothers, mothers, sisters, librarians, and teachers (Figure 2.1). Although there are cases of male primary teachers and devoted fathers teaching girls to read (Wendy S described her father's 'Look, Say and Smack' with the Janet and John books, though other fathers took a less fierce approach), the overwhelming majority of my respondents, acquaintances, and friends report a female instructor.

Novelist Linda Grant is one of many women who recalled fondly the daily 'Listen With Mother' BBC radio programme for under-fives that ran from 1950 to 1982 with Daphne Oxenford's opening line, 'Are you sitting comfortably? Then I'll begin.'[2] Grandmothers with time on their hands, mothers who would read aloud at bedtime, a Sunday school or primary school teacher, a female lodger, a duo of mother and aunt reading to two sisters, swapping books and stories . . . time and again, women describe memories of that magical early learning process.

And it is full of tender memories. Kathy R sat on her mother's knee while she read aloud *Little Women* and both of them cried over the death of Beth March, while several correspondents recount weeping with female relatives over the beloved horse Black Beauty's witnessing the death of Ginger. At the end of Chekhov's *The Cherry Orchard*, Anya's words urging her mother to return soon capture well the longing many of us feel about reprising this intimate reading relationship: 'We'll read all sorts of books together, Mamma . . . We'll read during the long autumn evenings, we'll read lots of books, and a new wonderful world will open up before us.'[3]

At the heart of many early reading experiences (for men as well as women) is the process of reading aloud, and telling or reading the same story or book over and over. While I'm aware many children don't have this experience, for those who did, the practice of listening to and absorbing language and stories was the first step towards being avid readers themselves. In *Somewhere Towards the End*, writer and editor Diana Athill describes her maternal grandmother's reading aloud of the Bible, with its stories of Joseph, Shadrach, Meshach, and Abednego, and the nativity: '[T]hose stories are engraved in my imagination so deeply that they can't be erased by disbelief.'[4] Jane W sat on a carpet in the classroom while her teacher read aloud C. Day-Lewis' *The Otterbury Incident*, adding lots of different voices for the characters. Many of us have the voice of a woman or women reading in our heads as we recall that process of *hearing* stories (often many times) before being able to access them for ourselves. This memory may well explain why so many women re-read old favourites, and why audio books have become so popular in recent years— the latter now said by neuroscientists to be more engaging than film or TV.[5]

Women have long been responsible for the reading choices of girls, and so have created a tradition or canon of fiction that has a powerful hold on readers into adulthood. Girls used to receive books as school prizes (mainly chosen by female teachers), but they were also given books as birthday and Christmas presents—and we know who is mainly responsible for that shopping...Keen readers remember (even if rather fuzzily) those precious early books shared with women we loved and trusted, often at bedtime, when the words and images would linger in the imagination and encourage us to take control of our own reading. For generations of children, there was a gender divide in book choices: Jennings, Biggles, and Billy Bunter for boys, Susan Coolidge and Edith Nesbit for girls. Years ago, a (male) English teacher complained to me that boys who'd loved the *Just William* books stopped reading them when they learned that the author, Richmal Crompton, was a woman. Well into the twenty-first century, you'd expect a shift to cross-gender and -generational reading—and this has happened with a few writers, most notably J. K. Rowling. Novelist Susan Hill describes coming home late one night to find her two daughters, aged 23 and 15, and her husband, a good deal older, tucked up in bed all reading a Harry Potter.[6] But at a sell-out reading by Jacqueline Wilson in the huge Forum at Bath Children's Literature Festival, 2017, I was surrounded by young girls with female carers, hardly a boy in sight. When I asked a bookshop manager about gendered reading, he said writers and publishers were trying harder to target mixed readerships, but he conceded, 'Boys will always like their explosions.'

I expected to find a clear generational divide—women in their sixties enthusing over *The Famous Five* while younger women preferred *Matilda*. In fact, there is far more overlap than I'd imagined. Women in their twenties, thirties, and forties from very disparate backgrounds told me that—while enjoying contemporary writers such as Judy Blume, Philip Pullman, and Roald Dahl—they also loved those Victorian and Edwardian books of earlier generations: Louisa M. Alcott, *Little Women* (1868), Anna Sewell, *Black Beauty* (1877), Johanna Spyri, *Heidi* (1881), and Frances Hodgson Burnett, *The Secret Garden* (1911). The writer and humourist Caitlin Moran (b. 1975) was home-schooled and so able to read anything she chose. On her website she advises girls and young women not to read any books by men 'until you're older, and fully-formed, and battle-ready'. The books she lists follow a familiar pattern: '*The Railway Children, Jane Eyre, Ballet Shoes, What Katy Did, Gone with the Wind, Pride and Prejudice, To Kill a Mockingbird, I Capture the Castle* and, of course, *Little Women.*' Asked by *The Guardian* for her favourite book, she said: 'I owe everything I am to Jo March in *Little Women* and Anne Shirley in *Anne of Green Gables.*' She claimed she

> instinctively gravitated towards stories about girls, and women. Stories about their lives—struggling with money, wondering what their careers would be, reading books, learning skills, finding clothes that made them happy, learning how to have relationships with siblings, friends and parents, chafing against societal restrictions, getting angry about the injustices of a wider world. Grieving. Hoping. Carrying on.[7]

Women readers have passed on beloved books to granddaughters, daughters, and nieces, offering model characters and stories and creating an inter-generational reading community. Lynne Hatwell recalls a grandmother giving her Daphne du Maurier's *Jamaica Inn*, which Lynne calls 'my transitional', between reading as a girl and a grownup.[8]

Significantly, the majority are by white writers so—whether through availability or choice—women tended to give such fiction to young girls. And although writers of colour are now producing fiction reflecting the lives of the 32 per cent black and minority ethnic schoolchildren in the UK, a 2018 study of British children's books by the Centre for Literacy in Primary Education (CLPE) showed that only 1 per cent featured a black or minority ethnic main character, and a mere 4 per cent included BAME characters, usually on the margins.[9] Responding to the CLPE report, in December of that year the publisher Knights Of opened a pop-up children's bookshop in Brixton, featuring books with only BAME protagonists. It proved a huge commercial and cultural hit, with kids coming in saying 'Mum this is me, this is me!' As I write, there are crowdfunding plans to roll this out across the country.[10]

Predictably, white writers creating white characters dominated my correspondents' reading choices. Enid Blyton featured most, and individual titles (often translated into film or TV versions) recur; others include Charles Dickens' *Great Expectations* (1861), Beatrix Potter's animal stories, Arthur Ransome's *Swallows and Amazons* (1930), Dodie Smith's *I Capture the Castle* (1949), E. B. White's *Charlotte's Web* (1952), the thirty-nine *Just William* books, and all of Georgette Heyer. Helen Bannerman's once bestselling and very widely read *The Story of Little Black Sambo* (1899) is recalled by a few women, reminding me of my own childhood passion for a story that culminated in Sambo eating 169 pancakes—my idea of heaven. As a child, I had no idea this work was controversial, with African American poet Langston Hughes claiming Sambo was a classic stereotyped 'piccanniny' (even though he is Indian). This imperialist story was denounced both within American civil rights discourse and British anti-racist movements, especially for its grotesque illustrations. It is still in print, in various different versions, though (probably now for reasons of political correctness) the majority of my correspondents omitted it from their lists of favourites.

What struck me most, as women of all ages from their twenties to eighties proclaimed their love for these writers and books, is the fact that none of them is contemporary. Beatrix Potter published her animal stories between 1902 and the 1930s, and Enid Blyton her novels between the 1930s and 1950s. In the 1950s and 1960s, Blyton's popularity endured until challenged and overtaken by Roald Dahl's hugely successful *James and the Giant Peach* (1961) and *Charlie and the Chocolate Factory* (1964). Both of these were eclipsed by J. K. Rowling's Harry Potter series—beginning with *Harry Potter and the Philosopher's Stone* (1997)—which went on to become the bestselling book series in history, with over 400 million copies sold. During the 1960s, Victorian and Edwardian tales (including those by Blyton) were criticized for their colonial and élite class bias, inappropriate for a modern readership, and from the 1980s onwards a whole new genre of Young Adult and contemporary children's fiction—by Julia Donaldson, Philip Pullman, David Walliams, Jacqueline Wilson, and others—filled a gap that used to be plugged with 'classics' by British and American writers such as Robert Louis Stevenson, Rudyard Kipling, Harriet Beecher Stowe, and Mark Twain.[11] In the 1980s, there was an explosion of anti-sexist and anti-racist children's books, including progressive material about the environment, and changing class and family structures (Leila Berg was a key writer). Apparently, teachers admired these books more than children, who tended to leave them untouched.

The nostalgia for the world of those Victorians and Edwardians, including Enid Blyton, lives on. From 2015 onwards, along with the spoof *Ladybird* books aimed at adults who read those when young, bookshops and supermarkets were full of Enid Blyton reprints with 1950s-style covers (presumably for Baby Boomers eager to relive their childhood), and Blyton parodies—named 'Enid Blyton for Grown-Ups', to amuse sophisticated post-modern professionals who had long since denounced her writing (*Five Go On a Strategy Away Day*, *Five Go Gluten Free*, *Five on Brexit Island*, and so on).[12] Feminist publisher Virago established a Children's Classics series featuring many of my correspondents' favourites, from Edith Nesbit's *The Treasure Seekers* and *The Railway Children* to the *What Katy Did* series, with pastel-coloured nostalgic jacket illustrations and endorsements from novelists Kate Saunders and Jacqueline Wilson. Many a grandmother may smile to herself as she recalls Nancy Friday's nod to that girls' favourite with the name of her ground-breaking 1973 feminist study of women's sexual fantasies—*My Secret Garden*.

Women emerge from my correspondence as moral guides, censors, and also sometimes non-judgemental figures who allowed girls to read 'adult' material. One middle-class woman's grandmother read to her because she felt girls' education was crucial, while her *mother* feared reading was 'bad' for a girl (especially in the morning—ultimate indulgence), arguing her eyes would be ruined and thus her chances of marriage would go down the drain. Penelope Lively's Somerset grandmother warned her against excessive reading: '"You should be out and about."'[13] As I've suggested earlier, guilt at reading voraciously—among adult women—is often the result of childhood constraints, and this crosses lines of class, race, and ethnicity. Sometimes reading had powerful consequences for imaginative girl readers. One (anonymous) 60-year-old recalled reading 'very inappropriately' George Eliot's *Mill on the Floss*, to which she attributes a lifelong fear of millponds. Nicky B was given H. G. Wells' *Invisible Man*: 'I was so terrified by it that I couldn't walk up to my bed at night, convinced the invisible man was hiding beneath it, waiting to grab my ankles. So I used to do a running jump from the bedroom door.' One female member of a family sometimes encourages reading frowned upon by another. Jane M's earliest memory is creeping downstairs against her mother's permission to sit with her grandmother who read *Brer*

Rabbit to her. Another woman's grandmother told her Kathleen Winsor's racy *Forever Amber* (1944) was unsuitable for her, but she read it anyway at her auntie's, until her mother removed the book. (My own mother recalled secretly reading this book as a young girl, with guilty pleasure.)

A woman in her seventies relates that her progressive mother banned Enid Blyton because of her 'sexist tendencies' so—unlike her sister, who read them in secret—she has never read a single one. At Tracey P's girls' grammar school, Enid Blyton was seen as rubbish, read only by idiots. Blyton's reputation has declined considerably, with many educationists deploring her simplistic use of language, xenophobia, elitism, racism, and sexism, but she is still recalled with huge affection by many readers. Susan Hill defends her: 'I was one of the Five and the Seven, I went to the Mountain of Adventure and Spooky Cottage, I was in the Fifth at Malory Towers. We all were.'[14] As Hill suggests, girls with restricted freedoms envied the adventures enjoyed by the Famous Five and Secret Seven away from parental control, and especially the apparent glamour of the Malory Towers boarding school life. Black British Esther W (in her mid-forties) told me: 'I was hooked on it at junior school and desperately wanted a pony and to go to public school', while white 67-year-old Gail W mused on how 'unquestioningly we entered into the world of "the hols," midnight feasts, ponies, boarding school japes, even nomenclature such as "The Fourth," when we were totally outside that class and that sort of life'. The Malaysian Chinese writer, Vera Chok, growing up in Malaysia, read Enid Blyton and dreamed (as I did) of midnight feasts.[15] And Nigerian writer Chimamanda Ngozi Adichie, reading British and American books, began to write the sort of stories she was reading. All her characters were white and drank ginger beer; she didn't think 'little girls with skin the colour of chocolate' could exist in literature.[16] Deirdre S, too, hankered after the Malory Towers life, 'but not in later years when we talked to other girls about the cold schools, horrible food and teachers, and loneliness'.

Memories of reading in childhood are often linked to specific places or times. One of childhood's great pleasures is the secretive spaces in which girls 'indulged in' their habit—the bathroom late at night (when bedrooms were shared), by torchlight or bike lamp under the

bedclothes, in corners of the home, under-the-desk school-time, and
so on. (Younger women now read on phones and tablets without any
need for extra illumination.) And if the book were sexually daring and
transgressive, it was often shared through underground sisterly loan
systems, with anatomically explicit pages highlighted or listed for the
impatient reader. Judie N's mother was a keen reader and 'got
through most of the classics in the outside loo, as if she read in front
of her own mum she was given something else useful to do'. Dawn
R-W read sitting under the table while her mother and female friends
had tea together after doing their chores, before their husbands came
home. When she was seven, Sandra J had measles, and had to stay in a
darkened room with curtains closed in case the light damaged her
eyes. She was forbidden to read: 'Some hopes. I had my book under
the covers and a torch . . . I wasn't going to be stopped from reading
my beloved books as well as being pickled in nasty spots.' Lynne H still
has grains of sand in her copy of *Rebecca*, read at the age of 14 on the
beach at St Ives.

The Library

However, the most referenced place for the early discovery of books
and reading experiences is the library. Jorge Luis Borges said that he
always imagined Paradise as a kind of library, and he is not alone.
Described by the charity The Library Campaign as 'the bedrock of
the nation's entire culture strategy', my correspondents dubbed it 'a
magical community space' and 'sacred pleasure palaces' which
'opened a world beyond where I was and allowed me to wonder
about lives different from mine'. These free, open places of calm,
quiet, and a cornucopia of choices gave girls, and then adult
women, the opportunity to go unaccompanied, sometimes with their
children, to an unthreatening place in which to browse and share
literary tastes with others without the interruptions of mundane life.
This has been especially true for women from homes where there
were no books and/or little money to buy them, and these spaces are
currently important for young and older Muslim women whose ability
to occupy public space is very limited. Margaret K describes a children's library opening around 1935 in Walthamstow, London. You
could join only when aged 8, and Margaret's mother made a big fuss

about signing her on: 'She thought I might catch diphtheria or scarlet fever. "Who knows where the books have been?"' Growing up in 1940s Scarborough, Susan Hill recalls the public children's library having labels on a book declaring it had been fumigated against infectious and contagious diseases such as chicken box, measles, mumps, and so on: 'Children died of them. Books that went into infected houses might be returned thick with germs, so it was necessary to report certain illnesses when books were returned, so that they could be put into special fumigation chambers to be rendered clean and safe again.'[17] This was an anxiety that lasted for many years, since Veronica C, growing up in the 1950s, recalls the label inside library books saying that if there was an infectious disease in the house, you must 'send the books somewhere for disinfection or bake them in the oven on a low heat. To kill the micro-organisms presumably.' Who knew libraries could be such dangerous places?

Women express pleasure in the mixture of generations, the swapping of books at mobile and other libraries, and presence of friendly (mainly female) librarians to suggest titles and point readers in new literary directions. The research project 'Sheffield Reading' recorded the use men and women born before 1941 made of the Boots subscription libraries, and the Red Circle franchise of tuppenny libraries (advertising 'Reading, your cheapest pleasure'). These readers then found their way to Sheffield's free municipal libraries, in the 1940s and 1950s transformed—by the inspired City Librarian J. P. Lamb— into international models of excellence (Figure 2.2). Children often went to a branch library on their own, spending Saturdays there while both their parents worked—seeing it as a second home. Alas, they were often allowed only one book a week, so chose a fat one to last (*Doctor Doolittle*, for instance).[18]

Women in their fifties and sixties recall the division of libraries into junior or children's and senior or adults'. Novelist Margaret Forster read her way through the alphabet, happily landing with 'B' on the Brontë sisters with whom she was enthralled. One of Sheffield's early readers took to Warwick Deeping because his alphabetical position was next to that of Dickens. Jean P was frustrated that, aged 10, she couldn't have an adult library ticket until she was 12: 'I remember the day I moved from the junior to the senior part of the library. It seemed very quiet and I remember the sloping tables. Then the whole world

Figure 2.2 Meg Young and two librarians, Sheffield Library, 1956
Photographer unknown

opened up to me.' When aged 11, Marjorie H nearly got locked in her local library for the night as she was curled up in a chair engrossed in a book. In the late 1950s and early 1960s, Veronica C's mother sent her to the local circulating library where, for an old sixpence each, she borrowed books. But several women told me they could hardly believe their luck when they discovered that libraries lent you books *for no charge at all*; free libraries were the salvation of many poor girls from homes without books.

Talking to librarians now, I'm struck by how the pattern of library use persists, and how much women—especially young mothers and the retired—value those spaces for themselves, their children and grandchildren, and have been at the forefront of protests against government and local council closures and cuts to the service. Those cuts have been challenged because libraries are a precious safe space for disadvantaged and minority groups (the poor, isolated, homeless, migrant, and refugee—many of them children). Although men, too, value libraries, librarians have suggested to me that they use them more for internet job and benefit applications, CD and DVD loans, and specific book selections such as graphic novels and crime. Lingering in the stacks, reading children's books to your child to improve your own English, joining mother-and-baby groups, reading groups, and so on, tend to be female activities. Recently, at a multi-cultural library and learning centre, I watched a 'Baby Bounce' in which fifteen mothers, tiny babies, and toddlers sang nursery rhymes and Christmas songs, then marched round the family space to 'The Grand Old Duke of York'. The group listened to stories read aloud by a librarian, breast-fed and chatted to one another in a welcoming space, with the babies learning to interact and explore with clumsy tiny fingers their first books. The library supervisor told me a family can take out twenty books at a time, a huge financial saving for parents who can't afford to buy books in shops or online.

Hilary Mantel described her school library:

> When I went into the second class, rising six, we had what was called a library, but it was a fold-out box the size of a suitcase, little tiny books with very simple words. The teacher gave me *The Little Speckled Hen*. I was stupefied by boredom and I took it to her and said I'd read it, and so it was my first lie as well...What I didn't know was the suitcase library was as good as it got. There were no books other than the ones you were using, and they were taken away at the end of the lesson.[19]

It is a shocking fact that, in twenty-first-century Britain, there is a statutory requirement for every prison to have a library, whereas there's no such requirement for schools. The notorious Ofsted inspections don't look at library provision, nor does it have any effect on a school's rating.[20] Ideally, schools should be the place where each child learns to read with fluency and pleasure, and in the most affluent schools children are introduced to a range of texts and encouraged to read as widely as possible. The problem for many less privileged children in schools with large classes and over-extended teachers is that reading is made to seem a chore and a bore, and the literature shared with children can put them off reading for life.

Favourite Books

So how do women think about childhood reading? Journalist Lucy Mangan has retained all her childhood books, and lovingly spent hours rearranging them on bookshelves she designed for them, claiming they 'made me who I am'. On a family holiday waking to find on the sideboard a pile of Milly-Molly-Mandy books, she claims that—at 43 years old—she is still waiting 'for a moment of greater joy'.[21] Childhood total immersion in reading, making everything else invisible and irrelevant, is something many of us look back on with nostalgia—remembering that sense of possessing a world that was both joyous and also a bulwark against difficult or painful times. For many adults (not just those who, like me, grew up in the 1950s and had never travelled abroad), memories of our girlhood books tend to focus on exotic places—the America of *Rebecca of Sunnybrook Farm* and *Little House on the Prairie*, Heidi's Swiss mountains, the Swedish village of *Pippi Longstocking*, the non-specific jungle of *Babar the Elephant*. Of course, there are also the mythical places fiction takes us: C. S. Lewis' Narnia, Richard Adams' Watership Down, J. R. R. Tolkein's Middle-earth. Illustrations—on book jackets and throughout the books—remain in our memories; Linda P loved visiting the library to see beautifully bound volumes of *Lord of the Rings* with maps of Middle-earth to help orient the reader. There are favourite animals, real and mythic—Winnie the Pooh, Babar the Elephant, the Gruffalo, and Iorek Byrnison. Then there is food, especially lavish, unusual and sweet treats: the cheese in *Heidi*, Famous Five picnics, Sambo's pancakes. And finally, for girls who felt and feel discouraged from derring-do, there are the physical challenges to female characters—ballet dancing, horse riding, and sailing. One woman echoed my own vivid memory of Katy going too high and falling off the swing. Hilary D, however, said reading this made her 'long to be crippled!'

I asked some Bristol reading groups to re-read novels they loved in childhood, to see if they still felt the same about them.[22] They chose the novels themselves, three by women and one by a male writer. Many of the comments revolve around class and gender expectations and aspirations. Some of the older women recall that their mothers didn't feel reading was suitable for girls because education was for boys, and one was frowned upon for reading the Jennings and Biggles books because they were categorised as stories unsuitable for girls. Other mothers—like my own—were anxious to encourage reading precisely to give their daughters a better chance in life than they had had.

Little Women

A favourite novel that emerged repeatedly from my questionnaires was Louisa M. Alcott's *Little Women* (1868), a story of four sisters and their mother coping with life and helping impoverished families after their pastor father goes to help troops in the American Civil War. I, too, relished this, largely because of my identification with bookish Jo, the girl who loved her Uncle March's dusty, neglected library to which she would go eagerly to read poetry, romance, history, and so on, until a shrill voice would summon her to 'leave her paradise to wind yarn, wash the poodle, or read Belsham's Essays by the hour together'.[23] While several of the (youngish) Henleaze Library 'Love Reading Fiction Group' found the novel 'sickly, twee and mawkish' (its 'little-me' title doesn't help), the Southmead Library group of 40–50-year-old white women knew it well and discussed it enthusiastically. Hardly anyone commented on the Americanness of the book, though one woman said it stimulated her interest in the Civil War.

Several readers—most of them now mothers themselves—enjoyed its predominantly female household, with a strong inspirational mother (Marmee) and solidarity among the four sisters Meg, Jo, Beth, and Amy (Figure 2.3). Women without sisters were intrigued by the strong bonds between five very different women in a house without men where—as one reader put it—they were 'ahead of their time, always challenging the status quo'. Another noted the harshness of their impoverished life, and the balance between that and their warm family relationships, something which made her feel: 'This may well help women today to realise they, too, can still have some fun in their lives with other women (perhaps by going to the same keep-fit class or reading group together!).' It is curious that many of us recall weeping buckets over the death of Beth, an event that occurs in the *second* volume of the British edition, often called *Good Wives*. These novels, together with the other sequels, *Little Men* (1871) and *Jo's Boys* (1886), comprised the March Family Saga, probably one of the first sequences of fiction young girls had read (long before Harry Potter came on the scene). One respondent identified with Jo the writer: when Mr Bhaer hands Jo her published novel, she felt, 'Being able to write from the heart has brought her genuine success. In a strange way, this gave me affirmation as a reader—what I had enjoyed so

Figure 2.3 Louisa Alcott's Little Women and their mother (n.d.)
Chronicle / Alamy Stock Photo

much had been praised by a publisher albeit the publisher was part of the story!'

Little did any of us girl readers know that Alcott was pressured by her publisher to write a book for girls rather than the sensational thrillers of her early career. Nor did we know about her distinguished career as a feminist and abolitionist, documenter of Civil War hospital conditions, editor, and more. It took feminist publishing houses and feminist critics to remind us in the 1970s of the timeliness of this versatile writer's work, and to suggest why it has remained a firm favourite with girls and women (and an influence on writers such as Ursula K. Le Guin and J. K. Rowling). And even though it's said President Theodore Roosevelt admired it, I was surprised to read that writer and broadcaster Melvyn Bragg was also a fan. He had to hurdle the 'terrible barrier' of its (presumably girly) title and claims most men would adopt a rather apologetic stance about having read such a book: '[They] would qualify the admission by muttering on about sisters or cousins leaving it lying around or found books in the house or teachers "forcing" them to read it at school.'[24]

It's interesting to compare the perspective of an African American woman with that of those British readers. In her memoir about life in America's 'Negroland', Margo Jefferson discusses her own re-reading of *Little Women*. For a generation growing up in the 1950s, Jo was a role model...up to a point. Most girls, Jefferson argues, would want to be Jo some of the time, 'Jo of the restless impulses, the unruly luxuriant hair; shouting, grumbling, flinging retorts instead of answers; thrusting her body into unruly poses'. Looking for role models in her Negroland, Jefferson saw Jo's refusal to marry handsome, charming and rich Laurie as a cautionary tale for a girl like her contemplating a racially mixed marriage. To her, a white man would *'always be aware of...what marrying you cost him in the world...He couldn't help turning on you at some point'*. But she regrets the choice Louisa M. Alcott gives Jo, to marry 'kind and dowdy' Professor Bhaer, who exerts moral and intellectual power over his wife and forces her to burn the 'sensational' stories she has written.[25] By contrast, Hilary Mantel believes, 'I'm probably the only female writer who took a very sniffy attitude to Jo March because I just knew the kind of trash she'd write. Far from being my heroine, I thought she should get a big rejection slip.'[26]

Since silent cinema days, *Little Women* has been a favourite of screen and TV producers, adapted into multiple versions, starring actors such as Katharine Hepburn, Elizabeth Taylor, and Winona Ryder. As part of the 2017 BBC TV Christmas schedule, dramatist Heidi Thomas (known for Christmas versions of the hugely successful *Call the Midwife*) wrote a mini-series for a modern audience. Recalling her childhood viewing in black and white of the 1970 'Sunday tea-time' treatment, she claimed this was the book she 'lived inside', and cherishes more than others she has adapted. To the adult Thomas, re-reading the novel meant she now saw 'a study of the human condition so intricate and moving that it took my breath away', one that was 'truthful, brave and reflected life in all its imperfections'. In 2017, Marmee was no longer just 'a saintly, embracing matriarch'; she was 'a strong, complex character with challenges of her own'. This contemporary feminist interpretation is echoed by the 19-year-old actor Maya Hawke, who played Jo March. The novel was the first she—a dyslexic child—read by herself, and Jo's 'determination and love of words and poetry . . . inspired me to work harder and finish the book'. Everyone, she claims, wants to be Jo—'it's her independent spirit, her lack of self-consciousness; she's free, awkward and weird'.[27]

The Secret Garden

The Bramley Reading Group decided to reread Frances Hodgson Burnett's *The Secret Garden* (1911), a novel about an orphaned English girl whose isolation and depression are cured by befriending two young boys and sharing and caring for a neglected garden in her uncle's house. This novel was originally published as a general family story, but over the years it has become identified as a *girl's* book—despite the non-gendered title and inclusion of two central male characters. In 2011, celebrating its centenary as a literary classic, marketing via book jackets and endorsements emphasized the ideal reader as female, with soft pastel colours and intricate flower patterns, and 'chick-lit'-style images of the central female protagonist Mary. While some boys do read the novel, it is regarded by feminist critics and publishers as a girl's book. And this may be explained in terms of the familiar echoes of that novel beloved by girls, *Jane Eyre*—the mysterious wailing in the night, a large house on the Yorkshire moors, an orphaned and isolated female character, and a distant brooding male figure (in this case, the uncle). One reader described it in Brontëan terms as 'diluted Gothic horror'.

Unlike the other groups' familiarity with *Little Women* dramatizations, none of the group had seen any of the film or TV versions, most notably the critically acclaimed 1993 production directed by Agnieszka Holland, starring Maggie Smith and Kate Maberly as Mary. The women speculated about whether modern children would enjoy this novel, since the Yorkshire dialect was distracting and the animals and birds rather Disneyish. But overall they felt it had a great 'feel-good factor' with the sad, damaged children becoming happy and healthy through the forces of nature, communication with animals, kindly countrywomen, and the coming of Spring to bring hope and renewal. A few of the group thought Mary and Colin (both neglected and rejected) could bring out the maternal instinct in girls and women, a factor that might explain why so many remember the book. The magical, mysterious garden was their big secret ('children like having secrets, the more important the better'), and the three children's developing friendship kept adults well in the background. The moral lesson of the novel, that both Mary and Colin become better people thinking more of others than themselves, confirmed this as a 'good' children's novel that works also for adults. To my surprise, none commented on the very timely ecological theme of the novel, something which—despite its colonialist context which made her feel invisible—a young African American reader, Zetta Elliott, claimed helped find her voice as an urban environmentalist.[28] And none of them expressed the concern several feminist critics have had about the virtual disappearance of orphan Mary by the novel's end, with the reinstatement of recuperated Colin at the centre of his father's mansion and thus the narrative.

Lucy Mangan tells an amusing story of trying to incorporate this novel into her own life experience. She decided—to her mother's delight—that she would follow Mary's example and take up gardening. Enthusiasm turned quickly to disillusionment:

> [T]he thing about gardening, it turns out, is that it is very slow . . . You have to dig for ages and then you scatter the seeds and instead of just turning the page to find them bursting into bloom, fuck all happens for months. No robins come to visit you. Or sex gods. Just your mother and your sister, who are out every five minutes to see what you're doing and explain how you're doing it wrong. I began to understand why you needed a *secret* garden.[29]

The Magic Faraway Tree

One of my most treasured books was Enid Blyton's *The Magic Faraway Tree* (1943), a tale of three siblings who climb to the top of a magic tree, and meet new friends who show them how to visit and have adventures in strange and magical lands. One (anonymous) reader captured perfectly how I felt about it: 'My recollection was of sheer escapism, enjoyment in lands at the top of the tree, with a frisson of worry recalling apprehension when the lands were about to move away and the characters may not get down in time.' I asked the Bramley Reading Group to read it (some knew it, others not) to see whether it retained its magic. It seems it did, and several of them reported that their grandchildren adored it. They valued the fantasy and magic, and the pleasure of escapism from the real world for children able to go somewhere different on their own with parents very much in the background. They enjoyed the humour of names like Moonface and Dame Washalot, and Saucepan Man's deafness—which means he brings the Dame a lion rather than an iron. They commented on the hint of danger as not all the lands in the stories were good and they noted the 'naughtiness' of the character Rick contrasted with the 'goodness' of Joe who helps Rick out of scrapes.

This group fell in love again with *The Magic Faraway Tree*, but another reader, Anne F B, found a very different book on re-reading. Initially it was exciting and fun, but then became very repetitive, though she thought that might be a positive quality for child readers. To her, the elements that stood out were the total absence of the father, and the surprising number of tasks within the house and garden that Mother set for the children (something she said would not apply today). Anne was also struck by the frequent simplistic references to 'naughty' behaviour without much psychological insight into the children's individual growth and developing personalities within a diverse, tolerant culture. In her words, 'Good and bad, naughty and nice, easy and hard, up and down, a very black and white sexist view of the world.' To her, J. K. Rowling and Roald Dahl offer far more interesting 'word combinations and word-sounds' and complex, interesting stories than Blyton's.

Danny the Champion of the World

The book chosen in June 2017 by the Wick Road Library Group, comprising young mothers, was Roald Dahl's novel, *Danny the Champion of the World* (1975), about a young English boy and his father William who live in a Gypsy caravan and survive by fixing cars and poaching pheasants. All of them remembered reading Roald Dahl during childhood, and this was one of their favourites—which they were already reading to their children. Several of them remembered bits and forgot other parts of the novel, with some scenes standing out in memory (such as putting water into raisins to give to the pheasants). Danny, his father, and the nasty landowner were recalled, but not the minor characters. For most of the group, there was a generally warm nostalgia about the novel and Dahl's work in general, though they felt this particular book might appeal more to boys than girls: 'We probably felt it was normal for boy characters to be leading exciting lives, having adventures etc., but we didn't really relate to him.'

As mothers, they felt particular sympathy towards the motherless Danny, despite his close relationship with his father, but they felt there were no female role models. They dismissed the two women characters—the vicar's wife and the teacher's wife—as 'quite minor and silly (and nameless!)' and as adults they commented that a lot of (especially older) women in Dahl's work are portrayed rather negatively.

Those mothers who had read the story to their children described it as a fun read, with lots of characters for whom they could do different voices. They did, however, feel more moralistic towards William than when they were young readers, finding him somewhat irresponsible when he left Danny alone at home and then allowed Danny to drive a car through the countryside. They admitted to editing during reading aloud—omitting dated references to gendered roles for parents and strict teachers and corporal punishment at school (especially Danny's caning scene). Finally, they all noticed something they hadn't picked up on when reading as girls: the simplistic class judgements of the upper classes as 'bad [and] unpleasant', the poor working class as 'decent and good'.

* * *

Of all the reading experiences women have, informal connections between adults and children can be the most fulfilling—allowing a girl to hear someone read aloud or read for herself a story recommended by a female family member, librarian, or teacher. This interaction between readers gives grown women the opportunity to revisit and reassess with our children or pupils those early love affairs with iconic novels, to see how much these fictions have shaped our lives. Continuity between generations is enhanced by the sharing of fiction, and the incorporation of fictional figures into domestic conversations and routines. A friend of writer Diana Athill complained that many children's stories were about animals not people, so she had to 'feed her children on this pap of fantasy instead of on stories about real life'. But for Athill, the response of children to animal characters is 'to discover and recognize their own feelings' rather than 'real life'.[30]

Allowing children to follow a variety of human and animal narratives begins the long process of making sense of their world, and creating fictional memories to sustain them.

This anecdote from a correspondent rang true to me. When her family lived in Rhodesia, Wendy S recalled reading a novel called *Fourteen Fourteens*, by Violet M Methley:

> I had it as a birthday present and was fascinated by the premise of the story: a school for fourteen girls aged fourteen all called Margaret. Every girl had her own room which had been decorated especially for its occupant, and somehow the Head knew what colour scheme would delight. I remember wondering what would have been chosen for me! I discovered the book after years and years of looking for it and telling my daughter about it. Of course it is totally dire and my daughter's comments on the plot were justifiably scathing, but I was able to jump back into being the girl who read it first without criticism.

We remember fondly stories that—however eccentric or badly written—spoke to something within us as children. The disappointments of adult rereading can't eliminate that sense of early wonder and excitement that are vital for lifelong readers and advocates of fiction for subsequent generations. Katherine Rundell, winner of the 2017 Costa children's books prize, said: 'The only time that kids fully understand the world they inhabit is when they read, the rest of the time the world is so large and so frayed at the edges.'[31] In recent years, a development in literature aimed at girls and young women has exploded onto the scene, offering stories appropriate for a 'frayed at the edges' twenty-first-century market. As I'll discuss in Chapter 4, the Young Adult category—largely written, edited, and marketed by women and read by young female readers—is in the process of creating a whole new canon of women's fiction that will resonate among future generations.

However, for all too many children, fictional memories are denied them by various kinds of social and family deprivation, closure of libraries, and huge school classes preventing personal attention to an individual child's reading. Initiatives such as World Book Day, and organisations such as The National Literacy Trust, Reading Agency, The Reader, Shannon Trust and others, have drawn increasing numbers into the pleasure of reading. Some male prisoners can record bedtime stories for their children in order to sustain a relationship through fiction. What emerges from my interviews and questionnaire responses is how much importance women attach to reading as a way girls can escape from the constrictions of patriarchal expectations, and how vital we feel it is for girls to explore literature (especially in libraries), and to have fun with handling and devouring story books at their own pace. Of course schools, charities, and educational foundations support the business of childhood reading, but it is still mainly women who keep it alive within the home and create the readers of tomorrow.

The Poet on her Childhood Reading

U. A. Fanthorpe

On my first day at kindergarten I fell in love. After school dinner the younger children rested, and we were read to for a while by a teacher. The first book she chose was *The Wind in the Willows*. I was enraptured at once, and went home demanding, insisting on instant purchase of the adored object, so that I could live with it as soon as possible, and not have to wait for the teacher to reach the end of it [at] her own pace. My parents complied, and I had the heady experience of at once tearing through the book independently, and relishing it at the more measured pace of Miss Knowles. Why *The Wind in the Willows*? I think that part of its appeal was that it didn't appear to be a child's book. Childish things were not for me... But *The Wind in the Willows* had nothing in it about children. What it did offer was much more enthusiastic writing about food and drink, a gang with a quest to perform, and a river... These subjects have never lost their charm for me. I have loved such books all my life and always suffer as much as I did the first time when the gang, its quest achieved, splits up and goes its separate ways.

[Another book I remember] was in the year my mother rebelled against Bognor Regis... That memorable year she announced that she would decide where we went, and took us to a beautiful place: Lynton in North Devon... the Doone Valley. I was presented with *Lorna Doone*, as a sort of historical guidebook. My mother gave me the impression that it was written by a distant cousin by saying that, just as her branch, the Redmores, came from Exmoor, so the author's branch, the Blackmores, were from Dartmoor. I ought to have spotted the flaw in this: what was a Dartmoor man doing writing about Exmoor? But I was too busy eating cream teas and ingesting *Lorna Doone*. The idea that a book belonged to a real place fascinated me, and so did the story, with its stress on the violent and lawless Doone family, all of them well over six and a half feet tall, robbing, raping and killing all over Exmoor and finally . . . suppressed by law, order and mighty Jan Ridd, who as a boy climbed the waterfall to visit the kidnapped child Lorna, and as a man defeated the tallest Doone of all, Carver, who slipped and died horribly in the Exmoor quicksands.

There was some good stuff about Carver shooting Lorna through the window of Oare church as she and Jan were being married, too. I was rather cool about mighty Jan, who had dangerous ideas about the inferiority of sisters, and an irritating way of reporting his own exploits with such elaborate mock-modesty that they became even more heroic than they would have been if described honestly. Luckily my brother merely fingered the book, and decided it was too long for him to bother with. I became a secret Doone, riding with the band as they went out pillaging, and returning to meals of mysterious substances called collops and schnapps, which I took to be an up-market equivalent of cream teas. I had found another gang to join, and this time, though I was hardly aware of it, I sidestepped the author's intentions and was an enthusiastic recruit to the wrong side.

[Extract from an unpublished essay by U. A. Fanthorpe (1929–2009), 'Autobiography of a Reader', *c.*1984. R. V. Bailey kindly agreed to its publication.]

3

Pride and Prejudice and *Jane Eyre*, the Novels Women Love Best

Do not disturb: I'm reading Jane Austen.

Sign on Sophie's bedroom door

Jane Eyre *is so built into the shape of my imagination that I can hardly think about it critically; I'm always in among its trees—the sturdy, northern, low-growing hawthorn and hazel bushes of its terrain—and can't dispassionately estimate the size of the wood. The novel touches not one responsive note in me, but a whole sequence of them, each quite distinct.*

Novelist Tessa Hadley[1]

Of all the beloved novels mentioned by women of every age—in questionnaires, interviews, and private conversations—there are two that keep recurring: Jane Austen's *Pride and Prejudice* and Charlotte Brontë's *Jane Eyre*. Both have developed global iconic reputations; each has had huge influence on later writers, and been adapted into, imitated, and parodied in film, theatre, TV, radio, and social media. Both are at the heart of the British literary tourism industry. Especially since the mid-twentieth century, each novel has attracted acres of scholarly articles, books, media coverage, and online blogs and websites. In 2012, a Facebook fan community was created, 'Heathcliff, Mr. Darcy, Rochester—The Literary Heroes', with a description, 'All your favorite Literary Heroes from Mr. Darcy to Rochester at one place!' An American fan page, it has attracted thousands of 'likes' from all over the world, by (almost exclusively) women of all ages.[2] The 2018 British Library exhibition of its treasures in Shanghai Library suggested that *Jane Eyre* (*Jian Ai*) is even more popular

among Chinese readers than in the UK. And, despite the deadly effect
of being 'set texts' at school and college, which drives away some
young readers, their authors and these novels have a very special place
in the stories of women's reading.

I discussed the two novels with Austen scholar Margaret Kirkham,[3]
who reminded me that until well into the twentieth century these were
'classics' read in abridged versions in primary schools and much
taught in girls' secondary schools, with enthusiastic English teachers
proselytizing on their behalf. Parents or aunts keen on education
would give them as presents, and cheap copies in mock leather covers
were sold for Christmas in Woolworth's stores. So they were widely
read and owned by generations of girls in families with and without
many books. Each novel, she points out, appeals to an impressionable
young female readership, with a penchant for a romantic love story
and heroines who stand up for themselves and get away with it. And—
despite many differences—they share heroines without decent dow-
ries who end up married to landed gentlemen, asserting their status as
'ladies', and rejecting improper proposals of marriage by the hero to
demonstrate they are not 'adventuresses'. They also both reject alternative offers from conventionally respectable clergymen. They were
regarded as suitable books to give to girls of all ages (mine arrived
when I was around 11) and women within families passed on their
copies to daughters and granddaughters alike. If you wander round a
large London bookstore, you'll find abridged, illustrated, engraved,
and other versions of both novels. One company, Real Reads, retells
classic novels for young readers, fitting each novel into a sixty-four-
page book, claiming to capture the flavour and tone while 'simplifying
the narrative and dialogue'. The company produces a six-book boxed
set of Jane Austen, and two novels by the Brontë sisters, *Jane Eyre* and
Wuthering Heights.

Kirkham also reminded me that in films made between 1939 and
1940, England's most celebrated actor Laurence Olivier, with whom
so many young girls (she and I both) fell deeply in love, played
Heathcliff (*Wuthering Heights*, 1939), Mr Darcy (*Pride and Prejudice*,
1940), and also Maxim de Winter (the modern Mr Rochester,
Rebecca, 1940), thus ensuring a glamorous and erotic aura around
these works.

Pride and Prejudice

Jane Austen's *Pride and Prejudice*, published anonymously in 1813, has worked its way into people's hearts over the centuries—and become for women a compulsive text beating most others. The famous opening sentence, 'It is a truth universally acknowledged, that a single man in possession of a good fortune must be in want of a wife,' is embedded in our collective unconscious. In all polls, this novel triumphs. A 2003 BBC poll to discover the UK's favourite book named it second (after *Lord of the Rings*) and in another survey the top book written by a woman, for women readers over 40. The following year Radio 4 Woman's Hour listeners, encouraged by the novel's champion, Monica Ali, said it was the most influential book in changing women's perceptions of themselves. A 2007 poll voted the novel 'the book the nation can't do without'.[4] Feeding Austen-mania are books on almost every aspect of Austen's carriages, fashion, courtship rituals, juvenilia, and rejected screenplays. An iTunes interactive edition provides maps, timelines, interviews with critics and writers, quizzes, and clips from BBC adaptations. Despite all this, Austen biographer Claire Tomalin is sceptical as to whether the 'Jane Austen Industry worldwide' has helped people understand her writing.[5]

The bicentenary in 2017 of Jane Austen's death was a year marked by publications, special events, literary festival panels galore, and media celebrations. In July's *Literary Review*, Lucy Lethbridge reviewed no less than seven new books about the writer—including a biography tied into a BBC series, a book about 'The Banker's Sister', a comparative study of Austen and Dorothy Wordsworth, and an analysis of why Austen is a hit in Hollywood.[6] In July–August, the BBC punned on the title with 'Prejudice and Pride', its series of programmes to celebrate fifty years of the partial decriminalization of homosexuality. Also in 2017, a £10 banknote and commemorative £2 coin bearing her image appeared—though many Austen experts noted the irony of the 'Saint Aunt Jane' portrait of the writer, the image of her brother's stately Godmersham House rather than her own modest Chawton Cottage, and the quotation from *Pride and Prejudice*. The words, 'I declare after all there is no enjoyment like reading!', are spoken by Austen's bête noire Caroline Bingley, designed to show her in truly hypocritical mode.[7] A Christmas book promoted that year was *Pride and Prejudice and Emojis*.

However, 2017 was not an exceptional year. Anniversaries are key to keeping alive the Austen brand. The 2013 bicentenary of *Pride and Prejudice*'s publication saw, inter alia, the campaign to put Austen's face on the £10 note; *Austenland*, a film about an Austen theme park; a ring owned by the writer saved for the nation by a fundraising campaign run by the Jane Austen House Museum; and a revisionary version of *Pride and Prejudice* by novelist Jo Baker, *Longbourn*, which went below stairs to tell the story from the perspective of the Bennet household servants. In the same year there were also many newspaper features, with feminist critics playfully rewriting the story so that Mary Bennet—despised for her intellectual and artistic pretensions—marries Mr Collins, enjoying writing his sermons and playing music in church. Furthermore, Lady Catherine de Bourgh has an affair with Charlotte Lucas, a revelation that kills Mr Collins so the Bennets get back their estate, and the two lovers open a boutique hotel for Georgian lesbians.[8] In dozens of modern revisions of the novel, Elizabeth Bennet herself has become a lesbian, a cannibal, a zombie, and a serial killer.

From 2013 onwards, The Austen Project commissioned a series of contemporary reworkings of the novels by bestselling authors including Joanna Trollope, Val McDermid, Alexander McCall Smith, and Curtis Sittenfeld. These simply added to the growing number of revisions by established writers such as P. D. James and Emma Tennant, with titles like: *Death Comes to Pemberley*; *A Murder at Longbourn*; *de Bourgh's Revenge: The Haunting of Longbourn*; *Not Handsome Enough (Mr Darcy's Erotic Dreams)*; *Mrs Bennet's Menopause*; Pride and Prejudice and Zombies: The Classic Regency Romance, now with Ultraviolent Zombie Mayhem... Not to mention the four novels of a contemporary Elizabeth Bennet alter ego heroine, Bridget Jones, published between 1996 and 2013, and its celebrated film versions, reworking *Pride and Prejudice* with a modern Lizzie and the aptly named Mark Darcy (played by Colin Firth, his character killed off for the final novel).[9] Bizarrely, in the 2016 BBC Radio 4 Woman's Hour Power list, of seven women judged to have had the biggest impact on women's lives over the past seventy years, one was the fictional 'Bridget Jones'.

Austen specialists Hazel Jones and Maggie Lane note that film and TV versions of the novel have undoubtedly increased its appeal, and especially the attractiveness of the rather austere male hero,

Fitzwilliam Darcy—who has been played by heartthrobs such as Laurence Olivier, Colin Firth, and Matthew Macfadyen. Jones and Lane quote journalist, Max Davidson, writing in 1995 of the fact that Darcy was

> for generations of middle-class English schoolgirls . . . the great romantic hero. They have fantasies about sleeping with Heathcliff, but it is Darcy they want to marry. 'A fine, tall person, handsome features, noble mien . . . ' And all that money! It's like Mills and Boon translated into English.[10]

But Darcy's appeal as rich husband is only one of its attractions; it is the couple's interaction that is so appealing. One of my correspondents, Annie D, said: 'I love Elizabeth's wit and Darcy was probably my first love.' Marion G wrote: 'Elizabeth thinks of the appropriate and acerbic response immediately, instead of two days later, which is what I do.' This is also a novel that satirizes the whole business of marriage and patriarchal family relationships with an ironic lightness of touch that appeals to men and women, but particularly amuses women who also respond to playful sequels and parodies that have proliferated over the years. Most tellingly, the high-budget and lusciously filmed 1995 BBC adaptation by Andrew Davies and Sue Birtwistle—taking considerable liberties with the novel—attracted ten million viewers. Dynamic, sexy, and irreverent—featuring a damp-shirted Darcy (Colin Firth) emerging from the lake at Pemberley—it quickly became legendary, and was followed by a huge international demand for the book itself.

Despite the rewritings and reworkings emanating overwhelmingly from female pens, you might think there is nothing particularly *gendered* about this enthusiasm for *Pride and Prejudice*. But there is indisputable evidence for Austen being a woman's special writer, and this novel claimed for ourselves by girls and women. Many male critics and readers admire Austen (George Henry Lewes, Winston Churchill, and Harold Macmillan for three), though it's notable that the reasons they give tend to be somewhat cerebral—along the lines of 'linguistic precision', 'stylistic polish', 'moral vision', 'psychological subtleties and nuances', 'penetrating understanding of human nature', and so on. I have yet to read a male critic describing his emotional or sexual passion for or identification with one of Austen's characters.

By contrast, there's no doubt that Austen has a special place in the hearts of women readers, and they are all too happy to give vent to this. The 2017 Ipsos MORI poll of British reading choices, commissioned by the Royal Society of Literature, found that women named Jane Austen five times more than men.[11]

Poet and translator A. E. Stallings reflected: 'I can think of no writer who better understands teenagers and young people, especially young women, their earnestness and cattiness, extremes of joy and heartbreak, their boredom and intrigues.'[12] Reminding us that many women first read *Pride and Prejudice* in their early teens, Samantha Ellis (who read it aged 12) underlines that adolescent identification with the young Bennet girls:

> Growing up in a tight-knit, traditional community of Iraqi Jewish refugees, I understood the pressure to marry, and the terror that it would be impossible to square my parents' expectations with my own romantic dreams. Lizzy gave me hope. I wanted to be her, all muddy petticoats and defiance.[13]

Jane D (in her late fifties) wrote wryly: 'I always saw myself as a Heyer heroine, or Elizabeth Bennet, and thought I should find my Darcy with his great estates. I never did marry a hero with rolling estates but had to create my own matchbox version.'

My questionnaire respondents cite her as a favourite writer, and women constitute the majority of members of the Jane Austen Society, attenders of Austen talks, balls, parties, and other celebrations. Joanna Trollope, addressing the Cheltenham Literature Festival after publication of her *Sense and Sensibility*, argued that readers 'feel more possessive about Jane Austen than they do about any other writer', and she confirmed this by her observation that—at an Austen convention in Winchester—most of the (largely American) delegates wore Jane Austen period costumes (though I think this also has something to do with fantasies of a period 'Englishness').[14] Many a book about the writer has a pastel-coloured cover with women in bonnets and dainty high-waisted dresses, cashing in on a female readership interested in Austen's fashions, the places associated with her, and humorous reworkings of the novels. In the bicentenary of her death, the BBC reported on worldwide celebrations, including the Jane Austen Festival in Canberra, Australia, which offered balls, teas, and dressing up in Regency costumes, as well as a one-woman Austen show in Chicago, USA, and Regency dance lessons in Singaporean schools. Meanwhile in the UK, Bath has its own Jane Austen Centre, where a police officer gives Jane Austen tours, 'chasing the bonnet bucks' as the BBC has it.[15] A spokesman for the Centre admitted that the audience is predominantly female: 'We do find that boyfriends or husbands are brought along kicking and screaming—often in military uniform— but in the end they seem to enjoy it' (Figure 3.1).[16] I went along to the Summer 2017 meeting in Exeter of the Jane Austen Society South West (Figure 3.2), and among more than seventy people I counted only four male attendees (one handling the IT projector). But after a scholarly talk about the theme of persuasion in the novel *Persuasion*, the first two questions to the speaker came from men, both of them specifically about the novel's treatment of the Navy.

That bicentenary year was marked by BBC TV with a programme, *My Friend Jane*,[17] which—through the stories of a handful of 'Janeites'—showed how an imagined friendship with the novelist

Figure 3.1 Characters on the Jane Austen Parade in Bath, September 2014
TimLarge / Alamy Stock Photo

Figure 3.2 The Jane Austen Society South West, Exeter, June 2017
Photo by Helen Taylor

herself (she's a 'really good friend') motivates many passionate women—and a handful of men—and creates special friendships around her life and work. Joanna Starnes, a scientist-turned-fiction writer, noted that there are between thirty and sixty new Jane Austen Fan Fictions (JAFs) every month on Amazon and other platforms; to date she herself has contributed eight. A 21-year-old, Sophie Andrews, had struggled with bulimia through her life but found her collection of Austen books, memorabilia, shawls, and bonnets a lifesaver: 'The Austen love in common immediately connects us,' she says of her friends who don their period bonnets and dresses to picnic and hold eighteenth-century-style balls in Austen-related places. And these enthusiasts are not only white British. A Bangladeshi Indian woman finds that Austen's novels reflect the marriage market in which she grew up, the passing of women from father to husband: 'Reading the books, I thought "Wait, I've been there—I know this situation."'[18] This is familiar to novelist and university teacher Sarah Moss, who says that the novel speaks directly to students from strict Islamic or Christian backgrounds about the constraints on female sexuality and marriage.[19] Gurinder Chadha's internationally co-funded 2004 film *Bride and Prejudice* gave a multicultural 'Bollywood meets Hollywood' twist to the story, translating the socio-cultural constraints of eighteenth-century Longbourn to contemporary Amritsar, 'swapping corsets for saris, and polite pianoforte for the bhangra beat . . . reinvigorat[ing] Jane Austen's *Pride and Prejudice* with fun and flamboyance'.[20]

Re-Reading Pride and Prejudice

American novelist Allegra Goodman describes a trajectory familiar to many a British woman: reading the novel when 9 years old, then again in high school (as a set text), and a third time in college when studying English literature. As a child, she was influenced by her mother, a teacher who loved Austen, and while not understanding some of the language, she appreciated the wit. The second time she was recovering from oral surgery, was being bullied by other children, and felt intimidated by the fair-skinned Bennet girls. The college reading was informed by her sophisticated Harvard training and gave her a disdain for Austen's contrived fairy-tale ending with an unbelievable hero. Her fourth and final reading is the most interesting. Returning as many women do to maternal favourites, she found herself reading the novel as an adult author, wife, and mother, recently returned from her mother's funeral. Alone in the house in pouring rain, with a young baby, she read the novel slowly and uncritically 'because my mother had loved Jane Austen and because re-reading it for solace was something she might have done'.

But that wasn't all. She read it because she claims her mother was like Austen—witty, a lover of irony, concise, shrewd, and ingenious. Like the writer she loved, her mother had died young 'with her work unfinished'. This reading led young mother Goodman to revise her original dismissal of Darcy as 'cipher' and 'figure of romance', now allowing her to see as 'inspired' the way Austen 'combines astute social satire with fairy tale'. But Goodman is clear that she needed to read the novel differently because of grief at her mother's untimely death at 51. While a student, having compared unfavourably the writer's 'sunny' art of watercolour with Henry James's 'chiaroscuro', in this re-reading she 'had never appreciated Austen's fairy tale so well, but perhaps . . . had never needed it so much'. For her, *Pride and Prejudice* is important for 'the memories and wishes I've folded in its pages—because on every reading I see old things in it'.[21] Here, we see many of the elements of women's reading histories which mark certain novels irrevocably for our own. The figure of the mother who pervades this story reminds us that those special texts we borrowed from our mothers, and thus in some way associate with them, carry us through a reading life and (when mothers ourselves) can revive memories and buried feelings that saturate our imaginative lives.

In 2017, I invited the Bramley Reading Group to re-read and discuss *Pride and Prejudice*.[22] Many of the group of eleven had read this book at school and suggested the famous first line of the book had held it in their memories over the years. They all loved it and felt it resonated with women readers for many reasons. First, it's easy to read and has short chapters that make it easy to pick up and put down—an attraction for busy women. Most significantly, it was seen as a 'classic love story' with the now-familiar romance plot of hero and heroine initially disliking each other then gradually moving towards love and inevitable marriage: 'elegant nineteenth-century Chick Lit' or, perhaps, contemporary romantic comedy. The group felt Elizabeth Bennet was attractive to women readers because she is 'a modern woman—feisty, intelligent and caring in character'. They enjoyed the humour; one woman said she felt it 'made the men of her time realize that irony wasn't their preserve'. The social history of the period appealed to them—Austen's depiction of class, the importance of money and connections, and the entertainments (dances, parties, music, reading, travel). Finally, they all confirmed that the various dramatizations, especially the 1995 BBC TV version with its 'Colin Firth effect', had made the novel an erotic talking point among women and contributed to its enduring popularity.

'Gentle-Janeism' and 'Janeitism'

However much critics express admiration for Austen, somehow her gender, single status, focus on domestic life and the subjects of marriage and financial status all put her down among the women. Her brother compounded this in 1817 with his famous 'Biographical Notice of the Author', creating a priggish image of a pious, sweet, modest, 'faultless' woman without affectation. Critic Marvin Mudrick called this 'gentle-Janeism', while Henry James objected to the notion of 'our dear, everybody's dear Jane'.[23]

While rejecting that 'gentle' label, Austen scholar Claudia Johnson defines 'Janeitism' as 'the self-consciously idolatrous enthusiasm for "Jane" and every detail relative to her'.[24] Like other terms attributed to groups of women ('suffragist' or 'feminist'), this word has been used to celebrate or mock enthusiasts. Coined by George Saintsbury in his 1894 introduction to a new edition of *Pride and Prejudice*, it signalled a male enthusiasm among serious readers; indeed, Rudyard Kipling published a short story, 'The Janeites', about a group of First World War soldiers who were secret Austen fans. However, in the 1930s and 1940s, the term acquired pejorative meanings because of Janeite gatherings 'staged with campy anglophilia', with male enthusiasts regarded as unmanly. In May 1928, British scholar H. W. Garrod gave a lecture, 'A Depreciation of Jane Austen', at the Royal Society for Literature, attacking Austen because she was a woman; her male characters were all 'soft', and any man who liked the writer was effeminate, not a real man at all.[25]

Thus Janeitism acquired the most negative connotations of female heroine-worship. Balls, bonnets, and TV adaptations helped to soften and neutralize Austen's acerbic critique of her stiflingly hierarchical society that—as the writer knew to her cost—subjected women to patriarchal judgement and fate. Novelist Ian Sansom urged readers to return to the novels 'in the hope that they might flush entirely from one's mind the horrid vision of an endless all-star omnibus Austen, in which Hugh Grant, Colin Firth, Michael Gambon, Anne Hathaway, Emma Thompson and Alison Steadman are forever jumping in and out of chaises and dancing cotillions'.[26] But I fear it's too late for such a purist view; the celebrity cat is out of the bag and many readers find the film and TV versions of their favourite reads only enhance their pleasure. And, as Paula Marantz Cohen playfully argued, when describing 'The Essential Regency Bonnet Workshop' at the Jane Austen Society of North America annual meeting, Austen was 'both a moral heavyweight and a material girl . . . partial to a nice bonnet'.[27]

The Non-Janeites

Janeitism is also repudiated by other distinguished writers. Charlotte Brontë famously dismissed Austen's work in girly terms as 'a carefully-fenced, highly-cultivated garden, with neat borders and delicate flowers', and claimed that 'the Passions are perfectly unknown to her; she rejects even a speaking acquaintance with that stormy Sisterhood'.[28] Eminent critic Lionel Trilling echoed this, bizarrely focusing on the names of the two writers:

> [Jane Austen's] very name is a charged one. The homely quaintness of
> the Christian name, the cool elegance of the surname, seem inevitably
> to force upon us the awareness of her sex, her celibacy, and her social
> class. Charlotte Brontë rumbles like thunder and drowns out any such
> special considerations. But Jane Austen can by now scarcely fail to
> imply femininity, and, at that, femininity of a particular kind and in a
> particular kind of society.[29]

In 2017, the Royal Society of Literature auctioned handwritten items
on Austen by their Fellows, including Margaret Atwood, Hilary
Mantel, Sarah Waters, and Ian McEwan. The one figure who produced a handwritten treatise about not liking the writer was the male
crime writer, Ian Rankin. Women are expected to admire the writer
and enjoy her novels, so if they demur it's usually somewhat defensively. Susan Hill, for instance, acknowledges that 'there could
scarcely be a more key author for me to miss the point of than Austen'.
She was assured by an English teacher at school, when claiming lack
of enthusiasm, that Austen 'will seem very different when you grow
up'. But this never changed:

> I am bored by Jane Austen.
> There now, I've said it.

Echoing Brontë's words, she dislikes 'that formality and porcelain
veneer', writing that is 'too patterned, too much like one of those
boring formal dances they performed, all too stylised'.[30]

Hill feels she is breaking some unspoken rule when claiming to be
bored by the Blessed Jane, but she is not alone—and there are many
readers who claim to have ambivalent feelings about her, or damn
with faint praise. Joyce Carol Oates said: 'We love Jane Austen as the
white "feminine" fantasy that stirs even (some) feminists to nostalgia
for a world of good daughters, good wives, good mothers, and good,
poised prose that never falters, stumbles, decays or effloresces, or
soars.'[31] And indeed for a kind of Englishness which Austen enthusiasts seek in their bonnets and bows, what Deidre Lynch called 'a kind
of time-travel to the past . . . a sentimental account of Austen's novels
that presents them as means by which readers might go home again—
to a comfortable, soothingly normal world'.[32] In Linda Grant's novel
The Dark Circle, young Jewish working-class Miriam is introduced to

the novel by fellow TB sufferers at an NHS sanatorium; she throws her copy into a rhododendron bush, saying: 'Them girls should just get bleeding jobs instead of hanging around fluttering their eyelashes at rich fellers.'[33]

Pride and Prejudice *and the Woman Reader*

When an earnest teenage reader of weighty masculine texts, I felt some snootiness about the novels—a sense that the world of Austen was precious, protected, and what we now call fluffy. However, I have come round. Years of teaching Jane Austen to mainly female student groups has confirmed my impression that her novels speak volumes to readers about powerlessness, patriarchal values, and the importance of close reading—both books and human beings. When Sarah Moss taught the novel, half her students had never read Austen: 'Millennials expect it to be nostalgic and about frocks, and they're pleasantly surprised.'[34]

By placing a variety of women characters at the heart of her novels, and continually reminding us of the link between romantic yearnings and economic power, Austen creates an aspirational (albeit largely white middle class) woman's literary universe. This enables both reader identification and also objective judgement, and allows us to imagine ourselves—however unimportant and oppressed—at the centre of a world in which male characters are somewhat marginal. Furthermore, Austen was a compulsive novel reader, and she especially valued women writers—Fanny Burney (from whose *Cecilia* she got the title, *Pride and Prejudice*), Maria Edgeworth, Ann Radcliffe, Hannah More, and others—on whose works she drew for her own fiction. Jacqueline Pearson argues that Austen 'demonstrates the moral usefulness of fiction in the education of the woman reader', and shows how she uses the trope of reading as allusion, symbol, a means of characterization.[35] Although the Mint chose to quote those false words of Caroline Bingley on the £10 note, in one way they got it right. Austen appeals to women readers because she takes women's (and men's) reading seriously, and makes her reader feel that learning to read closely is a crucial life lesson. In *Northanger Abbey*, her authorial comment defends the novel against its many detractors, praising it for work 'in which the greatest powers of the mind are displayed . . . the most thorough knowledge of human nature, the happiest delineation of its varieties, the liveliest effusions of wit and humour ... conveyed to the world in the best chosen language'.[36] Austen's much-quoted advocacy of fiction increases our respect for the novel itself but also for ourselves as readers. In her hands, reading fiction becomes a key shaper of female intellectual, emotional, and creative life.

Jane Eyre

Pride and Prejudice reigns supreme as the nation's (and thus women's) favourite *novel*. But there is a trio of writers quaintly described as 'The Brontës' who are often cited as favourite *writers*. In the Royal Society of Literature Ipsos MORI poll, of the Top 20 named writers of literature (headed by William Shakespeare and Charles Dickens), and the Top 10 female writers, 'The Brontë Sisters' were listed as eighth and third respectively. What a strange listing this is. Where else does one find three very different writers lumped together, as if offering group fiction—a kind of literary Beverley or McGarrigle Sisters? Father and son Kingsley and Martin Amis are never 'the Amises'; Brontë admirer Daphne du Maurier and her novelist sister Angela don't feature as The du Mauriers; and sisters A. S. Byatt and Margaret Drabble can't be linked because conveniently they have different names (though their Yorkshire roots and affinity with Charlotte and Emily—but probably not Anne—often invite comparisons). And 'Brontë' isn't even their real name. The Reverend Patrick, father of this trio, changed his name and added an *umlaut* to sound more exotic and less Irish than Brunty; Daphne du Maurier's ancestors adopted a similar ruse to create a more aristocratic-sounding surname than 'Mathurin Busson'.

'The Brontës' appeal to readers and writers partly because of the works, but also because of their short, tragic, creatively successful lives. Much is made of the fact (emphasized by Elizabeth Gaskell's romantic biography of Charlotte) that all Patrick Brontë's children predeceased him, and their brief lives were lived in a Yorkshire village and a parsonage where—apart from some forays abroad and to other parts of Yorkshire—they remained until death. But for women, I suspect there is another reason why this group resonates. As I've shown earlier, women form a matrilineal community of readers, from grandmothers to daughters, sisters to one another, women teachers and librarians to girls eager for literary role models. The grouping of the sisters describes their female reading and writing community, one that both includes and also excludes their unbalanced, dysfunctional brother. And writers are endlessly drawn to this sororal grouping. Louise Doughty is not alone in describing her fascination with their childhood creation of a full imaginative world around a set of toy soldiers, and sewing together little books for them, full of their exploits and adventures. She said this writing about 'imaginary friends' appealed deeply to later writers because the line of their literary development could be traced as inspiration to others.[37]

'I am an Emily,' said Doughty, nailing her colours to the second sister's mast. Without a doubt, Emily's sole work *Wuthering Heights* (1847) is generally recognized as one of literature's finest expressions of overwhelming and destructive passion, a novel of particular appeal to youthful yearnings and romantic idealism (enhanced for both genders by Kate Bush's acclaimed eponymous 1978 song). Kim L summed this up when she wrote that *Wuthering Heights* 'appealed to everything in my teenage self—tragedy, doomed romance, and the idea that there is only one love. It has stayed with me.'

But it is Emily's older sister's novel that continues to have greater impact on the literary world. *Jane Eyre* (1947) holds pride of place in any canon of women's writing for women readers and writers. Establishing a romantic heroine who is—in her own words—'poor, obscure, plain, and little', the novel has been adapted, reworked, and parodied in film (including silent), theatre, TV, and radio. Dozens of women writers (though hardly any men) from Daphne du Maurier and Mary Stewart to Emma Tennant, Angela Carter, and Michèle Roberts have engaged imaginatively with the novel in prequels, sequels, retellings, and spinoffs, giving it new life for female readers of all ages—though Carter mischievously said the novel came as close to being 'alluring trash' as a masterpiece could.[38] In the twenty-first century, young writers have seized on the novel's possibilities for transformation into Young Adult, science fiction, vampire, and erotica stories.[39] Like the opening words of Austen's *Pride and Prejudice*, the first line of the book's final chapter, 'Reader, I married him,' has become one of fiction's most quoted and parodied. In 2016, Charlotte Brontë's bicentenary year, novelist Tracy Chevalier published a collection of stories with that title and a subtitle 'Stories Inspired by Jane Eyre', compiling twenty-one stories by women writers paying tribute to this novel. Celebrating Brontë's championing of the under-dog who triumphs (something with which she feels we all identify) and Jane's irresistible self-determination and independent spirit, she rec-ognizes the novel's powerful direct address and appeal to (women) readers. 'It is . . . flattering—and memorable—to be addressed dir-ectly. How many novels acknowledge their readers? Jane addresses us the Reader throughout, and by doing so brings us on her side.'[40]

In Chevalier's collection, writers describe their first encounter with the novel. For many, it was a childhood or adolescent read, even a school prize. It's a book that a great many of my correspondents read when young girls, then returned to in adult life—often experiencing a completely different text. Jane's childhood experiences at Lowood School were often included in anthologies and read aloud to girls (as some kind of moral training, or reminder of how lucky we were?) and many identified profoundly with that lonely, defiant Jane becoming a self-determining figure who gets her man. Novelist Emma Donoghue called it a book that 'made the world take a nobody seriously', while Namwali Serpell first read it in Zambia and found Jane 'has always seemed my spiritual double'.[41] Germaine Greer went on record as saying the novel made her feel 'the heartbeat of female desire you don't find in male writing', noting the continuities between Ann Radcliffe's Gothic stories and Jane Austen's *Northanger Abbey* (both of which, as Greer pointed out, featured a madwoman in the attic before Bertha Mason).[42] When I asked romance writer Emily Murdoch why she thought *Jane Eyre* was of more relevance to modern readers than *Pride and Prejudice*, she wrote: 'In Jane Austen, marriage is the agency. Marriage is the action. But in Brontë, almost always heroines have a profession: another option, agency, choice. The men they end up marrying are not their only choice . . . in today's romance women do not HAVE to marry/fall in love, they CHOOSE to do so because they have an alternative.'

Fifty-eight-year-old Jane L chose *Jane Eyre* as a favourite novel, but told me: 'A passage was read to me when I was a little girl (the excerpt when Mr Brocklehurst insists that the girl with curly hair has it all cut off—I was a curly-haired child). I was entranced and horrified.' Despite or because of this, she said that moment began a lifelong passion for the Brontës, explaining that the book 'says so much about the thoughts and feelings of women... [and] about class and social position as well as love and relationships'. She also identified with it because it was set in Yorkshire, her home county. A 31-year-old respondent, Laura H, admitted that *Jane Eyre* had been very influential on her 'perceptions of relationships (not in a good way!)'. Young Adult writer Lena Coakley, orphaned at 12, went to live with her grandmother who read the novel aloud to her, probably thinking it would comfort the child. But comfort was the last thing she recalled: 'Because of my age, it was the young Jane with whom I identified, the Jane trapped in the haunted "red room", the Jane forced to go to the horrible Lowood School.'[43]

For a Christmas present, Hilary Mantel received a set of books including *Jane Eyre*. She was told she wouldn't understand it 'and there's nothing more enticing to a child'. But the novel was abridged:

> I walked away with the idea that Jane Eyre is a much better book than it actually is... [What you lost in this version] was all the embarrassing stuff about Jane hearing his voice calling... I wasn't interested in the love story between her and Rochester and I'm still not. I was interested in Jane the child and the mad woman in the attic—the horror, the gothic aspect of it. I'd have been much more interested in Jane if she'd gone off with the missionary.

The reading of *Jane Eyre* and *Kidnapped* (her favourite childhood read) began a writing career informed by the Gothic heart of Brontë's novel:

> What I have taken from fiction is that, however painful it is, you have to go on a journey, you have to leave home and you have to make your way in the world. That is what I see as a life's work—making one's way in the world. Sooner or later you're going to have to open the doors with the monster behind.[44]

Re-Reading Jane Eyre

I asked three Bristol-based library groups (of very different class and educational backgrounds) to re-read *Jane Eyre* and discuss it.[45] All of them felt it spoke directly to them, about a female character who is 'plain and overlooked' refusing to accept her lot, highly valuing education, seeking new horizons, dealing with terrible injustice and unfairness by challenging the Church and those around her to get what she deserved. One of the group described it as 'gruesome', following Mantel's lead in tuning into its decidedly Gothic tone (despite the fact most readers see it as a romance). Two women identified with the child Jane sitting reading behind the curtain. One said: 'That's what I did—sat and read all day and hoped not to be found!' The terrible treatment Jane received at Lowood School, and Jane's poignant relationship with the dying Helen Burns, struck a chord in adolescence. One reader recalled Jane's plucky response to the cruel and hypocritical school inspector Mr Brocklehurst who asked what she must do to avoid going to hell: 'I must keep well and not die.' Another identified this unequivocally as a woman's read:

> I don't know any men who have read *Jane Eyre*. It is written from a female point of view about what it was like to be a woman and a girl growing up . . . Jane Eyre doesn't accept this is all she can have in life. She has aspirations—how can I go beyond this horizon? It is about finding ways to go beyond it, go against the social constraints of the day . . . Jane Eyre is challenging the status quo.

That memorable much-quoted line, 'Reader, I married him,' is remembered by one woman as the final line of the book—as would befit a classic romance, albeit with an assertive heroine. When she re-read it she realized to her surprise that the novel concludes with a long account of the fate of that husband not chosen, St John Rivers.

An older woman first read it at the age of 15 or 16 and related strongly to the romance between Jane and Rochester: 'Now I'm 72, it's the imagery and the use of language. It was very evocative, the description of nature—like a character itself, vibrant and lyrical.' One reader compared Brontë's sense of nature with contemporary 'mindfulness' especially when Jane seeks solace in the garden and feels better for it. Another said her reading had been altered by Jean Rhys' reinterpretation of the story, *Wide Sargasso Sea* (1966), and scholarly articles she'd read about the novel. The love story now leaves her cold, and the latter part of the novel with 'ridiculous stuff about the cousins' seems irksome. But most positively, despite a creaky plot, she found in it 'fascinating matters that are of social, historical and cultural significance in terms of women's education and women's rights'—something with which another woman in the group concurred. Several commented sardonically on Jane's discovery of her relatives and (a fantasy many of us share) the large inheritance enabling her to marry and live comfortably with Rochester.

This reminded me of the working-class mixed-race writer Kit de Waal, who noted Jane's opportune transformation into rich heiress, and asked herself who she would have been at Thornfield Hall. The answer is 'Leah, the maid of whom we are given few details and no sense of her life and passions or whether Charlotte Brontë considered her, like Jane, a "free human being with an independent will".[46] One woman commented that 'in the end the only thing that gets her out of her ghastly life is marriage, it is no different from Jane Austen, and all so convenient'. Contemporary perspectives on mental illness and treatment of orphans led to some anger about the issues raised. Several correspondents deplored the cruel and inhumane treatment of the young Jane and Adèle (the latter referred to as 'it' despite being possibly Rochester's own child), as well as Rochester's first wife, Bertha Mason.

One problematic, and rather unfashionable, element of the novel that emerged from this re-reading was religion. One reader saw the 'spiritual religious thread right through the book' that led Jane to reject Rochester initially because of her 'engrained belief in God and right and conscience'. A group member raised the fact that St John Rivers has the last word, and suggests that Charlotte Brontë's consciousness of her Victorian reading public (and need to be read initially as a male writer) led her to make it a Christian novel. On the other hand, some saw it as a deeply anti-Christian novel, especially because of Rochester's behaviour. The ending focusing on St John Rivers made the group uneasy, but in one case he was compared with the lone outsider figure on stage often commenting in Shakespeare's plays—a reminder that people aren't always able to couple, and they don't necessarily live happily ever after.

One of the group said this was a novel you could identify with at different stages of your life. As with other books, she read it with women in her family, including her mother: 'It was part of a shared family background.' As child or young adult readers, many of them read the novel as a love story ('a very romantic master/servant relationship') and they commented on the fact that TV and film versions focus on the Jane/Rochester love affair, omitting the many other social and economic issues in the book which older readers find most engaging. They all used terms so often used by feminist critics about Jane—'strength . . . strong morals . . . bright and feisty . . . a modern woman'. One mother of daughters said the novel reminded her she wanted them to be able to be independent but also to choose to share their lives. Another woman who became a doctor then counsellor suggested the book inspired her to 'help people to recognize their own strengths and be able to shape their own lives, rather than have someone do it for them'.

In 1966, Nicky B was living in Jamaica, where her mother gave her a copy of Jean Rhys' *Wide Sargasso Sea*, a novel set in that country and featuring as central protagonist the 'mad wife' Bertha Mason. She has re-read it more than any other novel, still cherishing the hardback her mother gave her, with its jacket cover 'portraying the lush jungle and the mood of the book'. It remains special partly because of her connection with Jamaica, partly because she finds the language extraordinary. She admires the way Rhys reworked the Ur-text, giving us a sympathetic understanding of Bertha and her final destructive act of burning Thornfield Hall. And she shared this passion with her mother; both of them—living in Devon—found their way via Rhys to Diana Athill. Nicky quoted from a letter written by Rhys to Athill from Cheriton Fitzpaine, Devon, on the day her husband Max was cremated in Exeter. This letter related a recurrent dream that she was going to have a baby, then that the baby was 'a puny weak thing' in a cradle—an indication to her that she must finish her book. That was how Jean Rhys described to her friend the completion of *Wide Sargasso Sea*. For reader Nicky, the personal connections she shared with Jean Rhys and her mother opened up the writings of another woman who remained important to their shared reading history.

Adaptation and Reinterpretation

Wide Sargasso Sea is often acclaimed as the best reworking of *Jane Eyre*, directly taking on the question of who the first Mrs Rochester was, and how she came to lose her sanity and freedom—challenging the reader's sympathy for Mr Rochester himself and his status as romantic hero. But Rhys wasn't the first to be troubled by aspects of this unsatisfactory 'romance' as we see in subsequent reworkings, from Elizabeth Barrett Browning's *Aurora Leigh* (1847) and George

Eliot's *The Mill on the Floss* (1860) to Margaret Drabble's *The Waterfall* (1969), and Angela Carter's (alas unfinished) treatment of Rochester's ward, Adèle. Popular novels (including many Mills & Boon romances) have drawn on the central themes of the novel for decades, and in 2002 artist Paula Rego created a series of twenty-five disturbing feminist lithographs based on the story. Finally, prefacing a whole stream of feminist literary criticism on *Jane Eyre* and other Brontë novels, critics Sandra M. Gilbert and Susan Gubar placed that central subversive figure of Bertha Mason at the heart of their groundbreaking feminist study of women's writing, *The Madwoman in the Attic.*[47]

But there is one *Jane Eyre*-themed novel that has captured imaginations since its publication and first film version, and that is seen as a modern reworking of its Gothic subtext. In 2017, to celebrate their 225th anniversary, W. H. Smith asked readers to vote for their favourite book of the last 225 years. Daphne du Maurier's *Rebecca* (1938) won the vote against both Austen and Charlotte Brontë. This novel engages intertextually with Brontë's text, taking key figures—the young penniless governess, the older sexually experienced landowner, the figure of the first wife haunting the second, and finally the symbolic burning of the house of terrible secrets. But du Maurier startles her reader, subverting romantic norms by making the Rochester figure, Max de Winter, the murderer of wayward first wife Rebecca, and his second wife (carefully never named) an accomplice through silence, with the post-conflagration life a living death in exile from their English home. On first publication, *The Times* referred to *Rebecca* as a 'novelette', a term Alfred Hitchcock also used dismissively to François Truffaut about the 1940 film version he made under producer David O. Selznick, in which he made the eponymous character's murder a tragic accident to produce a happy romantic ending for female audiences (Figure 3.3).[48]

But in recent years, as novelists Susan Hill, Sally Beauman, Maureen Freely, Mary Wings, and Justine Picardie have reinterpreted *Rebecca*, and feminist critics have revisited her fiction, du Maurier's reworking of Gothic and romance themes have enlarged her reputation as an innovative and challenging writer around issues of class,

Figure 3.3 *Rebecca*, 1940, Laurence Olivier and Joan Fontaine
Photo 12 / Alamy Stock Photo

gender, and sexuality. And as with the growing status of those key novels by Jane Austen and Charlotte Brontë, du Maurier's *Rebecca* now enjoys the status of classic text following acclaimed film and TV versions, stage and opera productions, serious biographies and critical studies, as well as tourist locations (Cornwall's 'Du Maurier Country').[49] It is no coincidence that, a keen reader herself, Daphne du Maurier was deeply influenced by all the Brontës at different stages of her writing career. Indeed, she chose a line from an Emily Brontë poem for the title of her first novel, *The Loving Spirit*, wrote a biography of Branwell, and used motifs from Brontë novels in all her work. In 2017, director Paul Thomas Anderson claimed inspiration from *Rebecca* for his film, *Phantom Thread*, with the Jane Eyre/second Mrs de Winter figure, waitress-turned-muse Alma gaining awesome power over her charismatic but increasingly vulnerable and diminished husband.

The Legacy for Women of Pride and Prejudice and Jane Eyre

Jane Austen and 'The Brontës' have donated a precious legacy to women readers. Proving irresistible to artists of many kinds, their works have been repeatedly adapted into films, TV and radio versions, and fanfics, and have been reinterpreted and parodied by women writers. This in itself has reinforced a playful and affectionate familiarity with their works, and kept them fresh in audiences' minds. Their most renowned works have both received fresh contemporary significance via key twenty-first-century productions—with Andrew Davies' *Pride and Prejudice*, and Sally Cookson's feminist Bristol Old Vic Theatre's *Jane Eyre* (2014), that became a nationally acclaimed touring production. Because both novels focus primarily on women characters struggling with unmanageable desires within the tight constraints of their societies, and because passion, love, and marriage provide the framework for the narratives, women readers and audiences accord them a special place in our emotional lives and histories.

Besides, both novels take seriously the practice of reading well, be it Fordyce's *Sermons* or the Bible. And while self-conscious reading in *Pride and Prejudice* is satirized—as with affected Caroline Bingley and Mary Bennet—Elizabeth's reading, facilitated by having free run of her father's library (something unusual at the time), comes into its own when she scrutinizes and understands the truth from Darcy's two crucial letters. Jane Eyre, by contrast, is a passionate and thoughtful reader who is punished by having a book hurled at her head. Aged only 10, she tells Brocklehurst her opinions of the Psalms, Revelations, and Job, and discusses literature with the dying Helen Burns. Specific literary choices are named, perhaps to indicate her eclectic, sophisticated taste and intelligence (Beswick's *Books of Birds*, Jonathan Swift's *Gulliver's Travels*, *The Arabian Nights*, and Walter Scott's *Marmion*). Brontë seems to signal that, for a vulnerable young girl and woman without wealth or beauty, *being a good reader* is a bulwark against exploitation and cruelty, a protective inner strength throughout life. A salutary tale for female readers of all ages.[50]

There is another link, too. Both Jane Austen and Charlotte Brontë have thriving societies dedicated to them, holding major national and smaller local meetings, exhibitions, talks, teas, and visits. Their homes provide significant sites for literary pilgrimage. Any day of the week, you may see Janeites flocking into the genteel parts of Bath, where she visited and then lived for five years; Lyme Regis, because of the famous episode in *Persuasion* in which Louisa Musgrave is helped by heroine Anne Elliot after falling on the Cobb; and Chawton Cottage, Hampshire, where she revised the novel she called her 'darling child'.[51] And then there are the film and TV locations which allow visitors to enter into and imagine themselves part of a fictional Austen world: Lyme Park and Chatsworth House, Derbyshire (Darcy's Pemberley), Belton House and Burghley House, Lincolnshire (Lady Catherine de Bourgh's Rosings) and Luckington Court, Wiltshire and Groombridge Place, Kent (the Bennets' Longbourn).[52] Almost all of these sites offer the middle-class visitor tea and cakes, together with 'I love Darcy' totebags, Northanger Abbey tea towels, fridge magnets, and quill pens.

Brontë pilgrimages are even more popular, largely because there is one key destination, the Brontë Parsonage Museum, in Haworth, West Yorkshire (Figure 3.4), which has acquired mythic significance as the inhospitable breeding ground for four creative minds (brother Branwell gets included in this). Run by the Brontë Society, established in 1893 to act as guardian of the family's papers, possessions, and reputation, the Museum attracts thousands of visitors annually with its regular exhibits such as Charlotte's wedding bonnet and Emily's paintbox, and also hosts special exhibitions, talks, family activities, a dressing-up box, and a museum shop. There's often an anniversary to celebrate—the bicentenary of Charlotte's birth in 2016, and of Branwell's in 2017, Anne's in 2020—and guest curators such as Simon Armitage and Clare Twomey are invited to create original projects around their chosen Brontë. Anticipating Emily's bicentenary in 2018, Twomey invited each visitor to the Museum to copy one sentence of *Wuthering Heights* into a handmade book, on display during that year. Film and TV adaptations give it regular visitor boosts, and pride of place in 2017 was the exhibition of photographer's stills, costumes, and props from the celebrated BBC TV drama about the family, Sally Wainwright's *To Walk Invisible* (2016).

For many female critics and readers, it is a matter of celebration that Austen and 'The Brontës' have attracted so much popular acclaim and readerly engagement. But on a Brontë coach tour to

Figure 3.4 Haworth Parsonage, Yorkshire
Ken Biggs / Alamy Stock Photo

Haworth, I was surprised that our guide, a Brontë specialist, set them up in opposition, as if we had to side with one or the other (perhaps as Louise Doughty did, by naming herself 'an Emily'). Following Charlotte Brontë's tired and much-derided description of Austen's work in terms of a neatly bordered garden, the guide lauded as infinitely superior the high passions and great romance of the Brontë oeuvre. Surely the achievement of the last half-century of feminist scholarship is to recognize both these writers' ability to give voice to female needs and aspirations, and to explore emotional, spiritual, and financial anxieties in ways that have spoken vividly to women readers of many kinds. They make a formidable, complementary duo.

4

Romance and Erotica—Fiction by Women for Women

MYTH: Romance readers are obsessed with wine, chocolate and Pride and Prejudice.

FACT: You say that like it's a bad thing.

Maya Rodale, Huffington Post

'All young females are romantic novelists, feverishly plotting their own futures,' reflected novelist Allison Pearson, admitting that Fitzwilliam Darcy satisfied her own childhood fantasies.[1] As we've seen, Darcy and Edward Rochester remain the prototypes of popular romantic heroes—rich owners of grand houses, older and more experienced than their love interest, somewhat mysterious and unreadable until the heroine sees their true worth, transforms them with her innate powers, and accepts true love. Both *Pride and Prejudice* and *Jane Eyre* address the socio-economic and emotional reasons why women are so engaged in matters of love and marriage, in such a way that they have wrapped themselves into many women readers' life narratives.

Romance is one of the oldest and most enduring literary genres. An ever-popular form in Western literature, the term itself encompasses Greek romances, medieval romance, Gothic bourgeois romances of the 1840s, late nineteenth-century romances and modern mass-produced romance. The term 'Romantic' can allude to a literary period in the UK, 1785–1830, covering some of our greatest poets, from Keats to Wordsworth and Coleridge, and in the USA 1830–65, Emerson and Hawthorne to Whitman. 'Romance' describes a wide variety of texts, from Chaucer's *Troilus and Criseyde* and Spencer's *The Faerie Queen* to Keats' *Endymion* and Hawthorne's *The House of Seven*

Gables. It suggests heightened imaginative intensity, ideal worlds, often set in the past, associated with mystery, the remote and exotic, characterized by emotional extremes. Until the late nineteenth century, romance was a respected, revered, and ungendered—even masculine—literary form.[2]

The modern popular romance is the culmination of a long tradition from the eighteenth century of novels of sensation, the Gothic, erotic, and pornographic.

From the second half of the nineteenth century, it became a bestselling genre through Charlotte M. Yonge's *The Heir of Radcliffe* (1853), followed later by three huge popular successes that are now long forgotten—Florence Barclay's *The Rosary* (1909), Ethel M. Dell's *The Way of an Eagle* (1910), and E. M. Hull's *The Sheik* (1919). Ethel Dell was a major influence on the twentieth century's most successful romance writer, Barbara Cartland, who favoured aristocratic or royal landed heroes and sweet virgin heroines ('marrying park gates' as she put it).[3] Originally written and read by both genders, and despite the many male writers still reworking romance, from the late nineteenth century onwards it has been defined as a genre about love written by women, aimed mainly at female readers. As I quoted earlier, in 2017, 92 per cent of romance and 94 per cent of family/ historical romance saga purchasers are women. Authored by main-stream bestselling authors such as Catherine Cookson, Jilly Cooper, Danielle Steel, and JoJo Moyes, romance continues to be one of the publishing industry's success stories. Film and TV adaptations of romance are box office magic. Like other forms of fiction, romance has evolved through the decades, giving its heroines increasing agency and independence, with jobs, sometimes broken marriages and children, and developed lives that don't simply buckle when the hero enters the scene. He, too, is more likely to be a complex and vulnerable figure who craves understanding and love, and is ready to compromise his own life to suit his beloved. Romance is now seen in terms of a complex modern quest; as Norah Roberts puts it: 'Yes, there is a happy ending. But the book isn't about the happy ending. It's about the journey to that happy ending.'[4]

There is now a bewildering array of types of romance: online fan fiction, the family saga, historicals, sweet and sexy romances, paranormal, Christian and inspirational, BBW (big black woman), POC (people of colour), medical, MM (male male), MMF (male male female, also known as ménage), harem (one man many women), reverse harem (many men courting and attempting to woo one woman), and Cougar (younger man, older woman). There are Ankara Press' 'new and hip' African romances, and LGBTQ titles.[5] The Romantic Novelists' Association claims a romantic novel is sold in the UK every two seconds, yet it is the least critically respected genre. Known for their subject matter of (overwhelmingly white heterosexual) desire, fantasy, and sex, romances are loved by readers for their woman-centredness and liberating approach to sexual desire, but condemned by many others for their stock characters and situations, fuzzy utopianism, with clichéd concentration on the white male/female couple and inevitable Happy Ever After (referred to by aficionados as HEA) or—in romances aimed at younger readers—Happy For Now (HFN). The brand marketing, standard covers, titles, and subject matter have all led to this genre being dismissed as 'formulaic'.

Crime, by contrast, suffers no such fate—almost certainly because it is read by both genders (see Chapter 5). Romantic novelist Nora Roberts complained that 'mystery novels are socially and culturally acceptable reading material; they are not the victim of the "scribbling for silly women" reputation that romances endure'. Those 'silly women' were demeaned in 1970 when Germaine Greer referred to 'sexual religion' as 'the opiate of the supermenial'—crudely parodied as 'dope for dopes'. Alan Boon (of Mills & Boon) called his romances 'a drug, a form of Valium for women'.[6] In their book, *Beyond Heaving Bosoms: The Smart Bitches' Guide to Romance Novels*, American romance enthusiasts Sarah Wendell and Candy Tan describe the stereotyped romance reader as 'rather dim and kind of tubby—undereducated *and* undersexed—and she displays a distressing affinity for mom jeans and sweaters covered in puffy paint and appliquéd kittens'.[7] British commentators harbour similar prejudices about women readers in cardigans.

Taking Romance Seriously

In the 1980s, feminist academics (including myself) became intrigued by romance reading, partly because—paradoxically—the rise of the women's movement in the 1970s was matched by significant growth in sales of romantic fiction. Aware of dismissive or hostile attitudes to the

Figure 4.1 Barbara Cartland at home

Stephen Shepherd / Alamy Stock Photo

genre, Marxist, Freudian, and feminist psychoanalytic critics debated issues around mass readership, cultural representations of desire and fantasy, and the conservative or transgressive nature of popular fiction.[8] This was also the shoulder-pads decade of career feminism and the UK's first woman prime minister, Margaret Thatcher. Throughout the 1980s, the British were captivated by the doomed marriage in 1981 of 33-year-old Prince ['Charming'] Charles and 20-year-old Lady ['Cinderella'] Diana, step-granddaughter of 'Queen of Romance' Barbara Cartland (Figure 4.1). Diana was believed to read little except her step-grandmother's novels which—as Cartland later admitted—did her little good. Cartland herself became a much-parodied figure colouring public perceptions of romantic fiction: as romance writer Veronica Henry suggested, '[romance] has suffered from the clichéd image of the eccentric novelist dressed in pink dictating her novels from the chaise longue'.[9]

This decade produced a new batch of bestselling blockbusters which I have called 'the sexy greedy saga', by writers such as Susan Howatch, Jackie Collins, Shirley Conran, and Zoe Fairbairns. Strong, career-driven female characters have many a sexual relationship, but this no longer defines them—and a healthy bank balance makes up for lost love. The 1980s also saw re-imaginings or pastiches of romance by writers like Margaret Atwood (*Lady Oracle*, 1976), Marilyn French (*The Bleeding Heart*, 1980), and Jeanette Winterson et al. (*Passion Fruit: Romantic Fiction with a Twist*, 1986), with lesbian characters and themes entering the scene. Critical studies of romance by American critics such as Tania Modleski and Janice A. Radway, and British academics Alison Light, Cora Kaplan, and Jean Radford, signalled a new serious attention to the genre, and put the subject on the academic curriculum and thus national cultural agenda.

Critics have suggested the romance provides women with the opportunity for self-transcendence, to imagine being ravished, adored, protected, and loved. It also enables women imaginatively to resist the constraints and excesses of a male-dominated society, and to find a cathartic space in which to explore fear and guilt, as well as revenge fantasies, around fathers and husbands. Radway's *Reading the Romance* analysed the romance reading habits and preferences of forty-two women in a small US town, and confirmed what critics had argued about the complexities of romance reading. As I, too, discovered when discussing *Gone With the Wind* with readers, women gregariously swap romance books, memories, and ideas, and exchange with each other on and offline favourite lines, narratives, and playful comments on characters and endings. Women can be fierce critics but also enjoy banter and erotic fantasies around the stories. Readers devour romances actively, discriminating between texts and having a shrewd sense of how to find stories and characters that appeal—often via recommendation from friends or family members. *Gone With the Wind* enthusiasts were acutely aware of the shortcomings of the central characters, and were able both to understand and also criticize the flawed heroine Scarlett O'Hara, and they spent many a long hour debating with other girls and women whether Scarlett ever gets back bad boy Rhett Butler (and if not, why not). Romance, it seems, allows a declaration of independence (this is 'my space, my time, my choice of books').

The romance story is owned in a special way by women—in novelist Violet Winspear's words, 'a dream world for women only. An escape from the ironing board and the frying pan.'[10] Books of simple plots with single narrative strands and strong central characters can be picked up and put down between bouts of housework, breast-feeding, demands of a job or caring, chemotherapy, and more. Three of my correspondents summarized the self-deprecatory or sardonic attitude to this kind of reading. Amy W (aged 26) told me of her mum: 'A large body of free escapism has lured her into Mills & Boon... something you can read and be absorbed in without engaging the brain.' Sixty-year-old Lucy M's enthusiasm for romantic fiction 'waxes and wanes. It's never been a substitute for the real thing, and when a relationship is going well, I don't need to retreat into a book.' Liisa [*sic*] O (aged 36) wrote to me: 'I read a lot of what I call trashy fiction, something that takes me out of the real world and into the dreamy world of happy endings...I read more women [Sophie Kinsella, Susan Lewis] as they tend to write the soppy romances I enjoy.'

Successful romantic novelist Katie Fforde told me she read romances obsessively while a young mother, when all she could talk about was nappies, and so her reading was 'a place to be away from [my] own life'. Although she was 'addicted' to these books, she claimed that the fantasy of a powerful man sweeping her up and taking her away from all this was a pleasurable fantasy: 'I'd say most women know the difference between these and their real lives and I don't think they think they'll marry a millionaire. They know the difference between fantasy and reality.' For her, these novels were a 'prop, like anything that's easy to digest'—but she admitted that eventually 'you get fed up with junk food'.[11] As I've already suggested, the 'escape' element of reading is often equated with secretive indulgence in sweet things, the easy palate-pleasing power of forbidden ('junk') rather than improving food. As one woman commented online: 'Reading a general fiction book is like a five-course meal with dessert afterward. A romance novel is like a tub of ice-cream eaten when no one's looking.'[12] The greedy pleasure, guilt, and slight self-disgust, women feel as binge-eaters and romance readers are a reminder of the ambivalent attitudes women have towards 'naughty but nice' food and fiction.

Writers like Fforde get irritated by the 'massive snobbery' of critics towards the genre, while one romance writer I contacted (whose website is scattered with references to her long- and short-listing for romantic novel awards) claimed defensively neither to write nor read romance, and instead to be a writer of 'contemporary novels for women'. Most romantic novel writers use pseudonyms, perhaps as a way of distancing themselves from what they know to be a discredited literary form. Emily Murdoch (a pseudonym) told me she describes herself to *women* as a romance writer, while to *men*, a writer of historical fiction. Veronica Henry, on the other hand, claims that people are coming round to the notion that romance 'boasts some of the best writing around', and observes wryly that 'there will always be prejudice against anything that has commercial success. Who's laughing, though?'

Along with erotica, the only fictional genre written by women for women, modern romance puts women at the centre of the narrative, addresses our deepest desires for love and committed and sustained relationships, and also speaks strongly to us about our dreams and fantasies (two words that crop up repeatedly). In real life the Second Sex, in romance women are never just someone's daughter, wife, or mother. Instead they are the central drivers—and in Emily Murdoch's words, 'the prize'.[13] Although a woman reads a romance alone, often in secret away from male family members and workmates, she joins a virtual communal realm of female readers who share experiences and thus understand one another's responses. On the allaboutromance. com website, a retired rabbi and marriage counsellor (sounding like *Woman's Own* circa 1958) claims that women love romance because 'it made them anticipate sex/caring/love in a fictional context' and neuroscientists and many agony aunts claim that the anticipation of sex is more erotic than sex itself. Cultural historian Alison Light wrote wittily: 'The reader is left in a permanent state of foreplay, but I would guess that for many women this is the best heterosexual sex they ever get.'[14] Given the plethora of sexologists' accounts of female disappointment with sexual partners (usually around an inability to achieve orgasm), and women's increasing knowledge about their bodies and sexual potential, it's not surprising readers are turned on by narratives of male characters who understand, and know how to excite and satisfy, women's bodies. Benedict Nightingale suggested that the fantasies in these books were 'actually complaints about men',[15] so here is a unique space in which a woman can voice such complaints to herself and others, and dream of the ideal partner who will—in the HEA— appreciate her for everything she is and cater to her every physical and emotional need.

And of all genres, romance (like romcom films) allows women a form of expression associated most closely with femininity—namely, crying. My own research on *Gone With the Wind* found many women referring to it as a 'twelve-hankie' book and film, while the blurbs inside Jojo Moyes' dystopian bestseller *Me Before You* praise it as 'a real weepie', with reviewers urging readers to devour it 'like candy, between tears' and to 'Make sure you have a box of tissues to hand!'[16] This emphasis on great romances (often with Gothic themes or subtexts) as 'weepies' suggests they're designed to arouse in women bittersweet emotions and internal conflicts, best indulged in private away from the real people in our lives.

Mills & Boon

The best known and largest UK romance publisher is Mills & Boon. In 1997, the Oxford English Dictionary added 'Mills & Boon' to its canon, giving it the generic meaning 'romantic story book'. The firm was established in 1908 by Gerald Mills and Charles Boon as a general fiction publisher, including names such as Robert Lynd, Hugh Walpole, and P. G. Wodehouse. Its first bestseller, however, was by a woman, E. S. Stevens' *The Veil: A Romance of Tunisia* (1909)— the earliest of several 'sheikh and desert romances' produced by the firm and leading eventually to their specialization in fiction aimed at women. By the Second World War, the novels were standardized with trademark covers—stressing the *brand* rather than author's name, supplying new titles fortnightly to weekly, twopenny libraries (though paper rationing limited size and availability). After the war and the end of rationing, Mills & Boon started a direct mail catalogue operation, linked into thriving magazine fiction publication—most notably *Woman's Weekly*—and it established a personal relationship with authors that remains today. During the 1960s, as the women's liberation movement gained pace, the company thrived in the paperback revolution, and produced some of its most profitable writers; commercially successful Violet Winspear's erotic tales pushed the boundaries beyond the hitherto most popular doctor–nurse romances of the 1950s.

In 1971, the American Harlequin company merged with Mills & Boon to create a huge lucrative global market and a user-friendly mail order operation delivering books to women's own doors or (in later years) e-books onto electronic devices, together with special offers, 'surprises', and in recent times a hub within the website, 'Socialise', where readers can post blogs and reviews, enter competitions, and get details of events. By the mid-1980s Harlequin Mills & Boon were selling roughly 250 million books worldwide.

> In 1989, to mark Harlequin's fortieth anniversary, each of the company's 100 foreign markets published the same title on the same date, *A Reason For Being* by [British] author Penny Jordan—their most popular writer. When the Berlin Wall came down in 1989, staff from their West German office handed out 750,000 free copies to women from East Germany. [Free at last!?][17]

Today the leading world publisher of romance fiction, Mills & Boon publish 120 new titles per month, and—with sixteen different series—claim to sell a new book every five seconds in the UK, approximately 87 per cent to women.[18] They receive thousands of submissions annually; those who sneer at the imprint and feel they could easily knock off a novel or two soon learn there is ferocious competition. Novelist Emma Healey, author of bestselling *Elizabeth is Missing*, recalls being self-harming and suicidal while at school until she turned to romantic fiction: 'Mills & Boon saved my life . . . I don't think I'd have been able to get through life had I not been able to read one book, and then a few hours later pick up the next one.' For her, the escapism and the happy endings helped—'that's what you want when you are feeling shit'—but she also credits the novels with making her a better writer: 'There's a lot of emphasis on good dialogue, on being snappy. They are not total trash.'[19] She is by no means the only writer to have learned from reading, and indeed writing, Mills & Boon novels, nor the only woman to have found them a lifesaver. Linda W told me she turned to them 'trying to read when unwell mentally. You really need to read books that feel safe.'

Over the decades, like other romance publishers, the firm has adapted to social change and evolving reader expectations. The novels have had to respond to women's changing roles, developments in contraception, the feminist movement, progressive social attitudes around sexuality and sex itself, and shifts in attitudes to class (especially to royalty and the aristocracy, who once constituted the most desired heroes). In the 1990s, as 'date rape' was recognized as a crime raising important social issues, writers avoided those ubiquitous scenes of rape and sexual violence that had prevailed in past decades. However, intersectionalism is stubbornly ignored; the standard Mills & Boon is still overwhelmingly white and heterosexual, with mixed-race and LBGTQ couples hardly figuring. A standard format of 180–200 pages has remained in place, but the books' designs have evolved to include fewer soft-focus pastel landscapes with feathers and brooches, more images of men on the covers, and less clichéd 'clinches'. In a 2018 radical revamp, design company Hyland changed the shape of the logo, replaced the rose symbol with a heart, and/or adapted colour palates, typefaces, and images to suit the sixteen different series—a brand in tune with the times. There is now an imprint, Carina, which invites erotic short stories (one recent collection is called *The Dirty Bits*) and—as they court younger and more diverse readers—the direction of travel appears to be ever steamier.

Big Business

However, romantic novel publishing is by no means confined to the Mills & Boon company or imprint. Romance is a global business, and its writers must pitch to international markets. Business models evolve all the time, along with the jacket designs, subject matter, and a shift from 'Plain Jane' to 'Alpha kick ass' heroines, and so on. In the USA, it's said one in every five people reads a romance, while one in eight fiction books purchased in the UK is romance. One of the warmest invitations I received while researching this book came from Katie Fforde, president of the Romantic Novelists' Association (sister to the powerful Romance Writers of America). I joined the RNA as an associate member, and she took me as her guest to the Winter Party. Here, amid a sea of perfumed, glamorously dressed and coiffed writers (mostly women, with male publishers and agents circling the floor), all enjoying champagne and excellent canapés, the air fizzed with everyone's ambitious plans for and commitment to a maligned but lucrative literary form.

Opening my RNA newsletter, I discovered confirmation of the strong networking demonstrated that night. 'Romance Matters' details meetings of regional chapters, a summer conference and party, RNA Industry Awards, and author profiles. Here I learned that the term 'chick lit' was being replaced by 'romcom', and 'grip lit' is the new term for fiction with a dark edge. I gathered tips on plotting, getting reviewed, self-publishing, and writing good sex (common advice is to get drunk so you don't worry about what the vicar or your mother might think). I also read with awe an interview with bestselling American writer Eloisa James, who—beside writing romances—is a professor of Shakespeare at Fordham University, mother of two, wife to an Italian count, with homes in New York and Florence. A romantic heroine in her own right . . .

Writers of romance are a very mixed group, and—as Eloisa James demonstrates—increasingly highly educated and sophisticated, aware that (unlike 'literary' fiction) success in this field will secure the pad in Florence and a steady income for life. But *readers* are also a surprisingly heterogeneous group, and proliferating websites devoted to romance indicate the commitment of such readers, as well as their detailed knowledge of writers and their works. Of all publishing categories, this one reaches out to bring its readers and writers together—with advanced copies, downloadable freebies, author swag gifts (book-marks, tote bags, etc.), and female-friendly author websites, inviting dialogue on Facebook and Twitter and by email with a 24/7 demand on writers' availability. Readers are encouraged to share online intimacy to make them feel a valued part of a female secret society—the romance community. And in 2018, in order to 'increase diversity in romance and relationship-driven fiction', the RNA announced the formation of a Rainbow Chapter for members who identify as and are writing novels featuring characters who are LGBTQIA+.[20]

Erotica—The Success of *Fifty Shades of Grey*

Romantic fiction's increasing boldness in the area of erotica is fuelled by women's changing roles and life choices. Rarer now are closed-door romances featuring virginal young heroines falling for older, richer, sexually experienced heroes (commoner and duke or lord, doctor and nurse being classic couplings). In recent years, erotica (or 'romantica') has produced new series aimed at a more confident, egalitarian, and worldly reader who works outside the home and cannot be demeaned as 'just a housewife'. Women can select from many sub-genres or categories—with 'heat' or 'steam' ratings 1–5 from clean, sweet, and mild to hot and erotica—the kind of romance they prefer.[21] Mills & Boon publishes series called 'Sensual', 'Desire', and 'Blaze', the latter described as: 'Sassy heroines and irresistible heroes embark on sizzling sexual adventures as they play the game of modern love and lust. Expect fast paced reads with plenty of steamy encounters.'[22] A long way from doctor–nurse power play, with the accompanying female virginity and passivity required in the heyday of 1950s and 1960s romances. Targeting a wide range of age and class groups, the publisher is now catering for contemporary women's erotic tastes and social preoccupations: both partners usually have jobs, sexual and other life experience, even children, so the HEA ending may be bittersweet and isn't necessarily marriage.

The rise of erotica is partly a result of the digital age, in which online self-publishing, fan fiction, and blogging have produced a body of fiction that has defied the caution and censorship of publishers, been downloaded onto electronic devices for private reading, and thus produced new stories and readers. Kindles and iPads have been described as 'the ultimate brown paper wrapper' (as with earlier generations' furtive reading of Radclyffe Hall's *The Well of Loneliness*, Kathleen E. Woodiwiss' *The Flame and the Flower*, or Jilly Cooper's *Riders*). Mischief Books launched with a suggestive tag line, 'private pleasures with a hand-held device'—what one woman's daughter called 'mummy's naughty reader'. (*Plus ça change*—remember the Pierre-Antoine Baudoin painting of a masturbating reader? See Figure 0.3.)

E. L. James' *Fifty Shades of Grey* reflects a growing confidence among women writers, spurred on by new female readerships for online reworkings of earlier novels or more daring narratives. James first published fan fiction online as *Snowqueens Icedragon*, inspired by the series adored by young women readers, Stephanie Meyer's *Twilight*, as well as chick lit and erotic romances. Her tales of Ana Steele, an innocent young virgin who tames her psychologically disturbed and sexually violent man, Christian Grey ('Mr Darcy with nipple-clamps'[23]), has sold more copies of her trilogy than almost any author in recent times (at least 4.7 million copies in the UK alone), with the publishing industry amazed that women responded so powerfully to rather tame erotica. This *succès de scandale* is probably the most talked-about literary event since the sensational 1960 trial of *Lady Chatterley's*

Lover. All the books and film versions were successful, and became the subject of much media commentary and academic research, as well as a host of imitators. In *Book Club* (2018), a romantic comedy starring a group of Hollywood's top actors (Diane Keaton, Jane Fonda, Candice Bergen, and Mary Steenburgen), four mature friends read with shock and awe *Fifty Shades* in their longstanding book club. This revitalizes their libidos in such a way that each opens up to new emotional and sexual possibilities. Vivian, the most sexually liberated character (Jane Fonda), urges the book club to read it as an updated version of that earlier sexy feminist classic, Erica Jong's *Fear of Flying* (1973). The film therefore alludes (albeit clumsily) to a trajectory of women's erotic writing from Second Wave feminism to the MeToo generation.

This 'mommy porn', the fastest-selling paperback and e-book of all time, is a rare example of a romance novel going mainstream, and a first for self-published, fan-fiction romance. Its impact has gone well beyond the romance-reading community.[24] Whispering word of mouth has led to a viral female marketing campaign, with large numbers of women (and a scattering of men) discussing it with family and friends, laughing at, and online posting about this much-hyped phenomenon. One journalist called the first volume 'a nice girl's nasty book', and another noted that 'all over the country, groups of mums are discussing Christian's sexual motivations over a slice of Battenburg [a rather classy cake]'.[25]

Online support, reading and chat groups post sardonic and humorous material: 'Fifty Shades is my drug'; '50 Shades of Sarcasm—Grey's Crazy Fangirls'. Boutique hotels offer 'bed-and-bondage breaks' complete with Love Boxes and lists of 'saucy assignments'. And—as with Jane Austen's birthplace and Charlotte Brontë's Haworth—you may make a pilgrimage to the Seattle Escala apartments, the setting for Christian Grey's place incorporating the Red Room of Pain. There's a parody film, *Fifty Shades of Black* (2016), including a black Christian Grey, and a glut of post-*Fifty Shades* publications: *Tickle Torture, One Hundred Strokes of the Brush Before Bed*, and *Ultimate Spanking*. A Somerset Women's Institute group published a steamy short story collection for charity, and on World Book Day 2015, an 11-year-old male pupil scandalized his school by dressing as Christian Grey.

Critics and journalists expressed the kind of contempt reserved for formula romances, the 'shopping and fucking' novel, and indeed women's genres in general, as they patronized 'mums' and especially older women who giggle over Christian's sexual practices (even in reading groups!). Uneasy commentators warn of the threat this text poses to conventional female sexual life and practices—especially when so many other writers have followed her example, and 'slash' fanfiction has borrowed James' characters for same sex/trans-gender/queer characters and narratives. What on earth, they sur-mise, might this do for heterosexual relationships and marriage? The same anxieties had been expressed after the publication of Nancy Friday's sensational account from women's letters and interviews, *My Secret Garden: Women's Sexual Fantasies*, revealing that rape was a common fantasy; the success of this book and subsequent accounts opened the door to non-fictional and fictional treatments of women's transgressive desires.

However, many echoed Andrew O'Hagan's comment on *Fifty Shades* that the novels deploy 'every bonkbuster cliché in existence—powerful men, private planes and multiple orgasms', and there are warnings of the dangers of BDSM (bondage, discipline or dominance, sadism or submission, and masochism) in 'an instruction manual for an abusive individual to sexually torture a vulnerable young woman'. According to one journalist: 'Sex games do go wrong. Hospitals are full of people who have been injured this way. Deaths have occurred.'[26]

Fanny Burney, Jane Austen, Hannah More, and many of their successors would have recognized only too well those contemporary warnings of the dangers of reading such fiction—with psychologists arguing that the reading of *Fifty Shades* is 'normalizing abuse' and reinforcing negative emotional and physical behaviour. As in earlier centuries, the effect on women of sexually explicit or suggestive fiction is seen as a cause for moral panic. In an academic study of romantic comedy films and their audiences in three European countries, Alice Guilluy quotes critics' concern that young women will draw conclu-sions from the films' narratives that stalking is normal masculine behaviour.[27] It seems that vulnerable young women can't be trusted to distinguish between fictional and real scenarios, and may need protection (perhaps by censorship).

Feminist scholars have discussed the ways E. L. James has managed to tap into and subvert the romance form to make domesticated

pornography for a contemporary female reader. Ruth A. Deller
Clarissa Smith undertook a survey of *Fifty Shades* readers and—in vi
of the enormous media attention and voluminous worldwide sales
found that many readers were drawn to the books to see what the fuss
was all about. They wanted to be part of a wider conversation about
them, and so they were—with families, friends, partners, work colleagues, and book clubs. In the women's prison I visited, I learned that
the library had a long waiting list for the books. The contumely
thrown at readers was part of the fun. Women could claim they
were reading them to join in general mockery of the writer's style
and the absurdity of the story across three volumes, but also to give
themselves holiday or downtime 'trash' reading—as well as an erogen-
ous thrill. Who said women have no sense of humour? And these
books and films have become the focus for discussions among women
about erotic lives and fantasies; on Twitter and blogs you can see how
Fifty Shades has liberated sexual imaginations and given women permission to discuss and explore their sexuality as well as to dabble in
BDSM experiments (and blog/brag about it). As Lisa Appignanesi
said of romance in general and *Fifty Shades* in particular: 'Women . . .
just seem to be turned on by attentive love . . . however many guises
that might wear.'[28] However, some romance writers resent the fact
that, when writing about sex, they feel they're suspected of emulating
the sex scenes in *Fifty Shades*. Veronica Henry said her books used to
have 'quite a naughty edge' but, since the *Fifty Shades* phenomenon
and rise of erotic fiction, she has had to focus far more on the
emotional than the physical.

Fifty Shades has tapped into the imaginative pleasures of female
submissiveness to masculine force. This doesn't mean women are
literally inviting rape or sexual violence, but it does suggest that *Fifty
Shades* allows women to reconsider the perverse and diverse nature of
desire. One woman who spoke to Deller and Smith suggested that
what would be a nightmare in real life was—in fiction—a fine tale:
'She actually tames him, despite his attempts to dominate her—isn't
that women's real fantasy?'[29] This is often recognized as the central
fantasy of romance narratives, and writers have claimed this is what
they offer to female readers—an empowering fantasy of subduing
male power. But this is changing in the current climate of 'rape
culture' (Figure 4.2).[30]

Figure 4.2 Women campaigning against domestic abuse demonstrate at premiere of film *Fifty Shades of Grey*, Leicester Square, London, 12 February 2015
ZUMA Press, Inc. / Alamy Stock Photo

The Rape Scenario

Given that many young women read romances in early teenage years, commentators have suggested that romance educates women about their bodies, introduces them to sexual practices such as oral and (in recent years) anal sex, bondage, and *ménages à trois*, and helps them understand how to seduce men, turn on, and if necessary reject men's sexuality. Or, as *Beyond Heaving Bosoms* puts it: 'The Irresistible Woman's Magic Hoo Hoo Tames the Untamable Mighty Wang'.[31] However, in 2018, following the Harvey Weinstein scandal and global MeToo and Time's Up online movements, younger women became very vocal about the fact that a woman's hoo hoo taming the untamable wang simply conjures up scenarios of rape. A romance editor told BBC journalist Kirsty Lang that she had commissioned a book about an older couple's romance; when the male protagonist made a tentative sexual proposition inviting the woman upstairs, her younger female colleagues in the office called it 'a bit rapey'.[32] I wonder if the only romance bookshop in Los Angeles, The Ripped Bodice, established in 2016, may be reconsidering its name. The erotic charge of powerful men has taken a hammering in the face of women calling out domestic abuse and coercive behaviour, rape, sexual harassment, illegal female genital mutilation, and the objectification of women's bodies—especially poor, unemployed, disabled, and women of colour who have little economic or sexual power.

The dream of taming a man who wishes to dominate, especially via sexual practices that constrict and punish women's bodies, may once have seemed okay, especially when the relationship ended in the apparent safety of HEA marriage and motherhood. In the late teens of the twenty-first century, these non-vanilla sexual practices give pause for thought. The increasing sales of handcuffs and wooden paddles may seem innocuous enough, but at a time when record numbers of rapes and sexual assaults are recorded, and when coercive control is firmly on the legal agenda, all that 'kinky fuckery' can seem unwholesomely smutty and dangerous. In a 2018 high-profile case involving allegations of assault within BDSM relationships, the BBC quoted sex experts and practitioners defending BDSM on the grounds that 'full and free consent was a vital element of the practice, in which partners consent to inflicting or enduring pain or physical abuse'.[33] The way Christian Grey virtually stalks Ana, isolates her from other people by making her sign a nondisclosure agreement in regard to their relationship, tells her what to eat and drink, gives her a chauffeur-driven car so he knows exactly where she is, as well as dictating where, when, and how their sex takes place, all point to a non-consensual relationship. In *The Vagenda*, Holly Baxter and Rhiannon Lucy Cosslett read *Fifty Shades* as a modern fairytale:

> Prince Charming may not have whipped the tampon out of Snow White's bits before taking her up against the bathroom sink in a Hilton suite, but she certainly hopped on his stallion when he was ready for her . . . guys and gals, it's time to put the fairy tale to bed.[34]

'Cat Person' and Contemporary Sexual Politics

In case you doubt that the romance story has its finger on the button of contemporary sexual politics, look no further than the furore provoked by a short story published in *The New Yorker*, 11 December 2017.

Chiming with the MeToo generation, 'Cat Person' by Kristen Roupenian describes a casual and fairly disastrous sexual encounter between Margot, a 20-year-old white middle-class American student, and 34-year-old Robert (of whom she knows very little, and whose final message to her is 'Whore'). Written in the third person from Margot's brutally honest, intimate perspective, 'Cat Person'—a knowing joke about the prevalence of cats on the Internet—seemed to capture the tortuous nature of contemporary gender dynamics and etiquettes of dating and romance. An instant hit online, the story was praised and trashed in equal measure—the first mainly by women, the second by men—provoking 10,000 millennials to recount their miserable dating experiences, a Twitter account 'Men react to Cat Person', and a BBC short story from the perspective of Robert. Why did it hit a nerve? Commentators note that—because most people read it online—it was seen as an article or essay rather than fiction. This meant that readers, especially men, engaged with it in very personal and defensive ways. Its extensive use of texting draws on a long tradition of the epistolary novel and story, in which men and women both communicate and misunderstand each other in writing. The story also seemed to capture the zeitgeist of a climate in which the toxic masculinity of public figures such as Donald Trump and Kevin Spacey was being stridently challenged by both genders.

Playing with romance archetypes of the young naïve heroine and experienced older man, it alludes to the much-quoted Margaret Atwood claim that women fear men may murder them (Margot worries Robert will kill her), while men fear being laughed at (Robert is upset that Margot laughs at him when he asks if she's a virgin). The story presents a bleak picture of love. Kristen Roupenian herself commented:

> [I]t's an irony of heterosexual relationships, right, that you're searching for a partner who has experienced the world so much differently than you have, and whose romantic and sexual history is so different from your own? That's a pain a lot of women I know have felt acutely, especially in this past year, when all of these terrible shared experiences are becoming part of the public conversation. Women try to talk about these experiences with their partners, and they find themselves failing.[35]

Roupenian has tapped into the confusion and bewilderment young women are feeling about relationships. At a bookshop reading—

promoting *You Know You Want This*, her short story collection that includes 'Cat Person'—she told the audience she was now treated as a dating guru, with women claiming they too were Margot and urging the writer to tell them what to do.[36] *New Yorker* fiction editor Deborah Triesman claimed 'Cat Person' questioned 'people's inability to read each other, inability to read each other sexually'. As I've discussed in relation to Jane Austen, 'reading' a sexual partner is part of what draws women to, and keeps us engaged in, romance fictions. This story hit a nerve in uncertain times when issues of sexual desire, consent, and male–female communication and trust or distrust are high on the agenda.

Young Adult Fiction

As I've suggested, romance is a dynamic form that is constantly evolving. Since the early noughties, there's been a new development in the genre. Young Adult (YA) fiction, emerging from the USA with writers such as Judy Blume, Sarah Dessen, and Meg Cabot, came of age with the publishing sensations, Stephenie Meyer's vampire series, *Twilight* (2005–8, selling over 100 million copies), Suzanne Collins' dystopian post-apocalyptic trilogy, *The Hunger Games* (2008–10, selling 65 million), and John Green's *The Fault in Our Stars* (2012, selling 11 million). Following the huge success of the TV series, *Buffy the Vampire Slayer* (1997–2003), these novels place young women at their centre, addressing adolescent high school crises and concerns, focusing on early love affairs and coming-of-age emotional challenges.

YA looks like an ungendered name for a category that is in fact sold largely to a female market—67 per cent to 33 per cent male.[37] It's proved very successful with young women readers—college students as well as 15+ adolescents—telling stories to girls that address and give significance to their lives in a way few other cultural forms do. British writers are jumping onto the bandwagon, including very young writers. When only 15 years old, a University of Exeter student Beth Reekles from south Wales began posting for fun on Wattpad (an online story platform) chapters of her novel *The Kissing Booth*, set in an American high school. Very quickly she had three million hits, and then decided to tell her parents. Random House spotted and published her, to the annoyance of some Wattpad readers who condemned her for taking the money and no longer posting free material.

This genre is expanding already into 'New Adult' to suit a later teenage/early twenties YA reader. To date, there's little serious critical attention paid to the genre and—as with other female-directed fiction—much snide or hostile media commentary. In the *Times Education Supplement*, one academic dismissed the whole genre as 'gossip fodder' about 'petty anxieties'.[38] Petty as their anxieties may seem to academics, others recognize just why these novels matter. The critic Caitlin Flanagan defines the 'salient fact of an adolescent girl's existence' as 'her need for a secret emotional life—one that she slips into during her sulks and silences, during her endless hours alone in her room, or even just when she's gazing out of the classroom window'. The act of reading, she says, allows her to be 'undisturbed while she works out the big questions of her life, to be hidden from view while still in plain sight, to enter profoundly into the emotional lives of others'.[39] Doesn't this echo many of the reasons why adult women relish romance reading? One 30-year-old graduate student wrote of her pleasure in reading *Twilight*. She suggested that Bella and Edward's story offered 'intense, focused, and unmediated' simplicity: 'I think a lot of women long for those days when there was a magic to the mere thought of kissing someone and being madly, deeply destabilized by love. Where just one look from the parties involved can be enough to make you swoon.'[40] YA writers understand this, have a close, mutually appreciative online relationship with their young readers, mainly on Twitter and Booktube, and feel considerable responsibility for the current generation of vulnerable young women with their high levels of stress, anxiety, self-harm, and social media exposure.

I spoke to one young British YA author, Sara Barnard, who claimed the value of this literary category lies in its offer of counter-narratives to 'the limitations and expectations placed on women as they enter adulthood' and its provision of a 'safe space for girls in a society where they are rarely, if ever, centred'. She concedes that YA fiction is generally white (with a few honourable exceptions by writers such as Malorie Blackman), heterosexual, and somewhat bland, and that it's rare to find feminist stories, violent scenarios, topics such as lesbianism, abortion, and rape. Bucking the trend, her own first novel, *Beautiful Broken Things* (2016), and a few others, have tackled post-trauma narratives about recovery from abuse, incest, self-harm, anorexia, and so on. Despite works such as Holly Bourne's 'spinster club trilogy' featuring strong feminist protagonist, Lottie, and a few historical novels and lesbian tales by Julie Mayhew, Keris Stainton, and others, publishers tend to play safe and provide unchallenging sexual and emotional scenarios for a growing body of female readers, being careful not to preach to or patronize them. The YA sub-genre is still in its early years, but reader enthusiasm and author confidence are already pushing barriers and breaking taboos.

This new body of literature, providing young women with contemporary role models and narratives more immediately relevant than those of earlier generations' choices, from Jane Austen to Louisa M. Alcott, is following the trajectory of romance novels aimed specifically at adult women readers. The digital revolution has shifted focus onto the exposure of secrets via texts and online exposure, as in bestselling Sara Shepard's *Pretty Little Liars* (2006) and Karen M. McManus' *One of Us is Lying* (2017). Until the 1960s to 1970s, romances made suggestive references to female sexual desire and response, including many fade-to-black 'sex scenes' that left much to the imagination and didn't frighten the horses. Their output has become bolder in its representation of assertive and confident women prepared to challenge male power and express their own sexual desires and needs, and as a result has attracted a wider and younger readership. As I've discussed earlier, from Charlotte Brontë onwards, bestselling romances featuring women characters and female preoccupations, targeting female readers, have been pilloried, parodied, and seen by predominantly male critics as a frivolous or titillating literary form that can threaten women readers' well-being.

It seems that YA is following suit, and like adult romance and erotica is causing alarm because of its very popularity among the readers to whom it speaks directly. As these novels began to take on socially and politically sensitive subjects and moved away from soft-focus love stories, there were mixed critical responses to YA, accused first of offering gullible young readers escapism, instant gratification, and nostalgia, then of focusing too much on gloom, family breakdown, and gender uncertainty, and finally of excluding *boy* readers. As Sara Barnard points out, a body of work that has appealed to adolescent girls can't possibly be any good if the young male reader won't engage with it (though she points out wryly that once a male writer, John Green, achieved success in this field, more serious attention was paid). Once again, we see that the committed female fiction reader isn't to be respected or trusted as a literary critic; any kind of writing she and her sisters adore must by definition be of low value. Girls' and women's literary safe spaces—like other such spaces—are sometimes seen as temporary and inferior hideaways before entry into the grown-up arenas of 'literary' fiction or fiction focused on 'serious' (male?) concerns or non-feminine fantasies.

* * *

Romance in all its different forms, including erotica/romantica, remains a significant bestseller and favourite female genre—despite moral anxieties, scepticism, and snobbery by male partners and family members, critics, and educationists. Young and older women continue to buy, borrow, and lend romances to one another, enjoy reading about (often ordinary) heroines who experience the full adoration and attention of desirable partners, and relish the fact that romance writers invite them into a female literary community. In private, treasured spaces and moments, in between caring, domestic, work or school duties, female readers use romantic fiction to indulge in utopian erotic and emotional fantasies addressing dissatisfactions, unmet needs, and desires that are hard to satisfy in a patriarchal society. Whether this is a sop to women, keeping us quiet with fairy tales, or giving us imaginative tools with which to understand and gain power within relationships, is a moot point. What's clear is that romance and erotica writers deal with the subjects of love and emotional and sexual happiness in ways that speak directly to girls' and women's life agendas and preoccupations, and—most crucially—understand the importance of an intimate and trusting connection with their readers.

5

Women, Crime, Sci-Fi, and Fantasy

Crime

It has often amused me watching 'respectable' elderly ladies like me engrossed in the crime section of Colwall Library. Maybe we all have murderous tendencies which are sublimated in reading about others who really do it.

Marian P

One July recently, I sat on the train from Leeds to Harrogate, heading to the celebrated Theakston Old Peculier Crime Writing Festival. Opposite me were groups of women (many clearly middle-aged or retired) eating packed lunches from Tupperware boxes and thermos flasks, enthusiastically discussing the latest most violent novels and looking forward to seeing their favourite writers. Bearing out Marion P's words above, the (female) editor of *Women Crime Writers* said: 'There's a running trope that the gorier the serial-killer narrative, the more likely little old ladies are reading it.'[1] Note the assumption that there's something rather comical about older women enjoying a violent thrill . . .

Romantic fiction is the genre most associated with women, but it is by no means the only one. Crime has long been the most popular and commercially successful literary genre, and at the 2018 London Book Fair it was revealed that, for the first time, crime sales had overtaken those of general fiction. Crime fiction with all its sub-genres—locked-room mystery, thriller, police procedural, hardboiled, forensic, comic, etc. (many in translation from European languages)—has a long history. And as with romance, from the earliest days of cinema and TV, crime has attracted large audiences: gangster films to film noir, Hitchcock's psychological thrillers and Agatha Christie adaptations to

Midsomer Murders and Nordic noir. Read across all classes and genders, it remains the most borrowed genre from British libraries. In the 2017 Royal Society of Literature poll of reading in Britain, respondents were asked to name living writers; of the top eleven, six were crime or thriller writers.

A statistic bandied around is that 65–80 per cent of all crime fiction is read by women. It's sometimes assumed women write and enjoy 'cozy crime', the old-fashioned kind by writers such as Agatha Christie and Dorothy L. Sayers that avoids the grisly and gritty. Indeed, Minette Walters claims she was told in the United States that—presumably by association with those early writers—all British crime was automatically put into the 'cozy' category. But in recent years, there's been a notable increase in women writers and readers of crime that is definitely not that. At the 2014 Theakston Festival, crime writer Melanie McGrath estimated that 80 per cent of the audience and half the writers were women, and females over 55 are now said to be crime's most avid readers. Lee Child, no cozy crime-writer himself, described his reader as female and emphasized the relationship between reader and writer, 'actively interrogating the text and creating the story'. He even responded to one woman's question about whether he would ever write a 'non-Jack Reacher novel' by asking the largely female audience if they wished him to do so. They did.

As with all fictional genres, we know women are far more likely to be readers than men, and women read (indeed seek out) fiction by women far more than their male counterparts. As a result, some male crime writers have given themselves ambiguous names suggesting they are women. One, Martyn Waites, talked to his editor who was seeking a new female thriller writer to be the UK's Karin Slaughter or Tess Gerritsen (both very successful US writers). Waites suggested an idea he'd once read in a news story—a serial killer who targeted pregnant women and cut out their foetuses. His editor was enthusiastic, so he researched novels by popular female writers and *The Surrogate* (2009) was the result, published under the pseudonym Tania Carver. A big bestseller, it was followed by several male writers on both sides of the Atlantic publishing under gender-neutral names (A. J. Finn, S. J. Watson, J. P. Delaney, and so on).[2] Waites expressed surprise that women readers relished the brutality in his story.

Why Crime?

So what is the appeal of crime to men and women, and why are so many women now writing and reading it? Although dismissed and sniggered at far less than romance, crime, too, is sometimes characterized as trivial and unchallenging (note the critical uproar in 2018 when a crime novel, Belinda Bauer's *Snap*, was longlisted for the Man Booker prize). The genre's popularity has been explained in terms of its very predictability, driven by certain 'rules' that have been codified since its first practitioners and theorists such as Edgar Allen Poe, Wilkie Collins, and Arthur Conan Doyle. Crime fiction in all its forms offers puzzles to be solved, a clear and un-enigmatic, if formulaic, dénouement without loose ends—offering that over-used satisfaction of 'closure'. And in the words of Dayna J, one of my interviewees, 'I love Martina Cole . . . I like a twist, a surprise I never saw coming.'

But crime is becoming more sophisticated. Increasingly this genre—which includes 'true crime' (though ostensibly non-fiction, it uses many fictional techniques)—explores corruption, the state of the world, and the nature of morality. Crime writers such as Ian Rankin are hugely popular in prisons. For many enthusiasts, it is the genre that opens up social issues, warts and all, and—to paraphrase James Runcie's words about his *Grantchester* series—a secular space in which to explore the darkest recesses of the soul and human anxieties. Since we live in dystopian times, perhaps this genre best reflects our pessimism and terror of the unknown, our loss of innocence and need to understand evil.

A researcher at Lancaster Medical School established an empirical study of crime readers using that technique of 'Bibliotherapy' I've discussed earlier—reading as a means of improving mental health and well-being.[3] Usually, this technique is used with 'mood-boosting' books, lists of which are produced by The Reading Agency to include predominantly inspiring and uplifting texts. However, Dr Liz Brewster found that reading crime helped her group come to terms with and overcome long-term depression and other mental health problems. She argued that many people saw crime reading as a 'guilty pleasure' because it was seen as frivolous, a waste of time, not great literature. However, for her research subjects, its effects could be extremely therapeutic. All of her sample struggled with their mental health but, paradoxically, 'crime fiction made them feel safe and secure.

The coexistence of mystery and familiarity facilitated improvements in well-being and helped in the recovery process.' Crime's very predictability, the coexistence of the new and the familiar (since everyone knows all ends must be tied up) gave her readers much satisfaction—especially as, with any puzzle, they had to engage with the writer to work out how the narrative would conclude. Brewster's readers spoke of 'a refuge from the world'. This 'refuge' echoes that comforting space which the romance novel also provides as a respite from daily realities.

Women and Crime Fiction

Despite women's reputation for reading fiction that engages us emotionally through empathy with characters rather than ideas, it seems that for many women the *intellectual* challenge of crime (in Dorothy Sayers' words 'that quiet enjoyment of the logical'[4]) is what most appeals. Time and again, women describe their pleasure in crime as comparable with that of the crossword puzzle, jigsaw, and Sudoku: meaty brain-teasers that force you to think and engage all your cerebral resources, allowing you as reader to share the author's intelligence and omniscience. Recent developments in science and technology, the media interest in the bones of Richard III, and the successful long-running TV series about forensic pathologists, *Silent Witness*, gave forensic narratives great popular appeal. And of course there are the pleasures of the other quality cited, 'suspense'. Furthermore, these texts cater to our human desire for order out of chaos, our yearning for a world to be just and fair (despite all the evidence to the contrary), a restoration of decency and justice for heartbroken idealists. Because prolific crime writers offer series with the same plot structure and central characters (Philip Marlowe, Hercule Poirot, Martin Beck, Dr Kay Scarpetta), readers feel reassured, comforted even, confident in familiar characters, stories, and the promised endings (even if, as in romance, these are increasingly open or ambivalent). So far no clear gender difference emerges between women and men readers.

That said, there are particular pleasures and challenges for female readers. Dubbed by Val McDermid (Figure 5.1) 'the novel of social history', contemporary crime fiction focuses on real events of urgent importance to women—male violence, including domestic abuse and human trafficking, paedophilia, failures of psychological profiling, and

Figure 5.1 Val McDermid signing books, Liverpool Literary Festival, October 2018

Photo by Helen Taylor

race and gender expectations. Whether order is the same as justice is much debated, and resolution is seen by Denise Mina as not necessarily the same as justice itself—especially given all the uneven ways that works in terms of class, gender, and race. In a study of true crime readers, critic Laura Browder observed that many readers use these popular documentaries to 'help themselves cope with the patriarchal violence they have encountered in the past and fear in the present', using them as 'a how-to guide for personal survival—and a means for expressing the violent feelings that must be masked by femininity'.[5]

Melanie McGrath argued that women are accustomed to being appraised and viewed as vehicles for procreation or male pleasure: 'What better metaphor for the feeling of annihilation which follows the common female experience of being valued primarily as the sum of one's body parts than a murdered woman on a slab? No wonder we're so into forensics.' For her, such fiction allows women to access feelings of 'rage, aggression and vengefulness'. Her editor baulked at an incident in the novel *White Heat* when protagonist Edie Kiglatuk punched a persistent sex pest in the face. McGrath responded by saying this was something she had wanted to do herself but was squeamish about the repercussions. She also claimed that women find in crime a struggle for our own identities, especially if there is a female protagonist with whom we can identify, who is self-determining, and restores equilibrium by solving the crime.[6] Karin Slaughter, asked why there is so much violence in her books, wrote:

> I want to show violence for what it is. For so long, women weren't expected to talk about these crimes, even though we were more likely to be the victims. I think it's time we started talking about rape and violence against women. When I was growing up, these subjects were 'boys only' territory in fiction, so I find it refreshing to see authors like Mo Hayder and Denise Mina really opening up the conversation about abuse and sexual assault.[7]

Val McDermid claims a special power for women crime writers: '[W]hen women write about violence against women, it will almost inevitably be more terrifying because women grow up knowing that to be female is to be at risk of attack. We write about violence from the inside. Men, on the other hand, write about it from the outside.'[8] Terrence Rafferty seems to echo this when arguing women's novels 'are light on gunplay, heavy on emotional violence'.[9]

Killer Women and Cozy Crime

As I've discussed in relation to romance and erotica, in recent years the issue of violence against women has become a major moral, political, and cultural issue. The fact that domestic violence and the murder of women are overwhelmingly committed by male partners, and that the vast majority of murderers and murdered are male, raises fascinating questions about why female murderers and victims have become so central to crime novels and especially films and TV series. The Killer Women Crime Writing Collective (motto, 'Criminally Good Writing') is a group of twenty-one women writing predominantly for women readers with a focus on female victims. They organize an annual Killer Weekend in London, run a book club, and hold crime fiction debates and workshops, as well as Murder Mystery nights with cocktails. The Collective's Melanie McGrath became angry at the idea that they are writing about sexually motivated murder: 'There is only power and hatred.' She points to the considerable amount of casual sexism in crime novels (with stereotyped gender roles) and misogyny in TV and film crime: 'torture porn'. Crime writer Jessica Mann wrote—as George Orwell did in 1944 (so *plus ça change*)—of the rising violence in crime fiction. Receiving an increasing number of books for review featuring male perpetrators and female victims in situations of 'sadistic misogyny', she described the explicit details of young women who are 'imprisoned, bound, gagged, strung up or tied down, raped, sliced, burned, blinded, beaten, eaten, starved, suffocated, stabbed, boiled or burned alive'.[10] Mann argued that some of the most disturbing plots came from women writers, and Natasha Cooper conceded that the more graphic violence a novel contains, the more sales it attracts, and the more it can help 'establish their credibility and prove they are not girly'.

As I've suggested, the category of 'cozy' (girly?) crime—though not limited to women writers—is usually associated with them. Women in the interwar Golden Age of detective fiction excelled in procedural crime associated with small English towns, protected communities, neatly despatched murders, and tidy plots that tie up loose ends. One of Britain's best-loved and commercially successful writers is the original 'Queen of Crime' Agatha Christie. So revered is she that an annual crime writing festival is held in Harrogate's Old Swan Hotel, where she was found eleven days after her mysterious disappearance from her Surrey home. Although crime has moved on since her day, the works are still in print—now with retro covers capturing a nostalgia for simpler criminal tales—and she has been reinterpreted by a contemporary writer. Sophie Hannah is publishing four volumes featuring Hercule Poirot. Another female crime great (and one who shared an agent with Christie), Ngaio Marsh, has attracted the attention of novelist Stella Duffy, who completed an unfinished Marsh novel, *Money in the Morgue* (2018). Michelle Kirkby has returned to Conan Doyle, focusing this time on Mrs Hudson and the other forgotten women characters who were important to the stories but got left behind. All these writers reject the idea that their reworkings are 'pastiches', stressing the playfulness of Fanfic and intertextuality. Aficianados are excited by these new versions with their feminist perspectives, and they have raised questions about other classic female writers whose criminal record, as it were, has been overlooked. Stella Duffy argued that Daphne du Maurier should be included in any category of crime writing, citing not the most obvious crime novels (*Rebecca* or *My Cousin Rachel*) but the underestimated work, *The Scapegoat*.

Despite the variety of women's 'cozy' writing (some not so cozy at all!) there is a new genre named by crime writer Julia Crouch, 'domestic noir', psychological thrillers exploring women's need for constant vigilance in what feels like an increasingly dangerous world. These noirs feature abuse and murder within the home, as well as emotionally disturbed or transgressive female characters who defy the label of victim and are often unreliable narrators. Crouch herself argued that the monster is part of oneself as a writer: 'I'm a good girl so I like writing about bad women,' she told readers. Writing crime for women is seen as a way of exorcising fears, and of exploring toxic marriages in devastating ways. I return to those words of Margaret Atwood's (as relevant to crime as to romance) that while men's greatest fear of women is being laughed at, women's is being killed. However, in the new domestic noir, the tables are being turned. The cover of Sarah Vaughan's novel, *Anatomy of a Scandal* (2018) shows a woman peeping through a dark curtain—the classic male voyeur's pose—with the strapline: 'You want to believe your husband. She wants to destroy him.'

Trojan Horse Feminism

Focused on flawed marital relationships, there has been a group of novels such as Gillian Flynn's and Paula Hawkins' bestsellers *Gone Girl* (2012) and *The Girl on the Train* (2015), both made into successful Hollywood films, and Louise Doughty's *Apple Tree Yard* (2013)—a 2017 BBC TV series. These novels about affluent middle-class white women, appealing to film-makers, seem to be tapping into millennial women's weariness at trying to 'have it all' and keep their lives on the rails, while yearning at some profound level to relinquish agency, give way to their psychoses, and lose control. They have also been referred to as 'Trojan Horse feminism' confronting forces hostile to women, and contemporary feelings of injustice—exacerbated by social media—about 'gaslighting', victim shaming, and rage over the online abuse of children, sexual harassment, and bullying. The feminist critic

Jacqueline Rose demurred, however, commenting on the use of the word 'girl' in two titles, calling it 'their sly complicity with the diminishment of one half of the human race and a world that still permits it'. Wondering why hatred of women is so popular, she claims *The Girl on the Train* and *Gone Girl* 'turn abuse of women into a treat' and describes the ominous 'message' of the two novels: '[I]f women can take pleasure in what they have most to fear, then so can everybody else.'[11] I see the strength of her feminist argument, but it veers dangerously into an equation of reading with real-life actions. As with women's enthusiastic response to *Fifty Shades*, surely we have to recognize the need of both women and men to delve into their deepest imaginative spaces to confront and explore morally and socially dangerous and transgressive fantasies.

Alas, as many women writers testify, they are rarely granted the compliment of being seen to use their imaginations as much as men, and first-time crime writer Fiona Cummins said that mothers in the playground were now standing away from her, fearful about her criminal mind. One child hid behind her, and when his mother found him she told Cummins: 'Of all the people he had to stand behind, he had to choose you.'[12] But while there may be a playground standoff for a real writer, in the reader's imagination it can be reassuring that a woman writer is drawing on her own fears and anxieties to deliver a dangerous narrative that can be shared safely by readers in their own homes. Reading murder mysteries—as with that other popular form, the Gothic—may give us a frisson of excitement about the possibility of terrible danger, while paradoxically helping us feel safer in our little 'hygge' worlds, as we close the book, put out our bedside lamp and snuggle (we hope securely) under the covers.

However, in 2017, author and screenwriter Bridget Lawless claimed that violence against women in fiction had reached 'a ridiculous high', so she founded The Staunch book prize for 'A Thriller In Which No Woman Is Beaten, Stalked, Sexually Exploited, Raped or Murdered'. The Staunch website argues: 'That doesn't mean we're just looking for thrillers that feature men in jeopardy, but stories in which female characters don't have to be raped before they can be empowered, or become casual collateral to pump up the plot. If your story features a woman in a strong leading role, even better!' The launch of the prize had a noisily mixed reception, some claiming that at last women readers' revulsion towards excessively violent plots and characters was being addressed, while others saw it as dangerous censorship. Val McDermid conceded that some writers are guilty of exploitative and gratuitous violence towards women characters, but defended her own practice: 'My take on writing about violence against women is that it's my anger at that very thing that fires much of my work. As long as men commit appalling acts of misogyny and violence against women, I will write about it so that it does not go unnoticed.' Sophie Hannah concurred: 'Brutality is not the same thing as writing about brutality.'[13] The winner—Jock Serong's *On the Java Ridge* (about the scandal of modern policy towards migrants and refugees)—was announced on the day after the International Day for the Elimination of Violence Against Women, 2018.

Women Crime Readers

Many of my correspondents and interviewees have told me they reject fantasy fiction in favour of crime, which they feel addresses a real world, common sense, and rationality (as well as offering the suspense and thrill of a murder story). As is often the case, many of them got their first crime books from their mothers; they share them with other women, then take them to a charity shop. There is much swapping and discussing with close friends, and the page-turning quality of crime is felt to fit well into busy and fragmented lives. I spoke to two women who work in a bank. For them, crime is the perfect genre because—in a job that is completely predictable and logical—they like the unexpected and unpredictable nature of crime (though one really enjoys being frightened, while the other shies away from it). Another woman who reads all the time has a precisely forty-seven minute train journey to work each day, always sits in the same seat, and likes crime because it usually has short chapters that suit the length of time between stations.

One quiet, reserved woman told me she loved to fantasize about the violence and chaos not accessible to her in her own life, and approvingly quoted Lee Child's saying that we all have at least ten people we'd love to kill, given the opportunity.[14] Susie S echoed this when she said she'd been raised to repress negative and angry feelings in order to be fully feminine, and crime allowed her an outlet for anger and frustration. Helen R told me she believes men like to read crime for the violence, recollecting childhood games such as Cowboys and Indians, while women read for the characters and the romantic threads. In her view, certain writers, such as James Patterson, appeal more to men. But there is also the erotic appeal of private eyes and dysfunctional detectives. Lucy Mangan wrote of Lee Child's books: 'I am very much in love with Jack Reacher—as a man and a role model. If I can't shag him, I want to be him.' Karin Slaughter described Reacher as 'one of the sexiest characters in fiction'.[15] There are fascinating parallels of this kind between women's romance and crime reading.

Many of the discussions in the media about crime fiction, and of course TV and film crime, have centred on the misogyny or otherwise of depicting violence by and against women, notably female murderers and/or victims. Like eighteenth- and nineteenth-century anxieties about women being aroused by romantic and erotic narratives, or exposed to sensationalist plots that would disturb and perhaps derange them, articles galore describe reviewers' and novelists' concerns that women readers will be excessively distressed by forensically detailed, no-holds-barred thrillers that put women into terrible danger or allow them vengeance on those close to them. No one seems too bothered about male readers' distress or potential violence! As I discussed in Chapter 4, these moral concerns are echoes of those by commentators on the *Fifty Shades of Grey* phenomenon, with their astonishment that a darkly sadomasochistic fantasy relationship has struck so many chords with readers of all kinds, and concern at its effect on their sexual and emotional lives. As (feminist) critics of romance have reminded us, women have usually taken romantic novels or romcom films with a pinch of salt—knowing meet-lose-get happy endings don't exist or last, but feeling they satisfy some desire for a sweet treat in an otherwise mundane existence. The turn to bondage-obsessed erotic fiction and psychological thrillers has grown from developments in feminism that have allowed women to give vent vicariously to life's pains and traumas, as well as to explore rationally unacceptable and morally repugnant fantasies in new ways. And especially when *women writers* are offering such fare, readers can experience a feeling of safety and identification, an assurance that it is OK to go to dark places in your imagination in order to cauterize daily bitternesses and dissatisfactions.

Science Fiction and Fantasy

Despite my attempts to find them, few of my older (30+) correspondents claimed to be readers of science fiction or fantasy, though some admire John Wyndham and Isaac Asimov, and many have a soft spot for Philip Pullman's sophisticated *His Dark Materials* and prequel *La Belle Sauvage* (with intriguing female protagonist, Lyra), not to mention the Harry Potter series. Younger readers have taken to the fantasy, Gothic, horror, and vampire fiction of George R. R. Martin's *A Game of Thrones*, Anne Rice's *Vampire Chronicles*, Poppy Z. Brite's early vampire novels, and Stephenie Meyer's *Twilight* series. If we include the category of magical realism, I suspect there would be considerable enthusiasm for writers such as Gabriel García Márquez and Isabel Allende, since their works are grounded in family and community lives in a way many women enjoy. However, Avril H expressed my own feelings about a reluctance to engage in the 'hard' genres:

> Perhaps I like old-fashioned realist fiction best! I felt that sci-fi and fantasy worlds were too remote from the world I knew—both materially and (more importantly) emotionally—and they don't seem to do irony or nuance. They also seemed often to carry strong agendas and sacrificed character development to the exploration of ideas.

Another explanation came from the Bramley Reading Group, whose members claimed they were alienated by extreme violence and humourlessness. One reader described Tolkien as 'one b— battle after another' and another said the violence in *The Hunger Games* and *A Game of Thrones* put her off fantasy altogether—although several said their daughters were reading them and liked the easy-to-read escapism featuring strong female characters. Another said that since Terry Pratchett's death she didn't want to engage with new authors, and she resented longer books and multi-volumes that she 'couldn't be bothered to start'. Lynn F's reading group compared sci-fi with computer games, seen as a masculine preserve, while women want more emotional, plausible human interactions in worlds with human dilemmas and humour (they all loved Andy Weir's *The Martian*). One member of the group suggested provocatively: 'Women's lives are grounded in the everyday practicalities of family, housework, etc. It's true we like to escape through romance because these involve relatable relationships. Are we too practical to indulge or believe in fantasy worlds?'

The Sci-Fi Boys' Club

Discussing this with women, I've found much anecdotal evidence that—particularly middle-aged and older—women avoid science fiction ('a boys' club' as one woman put it to me) and fantasy in general—with the notable exceptions of Pratchett and Pullman. Science fiction by definition is concerned with science and technology which themselves are seen as masculine categories and enterprises, historically intimidating or uninteresting to a majority of girls and women. Fiction that focuses on these areas is thus seen to be aimed at male readers. Critic Sarah LeFanu points out that, until feminists engaged with the form in the late 1960s and early 1970s, sci-fi was dominated by men and masculine concerns: 'Women's participation necessitated becoming one of the boys, joining in on their terms, becoming a *Female Man* (this protective disguise is one of the subjects of Joanna Russ's classic *The Female Man*).'[16] The minority of female enthusiasts of sci-fi have often been introduced to it by fathers, brothers, or male friends, and are excited by its non-domestic, 'unfeminine' preoccupations, seeing it as an entrée into masculine discourses of identity, activity, and agency. Both utopian and dystopian, at its best sci-fi can offer androgynous visions that move between the twin poles of gender, and imagine different worlds in which women are no longer constrained and defined as lesser than men.[17] But all too often, women get short-changed and left out of this genre's play with alternative worlds.

The imaginative leaps made by futuristic fiction appeal less to female readers than those leaps made into romantic and erotic scenarios. One head teacher told me the schools inspector commented that in the twenty-first century school students described their reading in terms of *type* rather than writer or specific work. Girls, he said, did not choose adventure or science fiction. Seventy per cent of sci-fi writers are men, most of the key characters are male, and many of the 'cons' (shorthand for conventions), online bulletin boards and fanzines are male-dominated. Sci-fi has long had a reputation for being sexist, misogynistic, and saturated in sexual violence towards women. Is women's lack of enthusiasm surprising? If you look at STEM (science, technology, engineering and mathematics) subjects in schools and colleges, they are still—after years of apparent educational equality—studied mainly by boys and men, with a distinction drawn between 'hard' and 'soft' scientific subjects: scientific theories and physics versus more psychological and social issues relating to technology and science. In Karen Joy Fowler's *The Jane Austen Book Club*, the sole male group member describes his 'first love' as science fiction, 'books with rocketships on the spine' (126), and finally seduces book club fellow member Jocelyn ('I like books about real people') by persuading her to read one of the few women speculative fiction authors, Ursula Le Guin. Sarah LeFanu suggests this may have been 'a sort of in-joke with herself' since Fowler was also a highly regarded science fiction writer.[18]

Although probably the first, and one of the greatest science fiction novels, *Frankenstein* (1818), was written by a woman, Mary Shelley, and many major women writers in the field followed her lead (Charlotte Perkins Gilman, Ursula Le Guin, Marge Piercy, Joanna Russ, Sarah Hall, and others), they were always overshadowed and rarely acknowledged by 'hard' male sci-fi writers and critics. One *Guardian* critic reviewing Hall's *The Carhullan Army* dismissed women's dystopian fiction as a 'low-key subgenre'.[19] No prizes for guessing which category wins the prizes and gets listed in the MIT Technology Review's 'Top Ten Hard Science Fiction Books of all Time' (one by a woman) and Forbidden Planet's list of 'The 50 Science Fiction Books you MUST Read' (three novels by women, of which two are by Le Guin).[20]

'Soft' Sci-Fi

And yet, there are signs of changing writer and reader experiences. American novelist Dara Horn describes being hooked on science fantasy when a child, reading Madeleine L'Engle's *A Wrinkle in Time*, published in 1962 after multiple publishers' rejections, dealing as it did with evil in a very adult way, but also having a female protagonist—most uncommon at the time. She then started reading—but was too bored to finish—male sci-fi texts featuring dwarfs, wizards, and orcs, followed by *The Hitchhiker's Guide to the Galaxy*, Kurt Vonnegut, Isaac Asimov, and others (she never found her way to Ursula Le Guin). She asks:

Was the book off-putting because I didn't like science fiction? Or was it because of the description of a planet with three genders, where the one referred to as "she" was the literally squishy one that could only think in emotions? Or the pages about how life in zero gravity was especially wonderful for women—you know, because of their young-looking, free-floating breasts?[21]

These aliens were alienating. It was only when her daughter discovered a whole body of 'tweenage dystopia' fantasy writing—beginning, coincidentally, with that L'Engle classic—that Horn realized the literary world for girl readers was on the move. She felt something enormous had happened in the years between her childhood and her daughter's—a shift starting perhaps with *His Dark Materials*, or with novels by Tamora Pierce and Francesca Lia Block, and then accelerated with the runaway success of the *Twilight* and *Hunger Games* series that initiated the Young Adult sub-genre of science fiction and fantasy focused equally on girls as well as boys. The largely female fan following of TV shows such as *The X Files* (called OBSSE, 'the Order of the Blessed Saint Scully the Enigmatic')—focusing on its central character played by Gillian Anderson, regarded as 'saint, everywoman, and sexpot'—has created new female enthusiasm for the genre.[22]

From the early twenty-first century, women writers have gained a foothold in this masculine genre. Indeed, the African American sci-fi writer Octavia E. Butler rejected the sci-fi label for her acclaimed novel, *Kindred* (1979), observing on her website that 'there's no science in it. It's a kind of grim fantasy.' Some women are drawn to sci-fi mainly through reading speculative fiction writers, who include female characters and rely less on technological gadgetry and masculinist power struggles. Writers enjoyed by women include Doris Lessing, Angela Carter, and Margaret Atwood, with *The Handmaid's Tale* perhaps the most renowned text, adapted over three decades into film (1990), opera (2000), and TV series (2017 and 2018), and referenced frequently in post-2016 anti-Donald Trump demonstrations. To the excitement of her many fans, in 2019 Atwood published a sequel, *The Testaments*. And while *The Handmaid's Tale* has many new admirers, younger women—especially young adults and those in their early twenties—have flocked to these genres since the success of book and film versions of *Divergent* and the *Game of Thrones* series. Another triumph has been the 2017 Baileys Prizewinner, Naomi Alderman's

Figure 5.2 Naomi Alderman with her book *The Power*, winner of Baileys Women's Prize for Fiction 2017

WENN Rights Ltd / Alamy Stock Photo

The Power, a bestselling novel imagining men losing control across the planet, because of women's destructive force—described as '*The Hunger Games* crossed with *The Handmaid's Tale*' (Figure 5.2). The selection of Jodie Whittaker to be BBC TV's first female Doctor Who compounded this enthusiasm. It seems that a group of confident women writers are breaking through male sci-fi lines; the influential Amazon's Best Books List, 2017, named nine women out of twenty writers, with half of those women of colour. However, three of the nine—N. K. Jemisin, V. E. Schwab, and S. A. Chakraborty—used initials to signal ambiguous gender in order to fend off gendered criticism.

Online blogs and chat groups reveal that women relish female writers in the genre, the centrality of female characters, and foregrounding of women's issues and interests (what the sci-fi community would define as 'soft'—relationships including romance, feminist utopias, and domestic or family concerns). All of this may seem to respond to Donna Haraway's call in the 1980s for a 'comprehensive feminist politics about science and technology' in which feminist sci-fi writers would explore 'what it means to be embodied in high-tech worlds' using narratives to problematize both genders, all races, identities, and bodies.[23] There is a move towards greater involvement in the genre by women writers and readers, with feminists working to reclaim this most masculine of literary spaces by celebrating a canon from *Frankenstein* and Perkins Gilman's *Herland* (1915) to Zoë Fairbairns' *Benefits* (1979) and Suzy McKee Charnas' *The Holdfast Chronicles* (1974–99). Academics interested in promoting sci-fi for women have founded feminist zines, women-only rooms at conferences, and Internet discussion groups. In 2017, journalist Vanessa Thorpe proclaimed a 'brave new world of feminist dystopian sci-fi' with writers such as Atwood, her mentored writer Naomi Alderman, Ada Palmer, Sarah Hall, and Tricia Sullivan. Ada Palmer characterized the new feminist dystopias' distinctiveness from men's: 'Perhaps the ones by women have less often featured an isolated hero, while a woman author might tend to write more about a network of people, often with more complex roles...and a political context is unavoidable for a woman writer.'[24] As with other types of fiction, women readers appear to favour novels that avoid the solitary and extraordinary superhero/ine, ground us in relationships and communities, and address or compensate us for our position within patriarchal society.

The Literary Blogger

dovegreyreader

Dovegreyreader is a literary blogger who has become a significant go-to figure in British and international literary life. Her readers come from many countries and she's bombarded daily with responses to her idiosyncratic blogs. Her self-description is 'a Devonshire based booka-holic, sock-knitting quilter who was a community nurse once upon a time'. After an early career in the Health Service, and three children in quick succession, she wanted to focus on the fiction she found such a welcome escape after a day's work, housework, and childcare. Reboot-ing her reading life with middlebrow fiction by Mary Wesley and Susan Howatch, in 1996 she decided to do an Open University degree spe-cializing in literature. With the degree under her belt, in 2006 she read her way through all of Margaret Atwood's fiction. Looking online for critical reviews, she was horrified by what she saw: 'waspish, nasty, over-critical,' she said, and what she wanted was a 'nice space'.

She began to write an online blog, building on a reading journal she had kept for years and writing about books only if she liked them. 'Right book, wrong reader,' is her mantra when refusing to blog about a book. At first, there were very few hits. Ringing her father excitedly one day, she told him that she'd had twenty, at which he confessed he had gone onto it twenty times himself, so thrilled was he at seeing her in print. Gradually, her followers grew and publishers noted her observant and warm comments on books—recognizing she was a great marketing asset. One year, publishers sent her all the Booker short-listed books, so she was on her way, creating a 'Bookerthon' over many years. Dovegreyreader is now in demand by publishers and readers alike.

Int.2 dovegreyreader's tent, Port Eliot Festival
Photo by Tommy Hatwell

After some years of posting the blog, dovegreyreader scribbles, she knows that most of her readers are women and many of them latch onto her words for ideas of what to read. She thinks readers like her reviews because 'I write as if I'm talking', so she appears to be taking part in a conversation rather than delivering a verdict from on high: 'The oxygen of the blog is in the readers' comments.'

Dovegreyreader quilts while listening to audio books. For three years, she created a cozy feminine space in a tent at the Port Eliot Festival, Cornwall, where she set up a virtual sitting room with a sofa, cups of tea (made by her husband and friend) and spaces for knitting. To their great delight, she created 'knitsukes' as gifts for authors—a knitted hare with amber eyes for Edmund de Waal, three snow geese for William Fiennes, and a crocheted camera for photographer Martin Parr.

Here she is in 2015 on the first Elena Ferrante novel. Note her engaging call-and-response tone, the domestic imagery and family references to which women readers respond, and the gentle invitation to share female experiences through a particular work of fiction:

Reflecting on my own childhood in a post-war nation that had "won" the war I now realise that unwittingly we thought we were the kingpins here in the UK. Playing "wars" was standard fare even for girls on the streets and playgrounds of Britain, and none of us wanted to be the Germans or the Italians so I feel sure there is the legacy of World War II milling around in My Brilliant Friend too. And of course I now don't have my primary source to ask, but I do know we have pictures of my dad on board HMS King George V as it prepared for action stations off the coast of Italy prior to the invasion in 1943. I can read about it anywhere but it was always good to get a first hand point-of-view. I'd nip next door into Tinker's Cott, do my 'cooooeee' call through the door and ask exactly how the war and Fascist rule left the Italian people . . . humiliated and defeated, or defiant and bullish. My dad was well-used to me doing this; he would have had an opinion and it would have been fascinating. Funny how loss creeps in when you least expect it isn't it.

Anyway the upshot is that I have eventually warmed to My Brilliant Friend, especially as the Esteemed Readers tell me there are riches in store in the next three books, and the woman on the checkout at Waterstones intoned with some reverence that anyone who is anyone in the literary world is reading these at the moment. So I think I am reading the right book at the right time and now in the right format, but meanwhile I would love to know whether any of you have read it yet . . .

Have you been following the hype . . . Or are you waiting until the rolling boil simmers down a bit (sorry, too much jam-making)?

And what about childhood friends . . . ? How did we find them and keep them . . . and how and why did we lose them? Have you kept in touch with yours . . . ?

PART III

Writers and Readers

6

Women Writers on their Reading and Readers

On the BBC Radio 4 programme *Desert Island Discs*, novelist Margaret Forster said that growing up an avid reader in the 1940s, she didn't know any writers and anyway thought all writers were dead. Rarely did you see their photographs on book jackets, their profiles in magazines, or the creatures themselves on book programmes. Most writers seemed remote, uncontactable, mysterious. In 1975, Julie Myerson wrote a letter to Daphne du Maurier via her publisher, when the 15-year-old schoolgirl had resolved to be a writer. Not knowing whether it would reach the great woman, she describes being 'delirious with excitement when a small white envelope postmarked St Austell plopped through our Nottingham letterbox'. The novelist had sent a colour photograph of her home, Kilmarth, setting for the novel *The House on the Strand*, and wished young Julie luck with her 'O'-level exams. This correspondence continued for two years, and Myerson treasures the small collection of letters, cards, and photographs sent her.[1]

Today, this thrill of receiving personal communication has faded. On the whole, writers are no longer hidden-away, enigmatic figures inspiring awe in their readers. Now they have websites, Twitter accounts, blogs, publishers' profiles, and photographs online and in newspapers and magazines. Their publishers insist on author interviews and commentaries on the back pages of their novels. We know details of their childhood traumas, the names of their dogs and cats, and whether they handwrite, type or word-process their novels. They go to bookshops for signings and literary festivals to present their work, and appear on radio and TV where they are questioned by journalists and audiences. They receive feedback from readers who feel those writers are accessible to them, and communicate on a daily basis via social media—though some still find time to reply personally to ardent fans. As crime writer Mel Mitchell observed:

> Nowadays readers are looking for a more three dimensional experience from their reading and whether that is extra reading material—a reading guide at the back of the book—or whether it's meeting the author or whether it's a signed copy or whether it's asking questions of an author on Facebook or Twitter . . . I just think they're looking for slightly more.[2]

Most significant of all is that we know what these writers look like. In print features, on websites, TV chat shows and book award cere- monies, we can assess the gender, race, age, quality of beauty and hairstyle of any author in the limelight. We can decide if we like the look of them and wish to spend time in their writing company. For women writers this is especially hard. The focus in recent years on the visible author means that the women are certainly divided off from the girls—in Michèle Roberts' words, 'Bright Young Things or Wise Old Sibyls'.[3] As early as 1947, Agatha Christie complained to her pub- lisher, William Collins, about the author photograph they chose which made one reader express surprise to the 57-year-old Christie that she was 'such an old lady'.[4] These days, gorgeous young women writers attract considerable media coverage, while their older peers struggle for atten- tion or resort to cosmetic transformations to please photographers. This can, however, be a double-edged sword. When Sarah Howe won the UK's prestigious T. S. Eliot Prize in 2016, a Twitter hashtag 'deranged- poetess' tore into the poet for her youth and beauty. *Private Eye* suggested she won the award for 'extra-poetic reasons . . . as a successful and very "presentable" young woman', and many other critics followed suit. This emphasis on the appearance of a female writer probably also explains the relentless search for the real name and identity of elusive novelist 'Elena Ferrante' (a pseudonym); the fact that she refused over more than two decades to reveal this was interpreted as a perverse media tease.

Women Writers as Readers

It's easy to forget that fiction writers are themselves readers, except in those Sunday newspaper summaries of 'what I shall be reading on holiday/over Christmas/from the Man Booker Prize shortlist'. Writers are often expected to be original, thus not looking over their shoulders at their predecessors or contemporaries, and the 'room of one's own' is thought of as rather empty, with a view and a laptop but not littered with other writers' books. Of course, lots of writers choose not to read fiction when writing their own, and it's easy to imagine they read only those novels for which they give blurb recommendations ('The best novel I've read this year', 'Unforgettable and uplifting', and so on). But the best writers are usually the most prolific readers, and in my discussions with women writers I've found them to be generous in paying tribute to both male and female writers who've influenced them, careful to praise women writers who have been role models, and help younger colleagues along the way. And as readership itself becomes more of a focus in literary debates, they pay tribute to that complex relationship between writer and reader. At a 2013 Bristol Festival of Ideas event, Margaret Atwood told her adoring audience: 'The reader is the violinist of the text, interpreting it. Heathcliff hangs the dog but to each reader it is a different dog. I'm only the originator.'

Like other readers, women writers have often found their way through the baffling world of literature by inspired teaching at school or the serendipitous marvels of bookshops and public libraries. The 2014 Children's Laureate Malorie Blackman told a journalist that reading as a teenager meant she

> visited other planets, alternate dimensions, other countries, survived
> wars, obtained super powers, had numerous adventures, walked in the
> shoes and lived in the head of countless characters, laughed with them,
> cried with them, lived with them, died with them.[5]

Novelist Jeanette Winterson found liberating company in Accrington Public Library where 'every book was a message in a bottle' and 'I read on, past my own geography and history...The great writers were not remote; they were in Accrington.'[6] Blackman and Winterson aren't the only writers to devour the contents of a library as a way into new worlds and far from the constrictions of a book-limited household. Helen Dunmore (Figure 6.1) used reading to discover 'what life may be going to be like' and early on her novelist's ear and eye were being formed as she read:

> I can remember the reading books we had at school. *Janet and John.*
> I loved them, the rhythm of them. Do you remember? 'I walked and
> I walked and what did I see? I saw mother and mother saw me. Come

Figure 6.1 Helen Dunmore
Photo by Charlie Forgham-Bailey

home said mother come home with me.' I can still remember pages of it. And I don't know if you remember, but Janet had her red coat. They went shopping for a coat and there were all these very dull brown coats, but she chose a red coat and she pranced home in her red coat and I thought, "That's good." People mock Janet and John but I think there's plenty of narrative excitement in there if you look for it.[7]

Responding to Readers

Dunmore claimed to follow du Maurier's lead with Julie Myerson by responding to every letter or email received, though she and other busy writers have sent generic responses to students wanting their dissertations written for them or readers who demand extraordinarily detailed answers to long queries. Many women writers have followed this route (Margaret Mitchell famously never wrote a novel after *Gone*

With the Wind, so busy was she replying to over 20,000 readers' letters)
and I guess women share both a sense of duty towards, and also
serious acknowledgement of, the importance of that reader–writer
relationship.

Women fiction writers cannot fail to have a view on gendered
readerships and genres. For a start, there is a gender pay gap in
publishing (women writers earning on average 75 per cent of male
income), a situation which has grown worse in recent years.[8] Known
so often as 'women writers' while their male counterparts can claim
loftily to be 'writers' ('male writer' seems tautological), they know that
their readership is often skewed by women who choose female writing
and men who avoid it, or by the subject matter they choose. Sally
Beauman observed: 'Women are more catholic in their tastes. They'll
read *War and Peace* one day, and *Bridget Jones' Diary* the next . . . They're
prepared to try almost anything—whereas some men won't pick up a
book with a female author's name on the jacket.'[9] Both Helen Dunmore and Hilary Mantel have noted that predominantly *women* read
their novels with female protagonists or 'domestic' topics, while their
historical novels of political and social weight (Dunmore's *The Siege*,
Mantel's Tudor trilogy) attract enthusiastic *male* readers. In recent
years, numerous surveys have revealed that women's fiction, written
and read by far more women than men, is usually reviewed by
women, while male fiction is given a disproportionately greater
space in newspapers and literary journals and is usually covered by
male reviewers—with consequently higher status. Few women are
elevated to the '[wo]man of letters' status allowing them to cross
between men's and women's fiction—and even fewer BAME
women. Bernardine Evaristo commented on one notable exception:

> Straight, white male writers are considered normative and therefore
> don't have to be labelled. Toni Morrison is proud to be called an
> African American writer because this is who she is and the perspective
> from which she writes. The problem is really with the perception that if
> you're considered to write from a 'female' or 'BAME' viewpoint, your
> writing is seen as marginal.[10]

Sarah Moss objects to the way Oxfam bookshops divide men's and
women's writing into 'literature' and 'fiction' (guess which is which),
and she complained to one bookshop manager that on the front table,

'American literature' contained no book by a woman, while nearby 'romance' included nothing by a man. In 2013, Wikipedia's site for American novelists included so many names that they created a subcategory of 'American women novelists'. After huge opposition on social media, Wikipedia back-tracked, but the fact that an established company could consider such a move emphasizes the unthinking way heterogeneous women's writing is seen as some kind of separate, indeed lesser genre. At the 2013 Edinburgh Festival, Swedish crime writer Maj Sjöwall unfortunately seemed to endorse this when criticising her contemporaries for being too concerned with screen adaptations, and not focusing on police work and crime. Their work was, she said, 'very much about love and relationships—like girls' books'.

'Girls' books' became the subject of a controversy in 1991. Book prizes, traditionally open to men and women, often with predominantly male judges, usually selected a larger number of novels by men than women. That year, the Booker Prize shortlist consisted of only male writers, so publisher-novelist Kate Mosse and a group of people in the literature industry met to discuss the silence resounding around this exclusion of women. Securing sponsorship, the group established The Orange Prize, more recently The Baileys Women's Prize (or 'girls' tipple', as some of the press sneered) and now The Women's Prize, to honour women's fiction reading and writing, and stimulate discussion about the status of women writers in our culture.

From the start, this prize's board and judges have all been women, and it focuses on reading itself (the judges are selected as 'expert readers' passionate about books, rather than 'experts'). They ask what makes for the best fiction by this under-represented group of people. As Kate Mosse puts it, the Prize has been a 'lightning rod' for debates about whether men and women write and are valued differently, and has undoubtedly increased the visibility of women writers. In 2013, a sea change was noted when Alice Munro won the Nobel Prize for Literature, and all five Costa Book Awards were given to women (Hilary Mantel, Kathleen Jamie, Francesca Segal, Sally Gardner, and Mary Talbot). In 2016—despite the publishing industry again being accused of 'gender bias'—e-retailer Kobo revealed that its ten bestselling titles two years earlier were by female authors. And a 2018 *Times Literary Supplement* survey by a panel of critics, academics, and writers placed Ali Smith, Hilary Mantel, and Zadie Smith at the top of their list of best British and Irish novelists.[11] There's no doubt that this new prize alerted readers and critics to the wealth of women's writing and began to redress the balance. Furthermore, since 2004 it has helped shift the racial literary agenda by crowning BAME writers Andrea Levy, Zadie Smith, Chimamanda Ngozi Adichie, and Kamila Shamsie.

Little Woman-ing

I've spent my career fighting to keep stilettos off my covers.

Louise Doughty

Despite The Women's Prize, the derogatory label 'girls' books' is still a problem for women writers. Reaching the widest range of readers depends to a large extent on the way a novel is presented—crucially via its cover. Novelist Meg Wolitzer said in an interview that 'Books by men still have big letters on the cover so you feel this book is an event but books by women—even Elena Ferrante—still have covers that look like what I call "little girl in a field of wheat".'[12] Hilary Mantel objects to her writing being 'Little Womaned' and women's writing in general being signposted by pastel-coloured covers. 'No man's going to be seen on the underground reading a pastel coloured book,' she claims. This issue of jacket design gets women writers (and indeed some men) hot under the collar. On a BBC Radio 4 *Open Book* programme, novelist James Runcie described book packaging as 'disastrously gendered', and gendered cover design is cited by Danuta Kean as a key way in which women's writing is demeaned.[13] Journalist Alison Flood posed a challenge to readers to find a book jacket featuring an image of a woman over forty (citing novels about older women by such writers as Allison Pearson, Anne Tyler, and Elizabeth Buchan).[14] At the 2014 Appledore Book Festival, Michael Morpurgo told the audience he had wanted to use the title *Lucy Lost* for a novel eventually called *Listen to the Moon*. His publishers told him that—with a girl's name on the cover—boys wouldn't read it, while Kate Mosse claims that her novels covering a broad historical canvas are read by men as widely as women largely because she doesn't have 'a woman's jacket'.

Mantel's early work was marketed to appeal to a female readership, with images of women and children on covers with soft colours. By contrast, her later novels and recent reprints of the early work are defiantly confident and bold, using strong lettering, blood-red, gold, and shocking pink. However, Turkish writer Elif Shafak relates that the jacket of her novel *The Forty Rules of Love* was originally pink with a picture of a leaf on a tree (which she liked because it expressed the soul of the book), but then she had an adverse reaction from male readers who said they were embarrassed to carry it on public buses or boats. The publisher eventually produced a version of the novel for male readers, covered in smoky grey.[15] Critic Bidisha believes that a popular writer like Marian Keyes should be regarded more respectfully, citing the demeaningly girly packaging of swirly lines and pink, purple, and gold stars around a novel such as *This Charming Man*, which deals with domestic violence.

Margaret Atwood amused her audience at Bristol's Festival of Ideas, describing the first jacket her publisher proposed for the cover of dystopian trilogy *MaddAddam* (2013): flowers and a bee. The story concerns a small group of people surviving a man-made plague that has swept the earth. After she objected, the cover was changed to a pig in motion, not dejected but with eyes open, forward-pointing eyebrows, its hoofs taking off from the ground with dynamic wings taking it air-borne. Like Mantel's later novels, this cover has a bold chunky typeface unapologetically announcing its author and title. As these two writers have acquired unassailable international reputations, they can now call the shots in terms of their novels' presentation and marketing.

Illustrators' tendency to go for feminine pastels and pinks, young women's soft-focus faces, hearts and flowers, was challenged by the young American novelist Maureen Johnson, furious at the stereotyped cover of her serious novel about sisters dealing with a father's death. Agreeing with Jodi Picoult that this gendering of covers signals a difference between 'literary' (high-status) and 'commercial' fiction, she found support from paranormal romance writer Amanda Hocking: 'Women are the publishing industry's bread and butter, we are the backbone of the damn entertainment industry, but we are constantly demoted to "fluffy" to "light" to "meaningless".'[16] Johnson threw out a challenge on Twitter, called 'Coverflip', saying she wished

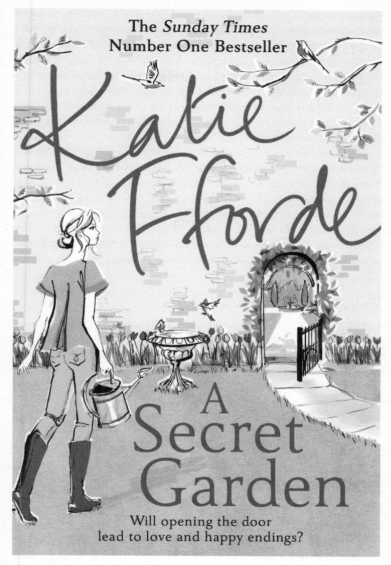

Figure 6.2 From *A Secret Garden* by Katie Fforde, published by Century, David O'Driscoll

she had a dime for every email that asks, 'Please put a non-girly cover on your book so I can read. – signed A Guy.' Hundreds of readers sent her mock-up covers, transferring the warm glow and light, fluffy beach reading promotions of women's fiction to male texts: from 'Jeanette' (Jeffrey) Eugenides's *The Marriage Plot*, with a bride and bouquet rather than the original Jeffrey Eugenides' plain white cover with a wedding band, to a lipsticked, smiling blonde on the cover of Stephen King's *Carrie*. The effect, of course, was to make these novels appear ludicrously simpering.[17]

That said, there is a successful body of fiction aimed specifically at a large market often dismissed by critics and commentators as frivolous. Katie Fforde has no problem with the fact that her covers—using ultra-feminine handwritten titles, pretty, young leisured heroines and lots of flowers and bees—signal to an overwhelmingly female readership her brand of bestselling romantic fiction (Figure 6.2). With writers such as Adele Parks, Joanna Trollope, and Fforde herself, the feminized jacket is a quick and easy way of asserting, 'Women, this is for you.'

On Being 'a Woman Writer'

In 2013, New Zealander Eleanor Catton won the Man Booker Prize, at 28 the youngest-ever winner—and the media went crazy. Catton cannily anticipated gender bias in media attention to come: 'I have observed that male writers tend to get asked what they think and women what they feel,' she told *The Guardian* two days after her win:

> In my experience, and that of a lot of other women writers, all of the questions coming at them from interviewers tend to be about how lucky they are to be where they are—about luck and identity and how the idea struck them. The interviews much more seldom engage with the woman as a serious thinker, a philosopher, as a person with preoccupations that are going to sustain them for their lifetime.

She even claimed that male reviewers over 45 felt outrage at being forced to read their way through her very long novel. Sally Beauman concurred. To her, the notion of 'woman writer' was belittling: 'It's one inch away from "lady novelists". I suspect women only get to be called "writers" once they're dead and canonised, though there are perhaps a few exceptions. Usually women of such considerable academic prowess that male commentators are intimidated—Iris Murdoch, for instance.' And I would add Pat Barker, who claims that because her early successes with Virago led to her being typecast as 'a northern, regional, working class, feminist—label, label, label—novelist', she left the feminist press and began her *Regeneration* trilogy about the very male area of traumatic warfare. Within a few years she had won general critical acclaim and—for *The Ghost Road*—the 1995 Booker Prize.[18]

Sally Beauman was pigeonholed very early, notably with her best-seller *Destiny* (1987). That novel, according to Beauman, 'was shoved into the "S&F" shopping and fucking category—a term I'd never even heard until after the book was published. The next novel didn't remotely fit that tag, so they made do with "blockbuster", and after that everyone gave up and consigned me to the swamp called "romance".' Possibly as a result of this, Beauman's body of fiction, reinterpreting genres and exploring original imaginative territory, has been critically neglected, missing out on a serious 'literary' readership.

A younger writer, Louise Doughty, who achieved considerable fame with her televised novel *Apple Tree Yard*, echoes this in her own critical history:

> My first novel, *Crazy Paving* (1995) was reviewed by, amongst others, Jonathan Coe and Jason Cowley and although three out of the five main characters were female and struggling with work, love, life in London, it was just treated as a first novel. Then along came the success of Bridget Jones and after that, I was only reviewed by women and my books were treated as books about and for women. When novel number four, *Fires in the Dark*, was published, one reviewer referred to me as 'previously the author of cheery chick lit,' despite the fact that *Crazy Paving* was about chaos theory and urban terrorism, *Dance With Me* about ghosts and mental illness, and *Honey-Dew* about a girl who murders her parents ... hey, I was a girl who wrote books, therefore ...[19]

Hilary Mantel (Figure 6.3) confirms this category issue to be one of the *reader* (often the male critic) rather than writer:

> My position is that, when you write you're not gendered, but when you're read you are gendered. And also when you're published. At the point of writing, of committing words to paper, I'm not gendered. Ten minutes before and ten minutes after, I'm gendered again, but when

Figure 6.3 Hilary Mantel
Photo by Els Zweerink

I'm writing—I may be wrong and self-deceiving—but it's not something I'm ever thinking about or conscious about. When I produce words, I feel erased as a person, as if I fall into a void. I did think at one time that it would be good to write wearing a mask, as a contribution to eradicating the self, and in recent years I feel I have got into that state, without needing the mask.[20]

Mask or no, Mantel is often asked why she has so many male protagonists. Her response is:

I can't fathom why should there be a problem. There's something the blessed Ivy [Ivy Compton-Burnett] says, about there being more difference within the genders than between them, and I really believe that. The difficulty starts when your book goes out to the world. If a house is being described, and the people in a household, then if the book is by a woman it's just about a household; but if a man wrote it, the household would be perceived as a metaphor for wider society... There is still a disposition to think that when a woman writes books, she must be commenting on The Woman Question, or on "What do women want?", as if she cannot pull away from personal preoccupations.

As Mantel describes, there is a lazy assumption that women are first and foremost autobiographical, writing always about themselves rather than employing their imaginations and using the writer's craft to create others. Ali Smith claims that because she is not a 'realist' writer she doesn't get labelled in the way other women are, and she believes she is read by men and women equally. Fiction-writer and biographer Sarah LeFanu often employs a persona, an 'I' to carry the narrative. She was teaching the final session in a short-story course at the University of Bristol:

> I gave them my twenty-year-old story, "Quail". As we were discussing it, I suddenly realised some of the people sitting there thought the "I" voice in the story was me—and I didn't know what to do about it. I can't just say it's not me. The story is about a woman married to a complete philandering bastard and splits up and ends up with someone else—and one of them said something that made it clear they thought it was me . . . There's an assumption women can only write "I I I" unlike men, but readers like to think this is the true story. You want them to believe it, but you don't want them to say "That's you, isn't it?"[21]

A celebrated writer who has unashamedly drawn on her own experiences for memoirs and fiction is Rachel Cusk who (like Julie Myerson) has attracted the wrath of some critics and readers for doing so. Memoir *Aftermath* (2012) described in forensic detail the breakdown of a marriage, and was strongly criticized as a betrayal of Cusk's husband and children. She has certainly been punished for her honesty; one review begins with the sentence: 'The observation that *some people do not like Rachel Cusk* is so omnipresent in criticism of her work that it's surprising no one's ever led off a review with "I, too, dislike her".'

In recent years, however, she has been acclaimed for a trilogy of 'autofiction'—*Outline* (2014), *Transit* (2016), and *Kudos* (2018)—that draws on Cusk's own experiences via the central character 'Faye' and interrogates the whole issue of storytelling about one's life.[22] Penetratingly witty and observant (with hilarious accounts of, for instance, a routine hairdresser visit and a grim literary festival in the pouring rain), Cusk is challenging our distinction between the mundane feminine personal and the resonantly and universally literary.

But it's not just what the writer is, and what she creates, that raises the question of gender. Readers themselves produce gendered readings and stereotypes that distort interpretation of a writer's work. One reviewer of Helen Dunmore's novel *The Lie*, about a veteran of the Great War, described her novel as a 'mum's eye view' of the blockade, one that was 'less Tolstoyan than suburban'. Dunmore's retort was: 'One of the great novelists of the domestic interior is John Updike. It's only when women do it that it's patronised.'[23] And British women, struggling with domestic lives in post-war Britain, were given a literary boost by American writers who made this their subject. In 2017, Margaret Drabble described the shocked excitement of discovering American novelist Mary McCarthy's novel *The Group* early in her own career:

> It had a great and liberating impact on my generation, with its bold confrontation of topics such as breastfeeding, orgasm, child-rearing, impotence, lesbianism and the etiquette of contraception. It educated us as writers, and it told us practical things that nobody else would tell us. These young women, the Class of '33 from Vassar, making their pre-war way in New York through marriage, housekeeping, and the search for meaningful employment, had a lot to teach the young women of England in the 1960s.[24]

Yet too little has changed. Sarah Moss is exasperated at the paucity of twenty-first-century novels about domestic family life. Despite knowing that as a woman writer focusing on the domestic and familial she risked critical dismissal, she set out to write a serious novel about living with toddlers and young children. Hilary Mantel cites a laudatory review in *Atlantic Monthly* of her Cromwell novels by the respected critic Christopher Hitchens, who uttered what he clearly regarded as the greatest praise, saying you couldn't tell they were by a woman. Mantel said this made her smile: 'She's finally come good, she's got it together, she's writing like a man, and you couldn't tell.' For her, the historical novels focus on periods of history when men dominated and determined the course of events and of course women's lives. She has encountered criticism from American feminists, Women's Studies advocates, and the blogosphere, all of whom wonder why she is not 'on the side of' Anne Boleyn in *Bring Up the Bodies*. For her, this is a form of ahistoric censorship:

> For a woman who writes historical fiction there is a problem you meet again and again. You have to accept that in the past, by and large women have not been the movers and shakers. If you want to write history you need to engage with that. If you want to assert the contrary then you're writing a fairy tale. I'm so tired of books about women in history who happen to have what's always called 'lore', with a terrific knowledge of herbs and medicines—and they're persecuted because of it, burned as witches.

With a wry smile, Mantel said: 'I don't see why, because I'm a woman writer in the twenty-first century, I have to be down with the witches.'

Sarah Dunant recognizes Mantel's take on women in history but adopts a different focus. Talking of the crude opposition between early stereotypes of women as 'crushed victims or above-the-parapet Boadiceas', she argues: 'Women live in many different shapes or cracks in which they forge successful, not so successful, blighted, covertly creative lives ... if you want to talk about history it's as interesting as what's going on in political hierarchies of men.'[25] There's no doubt this has contributed to the popularity of her bestselling Renaissance historical novels with predominantly women readers.

But Mantel by no means repudiates her gender. She claims that all women writers are 'yoked together in an endeavour', helping one another to be taken seriously, while some male writers are intensely competitive and spend much time and energy wondering what their competitors are up to. She recalls the 2010 prize-giving event for The Orange Prize. All the finalists were lined up and they held hands behind their backs. 'I think Lorrie Moore started it—we were like dancers about to execute a high kick, stabilising each other. You can't imagine the men doing that, can you?'

Nor can you imagine a collective of male crime writers sitting around a kitchen table. The Killer Women Collective I discussed in Chapter 5 began in this way, modelled on Sisters in Crime, American Sara Paretsky's group established in 1986. Initially the British writers met at that table to socialize and support one another in writing within a genre dominated by men who received the lion's share of reviews. Then—as they developed more confidence and profile—to share skills and blow one another's trumpets. Katie Fforde celebrates her active involvement with the Romantic Novelists Association, its programme of regional meetings, Christmas parties, and annual conferences to encourage and support young as well as established writers. Phenomenally successful herself, Fforde argues: 'I'm future-proofing my career, so when I'm no longer doing it or no one's buying my books, I can look at all the young things I've helped and say, "If it wasn't for me ... "' She also praises the RNA network for countering the sneering denigration of romantic fiction by journalists and critics: 'We have a jolly time, rejoice in one another's success and we're very supportive ... We keep one another going through hard times.'[26] Another line of high-kicking literary dancers ...

The 'Sari Count'

Most of the writers I've discussed—whatever their class and educational background—are white, a reflection of the current British publishing markets. Hard though it is for them to get into print, and be taken as seriously as male writers, for BAME (Black, Asian, Minority Ethnic) writers there are many more obstacles. Bernardine Evaristo (Figure 6.4) describes coming of age in the 1980s at a time when 'black British women were almost invisible in the literary landscape'. Founding a black women's theatre company, she turned not to the English canon on which she'd been raised, but instead to the African American writers making waves at the time—women such as Gloria Naylor, Alice Walker, Audre Lorde, and Toni Morrison who were placing black women centre stage. Told there was 'no market' for work by black British women, she and others produced their own anthologies, but with limited success in challenging 'the elite networks of power'.[27] She went on to become a prizewinning writer in many genres, and told me that, from the perspective of 'a black British, British-Nigerian, mixed-race' woman she writes 'into the otherwise silences'.[28] I quoted earlier Danuta Kean's 2015 report, 'Writing the Future', a damning commentary on the homogeneous publishing trade which, she claims, concentrates on 'People Like Us—White, aged 35 to 55 and female'.[29] Arguing that publishers should be preparing for a future in which—by 2051—one in five people in the UK will be from an ethnic minority, Kean urged greater recruitment of BAME writers,

Figure 6.4 Bernardine Evaristo
Martin Beddall/ Alamy Stock Photo

publishing staff, and internships. After speaking to 203 UK-based published novelists, she found they were urged to '[up] the sari count, deal with gang culture or some other image that conforms to White preconceptions' (p. 8), an indication of 'authenticity' and 'exoticism' many of them resent. The Arts Council England 2017 report on the state of literary fiction, 'Literature in the 21st Century: Understanding Models of Support for Literary Fiction', deplored the fact that BAME fiction had gone backwards in the previous fifteen years.[30]

Ironically, most BAME novelists write 'literary fiction' rather than the popular bestselling genres crime, romance, and Young Adult, but are expected by commissioning editors to address 'the tension of the ghetto or the fragrance of the mango grove'.[31] Not surprisingly, a growing number of these writers have turned to small independent publishers and crowd-funded self-publishing. In 2018, the centenary of women's (limited) suffrage, Kamila Shamsie's call to publishers for a Year of Publishing Women was answered by an independent press, And Other Stories, which published a range of fiction by new names, many of them (such as Rita Indiana, Alia Trabucco, and

168   *Why Women Read Fiction*

Norah Lange) in translation and/or from racial and ethnic minorities. This initiative, together with the Penguin Random House policy to reflect the diversity of UK writers and publishing staff by 2025, may signal a shift in publishing trends and open up a broader range of fiction for diverse readers.

The Restrictions of Gender

The sense of restriction within the identity of 'woman writer' is entirely understandable when writers of ambition wish to circumnavigate the metaphorical globe rather than be confined to a female-only corner. In a cultural climate that offers readers media and online author profiles with photographs and detailed biographies, it's hard to be read neutrally and without the trappings (an appropriate term) of gender and indeed race.

The complaints of older female TV presenters, actors, sportswomen, and indeed writers, that they are overlooked, unequally paid, and demeaned in the press and social media, remind us that foregrounding gender can be a risky and potentially harmful business. The oblique or direct questions about how they manage to juggle it all with the responsibilities of marriage and children place women rather firmly in the literary kitchen rather than sitting room. Jon McGregor, who won the 2017 Costa Award for best novel, commented sardonically: 'I have never been asked how I juggle writing and fatherhood. I'm not complaining; it's nobody's business, and nothing to do with writing. But I wonder what assumptions lie behind the question of juggling writing and motherhood coming up so regularly?'[32]

At the 2013 Edinburgh Book Festival, American novelist Rachel Kushner discussed her novel, *The Flamethrowers*, with a female protagonist who rides a motorbike in the American West to become a land artist. Hailed by some critics as a Great American Novel, it was also attacked for its 'macho' qualities and 'male material'.[33] Colm Tóibín introduced her to the Edinburgh audience by saying wittily it was as if she were announcing: '[I]f anyone thinks there is a "male novel", and anyone thinks that women should write a different kind of novel, I've just arrived on a motorbike covered in leather and I am ready to eat you all.' During the discussion, Kushner argued that if her material were to be defined as male, 'I guess there's part of me that's male, because I wrote the book that was in me and was natural for me to write . . . Growing up, I was not told that there were women's areas of preoccupation or male ones.' It seems to have surprised some critics that she felt herself to be a kindred spirit to great male writers such as Don DeLillo, 'a connection that was beyond gender'. Lisa McInerney, who won the 2016 Baileys Prize for her debut novel *The Glorious Heresies*, found it, too, was being dubbed a 'masculine novel'. She was puzzled as the novel contained themes specific to women and motherhood. 'I think it's something to do with the swearing or the language? . . . So is it the case that if you throw a few "fucks" in then it becomes a masculine novel? I don't know.'[34] I suspect she's right.

For writers who don't fall into the white and/or middle class category, perhaps all these protestations smack of a certain entitlement. Kit de Waal told me she would 'always be happy to be described as a woman writer and a black writer and a mixed race writer and a working class writer and a Brummie writer and an Irish writer and a new writer and an older writer and also just writer is fine'.[35] But Aminatta Forna dislikes those limiting labels applied to her, such as 'African writer' or 'transnational writer': 'We hyphenated writers complain about the privilege accorded to the white male writer, he who dominates the western canon and is the only one called simply "writer".' Of her novel, *The Hired Man*, she asked: 'So where should a bookshop shelve a novel set in Croatia and written in English by a Scottish Sierra Leonian author?'[36] Asked by trans writer Juno Dawson whether she has to speak for her 'community', Zadie Smith responded:

> Doesn't everyone exist in a Venn diagram of overlapping allegiances and interests? I'm a black person, also a woman, also a wife and mother, a Brit, a European—for the moment—a Londoner, a New Yorker, a writer, a feminist, a second-generation Jamaican, a member of the African diaspora, a *Game of Thrones*-er, an academic, a comedy-nerd, a theory-dork, a hip-hop-head and so on . . . no one calls Don de Lillo the "white American author Don DeLillo", so why should I put up with being called "the black British author Zadie Smith"?[37]

But it's not all bad news. Sally Beauman is one of many writers who welcomed the development of feminist literary criticism, claiming it 'revealed women's writing, exposed it to the light, demonstrated just how fine, subtle and important it is'. In their rewriting of literary history and definition of a tradition of women's writing, feminist critics 'made me see that a woman writing now is not alone: she has grandmothers, cousins, sisters, aunts...there are "ancestral voices" here, if you like...When you open your computer or pick up your pen, it gives you strength.' That dialogue between female writer and reader, boosted by critics and women's studies courses in universities and schools, has opened doors, flagged new creative possibilities, and reached large readerships within and beyond the educational academy.

A Feminist Agenda

The women's movement emboldened women writers. Sarah Dunant, for instance, embraces feminist thought and criticism: 'I have been forged by this secular religion of feminism.' She's unfazed by the fact she has more female than male readers (though pleased when men claim they appreciate and have learned from her). Beginning as a mystery writer, she turned to the Italian Renaissance with a very specific theoretical agenda:

> I went in asking a big question for feminism and the Academy. We can do our best to change the present but we can change the past—not the way it was lived but what we recognise it was about. So this means asking who were half the population—because I don't seem to find them very much in the history books and perhaps they were interesting too. I'm very happy for that to be part of my life's work because all of those three books came out of new research, the new scholasticism, feminism and new history and micro-history. I've been able to paint lives of women that we just didn't know before. So when you ask what the fifteenth century was about and people give you fifteen male names, you can ask, 'Well would you like to know what the whole fifteenth century was like?' In that respect I've been very consciously a woman writer.[38]

The confidence of women writers to assert their feminism was boosted in June 2017 when Naomi Alderman's *The Power* won the Baileys Prize. In her acceptance speech Alderman claimed: 'My life would be more possible with the women's movement existing and no running water than the other way round... the support and the power of other women has been more vital to me than electricity.'[39] She is probably the first major book prize-winner publicly to acknowledge the support of another named writer; Alderman was selected as the protégée of Margaret Atwood on a mentoring programme, and—in another example of that Tiller Girl line-up—she happily acknowledged a sisterly solidarity.

Anonymity, Pseudonyms, and Initials

Despite this high-profile feminist triumph, the literary world remains a muddle of gender obsession, confusion, contradiction, and double standards. Women writers have resisted over centuries attempts to restrict them on grounds of gender. From the earliest anonymous poets to novelists adopting pseudonyms, women have adopted ruses to avoid discrimination among publishers, reviewers, and general readers. Among the pseudonymous are George Sand (Armandine-Aurore-Lucille Dupin), all three Brontës (Currer, Ellis, Acton Bell), George Eliot (Mary Ann Evans), Louisa Alcott (A. M. Barnard), and Harper Lee (Nelle Harper Lee). The use of initials has also enabled many to escape from gender stereotyping, from H. D. (Hilda Doolittle) to M. C. Beaton, P. D. James, and A. L. Kennedy. Joanna Penn, successful author of *Pentecost* and *Prophecy*, blogs that she made a strategic decision to use the name J. F. Penn for thrillers, action-adventure, or any writing in a genre dominated by men. For non-fiction and other writing, 'Joanna' would remain. Romance writer Nora Roberts chose the 'masculine' name J. D. Robb for her ventures into suspense and crime, while Doris Lessing played a trick on her publisher by submitting a novel under a *female* pseudonym, Jane Somers, claiming she was testing the power of a name to get published.

J. K. Rowling is the most successful living female writer (across three genres—children's, adults', and crime fiction) and cannily maintained gender-neutral initials for her Harry Potter series, going one further by publishing a detective novel under a masculine pseudonym, Robert Galbraith. Her website joked she had 'successfully channelled [her] inner bloke' after her editor David Shelley said at his first reading that he would 'never have thought a woman wrote that'.[40] Within our celebrity culture, it's almost impossible to keep the identity of published writers secret for long, so Rowling's ruse was outed very quickly. Her claim that she chose a male pseudonym in order to 'take my writing persona as far away as possible from me' echoes that impatience expressed by many women writers about the labelling and thus diminishing of their creative imaginations. Perhaps the name of her film production company, Brontë Film and TV, is a gesture to her distinguished predecessors who struggled with this identity problem. When she appeared at the 2014 Harrogate Crime Writing Festival to promote the first Robert Galbraith novel, *The Cuckoo's Calling* (2013), Rowling playfully dressed in a suit and tie to signal her masculine alias.

However, women may protest too much. After all, romance novels, chick lit, erotic fiction, and other genres, sell better if authored by women. Because readers need to invest a high level of emotional trust in their authors, it's often claimed no *man* could publish a commercial romance with Harlequin Mills & Boon. Mindful of this, Bill Spence, who had already published a large number of westerns and a non-fiction book about whaling, turned to romance and was assured his name would not sell. Then the pseudonymous bestselling author Jessica Blair was born. Margaret Atwood satirizes this not-uncommon phenomenon (as rumour has it—publishers won't tell) in her *Lady Oracle*; an aspiring female writer is mentored for romance writing by a much-published Polish count.

As I discussed in Chapter 4, romance and the new erotica are very much a woman's sphere, a highly profitable genre dominated by women writers and supported by a vast market of mainly women readers. Writers protect their identity with initials and pseudonyms that avoid sounding too cosy and Home Counties. 'Bonkbuster' writer Victoria Cox adopted that name which sounded 'slightly naughty', classy, and friendly, and the surname of which came from the first half of the alphabet so it would appear high on bookshop and supermarket shelves. (Much research goes into the impact of names, titles, and alphabetical placement). And there are other women's markets that are now recognized as worth targeting. American literary critic Elaine Showalter argues there's a growing tendency for publishers to follow rather than lead women readers, marketing to specific groups:

> Fiction has adapted to become more directed to different reading groups or constituencies. For example, chick lit is now categorized in such a way that you can find a genre for each niche group (Amish, American Indian, Jewish, 'Born Again', etc.). Marketing is hipper to women's choices and there is a more complicated, sophisticated

understanding of women's lives—no longer one category of 'woman'. Just as African American writing broke a mono-cultural mould in the US, so in Britain there is Anglo-Indian, Indian, and Caribbean fiction, heterosexual and lesbian sexualities, with a real crossover and diversification of writing and readerships.[41]

In Women's History Month 2017, Loganberry Books in Ohio reorganized its 10,000-title fiction section so all books by male writers had their spines and covers facing the wall. The bookshop's founder and owner Harriett Logan said this was to illustrate the way women's voices were drowned out, highlighting the disparity between the genders and bringing more focus to women's books. This generated some anger, with cries of sexism and censorship, but the visual impact on readers of both genders must have been shocking. A year later, to coincide with International Women's Day, March 2018, Penguin Books made a more celebratory gesture by opening for five days the Like a Woman Bookshop in Shoreditch, London, selling titles by only female writers. Though accused on Twitter of sexist and divisive action, Penguin's Creative Manager Zainab Juma defended the fact that women 'are not allowed to take up room' so she gave women writers a room of their own for five days. Women readers and girls from local schools lolled on sofas reading, threw out recommendations to one another, pounced on the writers who came for signings, and generally relished the idea of a special space for women writers and readers.

And on another positive note, let's not forget that in the twenty-first century, three British women much admired by women readers—J. K. Rowling, Hilary Mantel, and E. L. James (two significantly using names with non-gender-specific initials)—turned the literary world upside down, and dominated the bestselling lists over many years.

7

Book Clubs in Women's Life Stories

Once a month I wake up with booze on my breath, guacamole in my hair and an ill-defined sense of shame. If I were 21, this might indicate a cracking night out. As I'm 43, it means I got drunk again discussing Jodi Picoult on a near-stranger's couch. Because like 99.9 per cent of middle-class, middle-aged women, I belong to a book club.[1]

For many women readers, the story of our lives is bound up with the membership of book clubs or reading groups. Guy Pringle, founder-publisher of book club magazine *newbooks*, dubbed them 'the female equivalent of freemasonry'.[2] These groups—dating back in one form or another to the seventeenth century—have proliferated to become central to both the lives of individuals and also writers' coffers and reputations, and the whole book trade.

In March 2018, the *Times Literary Supplement* carried a series of notes and letters about longstanding groups. The back-page column 'NB' noted with amazement that the Tayport Book Circle had lasted for thirty-six years. Jean Martin wrote to say that she and others started it 'to give us something to talk about except babies and nappies. Now we avoid talking about grandchildren, pensions and ailments.' Thirty-six years later, the group continues and she boasted they had read 350 titles. Favourite writers—leading them to choose five novels by each—were Penelope Fitzgerald and Carol Shields. But, lest Jean think Tayport stands alone in its longevity, others—all women—responded in subsequent weeks to claim similar distinction: Mavis Maureen Raper's Berwick-upon-Tweed Community Reading Group (thirty years), Judith Lafferty's Sheffield Group (forty-three), and Elizabeth Tanner's Epsom, Surrey (forty-eight). Mary M. Smith reported that her Bristol Book Circle had been meeting for forty years, while the University of Leeds Ladies Club is now in its fifty-second year.

All these groups contained some of the original members, and all had read annually at least ten books (usually novels).[3] A final addition to this list, Susan Jacobs of Teddington, was celebrating forty years of her group; this was the only one of mixed gender (with three married couples) and the only one that runs themed meetings 'with appropriate food or dress'.

I have to come clean and admit that—with the exception of a special poetry group—I've never joined a book club; as a lifelong teacher, I'd have an irresistible desire to chair and guide the discussion . . . not a good idea. But as Jean Martin's words about the journey from nappies to pensions show, reading groups document for passionate women readers the trajectory of their lives. In recent years I've spoken to many women in such groups and found similarities between their composition and practices. All around the country, book clubs have lasted for decades, like Jean's group coming together as young mothers with limited space in their days, now retired with more time to read. They have adapted to changing times, faced the loss of members through relocation, illness, or death, and have refreshed themselves with new blood. Some are intellectually very serious, interviewing new members and requiring a high level of commitment. Others are more laid back and informal. But groups are springing up all over, with ever younger and more diverse members. They're one of the fastest-growing social movements around.

Women's Book Clubs through the Ages

Over the centuries, women of all nations have come together to read. These include seventeenth-century Bible study groups, eighteenth-century Parisian salons, nineteenth-century American groups like Sorosis, and progressive era reading circles and suffrage groups. More than any other country, the United States has a distinguished tradition of women's clubs and reform organizations, which have fought against slavery, promoted African American and women's civil rights, and campaigned for universal suffrage and education. These laid the ground for the Women's Liberation Movement of the 1960s with radical confidence-building consciousness-raising groups, and by the new century a formidable widespread reading group movement. The Book of the Month Club started in 1926, but by the end of the century it began to look dowdily middlebrow. An unexpected focus on reading was initiated by American actor and presenter Oprah Winfrey, whose television Book Club (1996–2011, part of the *Oprah Winfrey Show*) became a phenomenal success, massively increasing book sales and author profiles. In Iran, as Azar Nafisi recounts in *Reading Lolita in Tehran*, a reading group met secretly in the late 1990s in order to discuss forbidden works of Western literature.[4] No one could possibly document all the groups meeting in recent times across the globe, so we can only guess at the scale of the phenomenon.

In the UK, the BBC Radio 4 Book Club began in 1998 and still holds eleven annual broadcasts; in 2010 Simon Mayo began the Radio 2 book club which continues (with a new presenter) to this day. The Daily Mail Book Club was launched in 2004, the same year as the Richard and Judy Book Club, which had Oprah-style success— for instance endorsing Karen Joy Fowler's novel *The Jane Austen Book Club* which became a multi-million bestseller. Other female celebrity-led ventures have followed: in the US, Reese Witherspoon's reading clubs and Dolly Parton's Imagination Library, and in this country Zillah's and Zoe Ball's ITV Book Club. Publishers haven't been slow to follow, with Reading Group pages on their websites, 'Reading Group favourites', 'Hubs', and 'Guides'. Websites to guide readers' choices are now legion, with feminist presses such as Virago and Persephone pointing the way to women writers, while in 2007 Amazon's Goodreads, the world's largest site for readers and book recommendations, hit the ground running. When I last checked, it claimed to have sixty-five million members, two billion books and sixty-eight million reviews. American women's reading groups (estimated at around five million real groups, over forty online) are currently so important to the publishing industry that readers can access booklists, reviews, notes for discussion, interviews with writers, and much more.[5]

British publishers have jumped on this bandwagon, though they are in competition with sites such as litlovers.com, MsLexia, Our Shared Shelf (led by Emma Watson), Mumsnet's various digital groups, Book-tubers, Book Talk, and—not least—the Vaginal Fantasy Romance Book Club, founded by *Buffy the Vampire Slayer*'s actress Felicia Day to focus on romance novels with paranormal twists. Launching in 2000, Guy Pringle's *newbooks* worked with libraries and publishers to promote mainly fiction, help groups get established and send them free books, questions, and ideas, including the odd brownie recipe for meetings.[6] One provocative suggestion for all group members was to name 'The one I loved, the one that made us talk, the one I struggled with, the one that surprised us, the one that divided us, the one that nobody finished, the one I wished we'd read.'

All of these focused and in some ways professionalized the reading experience, and gave a new impetus to book clubs, which on both sides of the Atlantic are now said to cover all age ranges, socio-economic groups and geographical sites, meeting in cafés, bars, libraries, residential homes, day centres, workplaces, prisons and—easily the majority—women's homes.

Just like libraries, bookshops, and literature festivals, the reading group is a secure and friendly place in which books may be investigated, experimented with, and cross-checked with others you trust. In 2001, academic Jenny Hartley published an account of British groups, finding that 80 per cent met in people's homes, with food and drink an essential part of the experience. She compares them with a 'well-functioning family' celebrating anniversaries and special occasions, pointing out that some groups have survived longer than marriages.[7] The readers are mainly women (even in mixed groups), with members inviting friends and neighbours to join in local neighbourhoods. Hartley found that 69 per cent were all-female and 4 per cent all-male, and I suspect those figures haven't shifted much since. Groups tend to select novels, with occasional short-story collections, and British publishers have responded accordingly, providing back page author interviews, questions, and discussion points for groups, while TV and radio programmes offer the writers themselves for scrutiny and questioning. Book prize shortlists and winners make easy selections for these groups, and some of the more enterprising or long-established groups invite writers to come to speak to them. Literary festivals invite and hold events for reader groups.

For women, this movement has been a natural development out of earlier networks—from the Women's Institute and Townswomen's Guild to post-natal groups and feminist consciousness raising groups, Tupperware parties to language, craft and cooking adult education classes. Scholarly studies of such groups have revealed how important these are across social and racial groups, translating 'written text into group talk, turning back the clock from literacy to orality, from the act of the individual reading to talking, from the solitary experience to the social'.[8] And in no way are the discussions bland; many readers claim their best meetings were when they strongly disagreed about the merits of a book and enjoyed heated debate. So popular are these groups that there's been a cluster of novels and films set within them, from Elizabeth Noble's *The Reading Group* to Mary Ann Shaffer and Annie Barrow's *The Guernsey Literary and Potato Peel Pie Society* (both book and film), Fay Weldon's play *The Reading Group*, and the film *Book Club*.[9]

The female book club is an easy target for jokes, with its connotations dating back to the much-derided 'bluestockings' or '*bas bleu*' of eighteenth-century England and France. It has been caricatured as an earnest, humourless bunch of unhappily married or sad singletons and wannabe scholars. But this has been perhaps the most successful group education project of the last few decades. For centuries, women were deprived of formal schooling and equal employment opportunities, so had to find ways to learn and better themselves in domestic environments; the reading group is a modern example of female self-help. This simple idea has been seized on as a way to create new friendship networks or revivify stale relationships. Broadening women's experiences, it's an informally structured way of keeping in touch with people, often in small towns and villages. Besides, it satisfies women's curiosity to snoop around one another's homes and gardens...

Reading together can help isolated readers (the elderly, disabled, visitors to day centres, or women in prisons) to feel part of a wider community. Various cities followed Bristol's example of a 'City Read' in which free copies of a novel were distributed and discussed in various sites. At their best, book clubs provide an unthreatening, companionable form of reading pleasure and bibliotherapy that shakes off the association with 'set books' and intellectual competitiveness at school or college. Unlike their predecessors in earlier times, few groups (except, perhaps, overtly feminist groups) have a political agenda; socio-political engagement now takes place elsewhere—via the media, especially online—so reading is the focus and pleasure is the aim. As many women have reminded me, literature academics like me are slow to join such groups as we're used to analysing books critically rather than reading for pure joy. Book clubs have given a new lease of life to local libraries that set up groups (open to everyone), suggest and stock titles, and loan sets of books. Selected fiction by women writers has gained huge cachet, as women readers have read and recommended titles. Much-cited examples include Audrey Niffenegger's *The Time Traveler's Wife*, Elizabeth Gilbert's *Eat, Pray, Love*, and Kathryn Stockett's *The Help*.

Groups have been dubbed 'Knit and Natter' or 'Knit and Bitch'. By contrast, men-only groups don't knit but they do cook—often very competitively with researched recipes, and they tend to have a more formal structure with elaborate websites and so on. They also select far more non-fiction—biography, military and political history. According to several of my correspondents, men who join mixed groups often dislike the fiction choices (usually those by women writers) and the feminized atmosphere, and gradually drift away. Leanne J told me the lone man in her group of eleven has never liked any book they've read, and she wonders why he still attends.

Talking to Book Groups

I wanted to get a snapshot of the more than 50,000 reading groups that exist across the country. My questionnaire responses and personal interviews indicated how varied and adventurous they are—and they are increasingly specialized (though there is no national register, so it's hard to find them). I set out to talk to some and correspond with others.

I was invited to tea with a group that started in 1983, so has been in existence for over three decades—covering five villages in Somerset. The Wedmore Book Circle (Figure 7.1) began as a branch of the National Housewives Register (NHR) (now the National Women's Register), and gradually turned into a reading group, meeting monthly on a weekday at 8 p.m. after children were in bed. It's worth describing at some length because it is typical of many other groups. The 15+ white members—mainly actively retired from various kinds of white collar or professional jobs, most with children and now grandchildren—meet eleven times a year and a coordinator sends dates, venues, and reading lists via email (what did they do before social media?). A few are also in other groups, such as University of the Third Age (U3A). They meet in one another's houses, and

Figure 7.1 The Wedmore Book Circle, May 2018
Photo by Helen Taylor

the hostess selects the book which she then introduces with a brief (usually internet-researched) talk to get the discussion going. They don't complain about 'spoilers' if they arrive without finishing and have to hear others arguing about the ending. After ninety minutes of discussion, there's an informal chat with refreshments.

They provided me with lists of all the books selected, and short-listed, since 1983; as I keep finding, the list-making capacity of women is awesome. Books must be available in paperback, and the group regards e-readers as inconvenient for discussions (since flipping back and forth is too cumbersome). They did consider the request of a male reader to join, but decided against. Most vociferously opposed was a high-ranking police officer who felt her working life was so male-dominated she relished the all-female book circle and argued they should keep it that way. In line with many other groups, the first novel chosen was by a woman, Anita Brookner's *Family and Friends*, and it has kept fairly steadily to fiction ever since. Like other groups, they rule out 'competitive baking'; tea and biscuits are provided—though wine is served at the July planning meeting and the December gathering provides mince pies and punch. (Sweetmeats, as I've described earlier, are never far away from women's ideal reading experience.)

From the beginning, they followed NHR advice to bring the names of two books each so that the group could select ten to eleven titles for the coming year; the also-rans are listed so they provide an additional reading list outside the circle. The choices are mainly contemporary 'literary' fiction, with few concessions to genre or commercial fiction—except by rather upmarket crime writers such as C. J. Sansom. In their first documented years, 1986–94, the group read 18 per cent more female than male authors, while in the decade 2007 to 2018, they read 26 per cent more female. The gender mix is typical of other such groups, but it's interesting that the number of female authors has risen sharply in the current century, probably an indication of readers' preference for the female voice, greater media coverage of women's issues and women writers, the Women's Prize, Feminist Book Fortnight, and so on.

They gather suggestions by word of mouth, book reviews, bestseller lists, literary prize long- and shortlists, reading mainly British or American writers—with a nod to 'classics' (Charles Dickens, George Eliot, Joseph Conrad). Choices cover both genders and a modest number of BAME authors. They favour works of emotional intensity about relationships, families, and children; one woman wryly commented: 'Men talk about things, women about people.' Almost to a woman, they don't enjoy sci-fi or speculative fiction (though—as I've argued earlier about women's dystopian futurist fiction—*The Handmaid's Tale* was a hit). As with many other groups, those classic 'reading group favourites,' narrative-driven A. S. Byatt's *Possession*, Louis de Bernières' *Captain Corelli's Mandolin*, and Barbara Kingsolver's *The Poisonwood Bible*, were their top reads. They all hated Virginia Woolf's challenging modernist novel *To the Lighthouse* until the woman who proposed it gave such an interesting introduction they were willing to reconsider.

When the group began, and most of them had young children, they had a saying, 'no baby talk until coffee', to keep focus on the book; many such groups deliberately avoid domestic and family chat to maintain that sense of serious purpose. They all agreed that their best discussions have occurred when there are strong feelings against a novel, and that the most admired reads often lead to bland praise. Each year, they go to the event for book groups at Wells Literature Festival. They invited writers Andrew Miller and Adrian Tinniswood to speak to them. New members have joined over the years, though three of the original group remain. Like other reading groups, they often laugh at the endnotes for groups included in some novels, finding them patronising or banal (though they admitted they can turn to the questions if discussion gets stuck).

For comparison, I agreed to meet a group of younger women who are still working, often with young families, in businesses—hairdressing, a children's shoe shop, creative media, a restaurant.[10] They all live in a city and describe themselves as 'a very close gang of girls with a long shared history'. Because they've known one another for some years, including taking family holidays together, they found the book club a good way to refresh their relationships: 'We've known each other for so long and it's same old same old and we're quite rude to each other (affectionately) but in the group we're sensible and grownup for once in our lives, and we have to think.' It allows them to escape from the domestic, everyday and—in the case of the hairdresser—'my girly, hairy, make-up life in the salon'. Their educational level and speed of reading vary considerably, so there's a fair amount of give and take.

Like Wedmore Book Circle and other groups, they avoid fancy refreshments. One member who asked her husband to provide nibbles and wine came home to find he'd prepared posh canapés; she told him these had to be abandoned as it would look like 'showing off' (and a reminder that escape from the kitchen is one reason groups were set up in the first place). They read mainly fiction, trying to vary the historical and contemporary, with a few non-fiction additions (for example, Obama's autobiography). Sometimes the novels chosen are too difficult for group members—Daniel Defoe's *Roxana* and George Eliot's *Daniel Deronda* had to be dropped. Most are working mothers who read late at night, which means they're sleepy and miss things which then get amended in their discussions; one member was left very embarrassed after misunderstanding the ambiguous ending of a book. At times the meetings feel like counselling sessions. One novel, Laura Beatty's *Pollard*, hit a nerve with them all (and was recalled vividly by members with whom I spoke) because it provoked discussion about the death of a father and child, post-natal depression, adoption, and autism.

Mary M. Smith whose group, you'll recall, was fêted in the *TLS*, sent me lists of their first 300 books, chosen between 1976 and 2008. Of these, 168 were by women; eleven were nineteenth-century 'classics'; eighteen were by Nobel Prize winners and nine by Booker Prize winners; fifty-nine books were non-fiction; there was an impressively wide global spread of writers, from Ireland to Chile and Hungary; and they read five titles by that favourite of reading groups, Margaret Forster, and four by Elizabeth Gaskell, Ian McEwan, Alice Munro, and Doris Lessing. The 'Wash Brook' Book Club, led by retired teacher Eila Huxford, has a more formal educational structure than many.[11] This group reads across genres, even some poetry, and like other groups they invite speakers and go to literary sites such as Jane Austen's Chawton and Thomas Hardy's Dorchester. They pay £5 per session for which they receive a pack including questions posed by Eila, newspaper articles, author information, and a monthly quote and cartoon. They meet in her house and keep strictly to the subject: 'No gossiping about local issues on my patch!' A group of readers in Kingston upon Thames, all with primary age children, read only literature in translation (current text, Mikhail Bulgakov's *The Master and Margarita*).

White writer Ian Thomson, award-winning author of *The Dead Yard: Tales of Modern Jamaica*, describes his invitation to address a high-powered middle-class West Indian reading group in Balham, London, where the elegantly dressed and coiffed members were served Pimms, jerk chicken, and avocado by a white waiter. Thomson agreed to attend, with considerable nervousness, and they proceeded to grill him rigorously about his book (with a Skype link to one member's sister in Kingston).[12] The fact that Thomson called his piece 'Why I'm now scared of book clubs' reveals his own unease as a white middle-class man being challenged by (heaven forbid) smart, informed, and networked black women readers.

Informal Styles

To date, I've described groups and clubs that take themselves fairly seriously, with a quasi-professional approach to the reading programme. Other groups are more relaxed and quirky. The one that meets in my neighbourhood openly admits to spending half the time sharing local political, street, and personal news, and (amid much mirth) has a book selection process that involves moving books up and down on the carpet. The Bedford Bookworms tell me they 'vote a book a hit, miss, or absticate (a made up word, I know, which means you didn't hate it but wouldn't recommend it)'. Helen R, who is in two groups—one in a library, the other a village hall—suggests that the latter 'tends to descend to local gossip and good snacks', while Ann C calls hers 'a wine and laughter group'. Some take the group beyond four walls. Birgit G's goes on outings: a Robert Tressell walk, a trip to Henry James' house in Rye, a forty-two mile walk along the Sussex Ouse to follow in the footsteps of Olivia Laing's *To the River*.

Emily Rhodes of Daunt Books, Hampstead, leads a monthly dog-friendly Walking Book Club on Sunday afternoons, which began with Muriel Spark's *A Far Cry from Kensington*. She explained to the BBC's Clare Balding that customers and bookshop staff walk together on Hampstead Heath, on the grounds you can 'wander with your feet while you wonder in your mind'.[13] At that time the group, open to all, consisted of nineteen women and one man, and Emily gives a quick opening talk to get things going. Conversation flows between people who mingle throughout the walk to create a relaxed and unthreatening atmosphere ('no worry about feminist or postcolonial readings', she promises). To Emily, members of the group 'travel with us, they accompany us through from our pasts into our futures, always with their present-tense ability'. Her example has since been followed by walking book clubs from Edinburgh to Exmoor.

Martina G's reading group has lasted for almost two decades. One time when she was hosting,

> The book was *Desert Queen* [the biography of Gertrude Bell, by Janet Wallach]. I set up a tent in the garden, had a low table with a beautiful red satin cloth, lots of gold and flowers. We had red and yellow peppers to dip into tahini, pitta squares to go with a cucumber and yoghourt dressing, lamb kebabs, couscous and baklava for dessert. It was over the top but it was great!

And finally, a bonkbuster book club, the Guilty Pleasures, focuses on bonkbusters over the decades—from *Valley of the Dolls* and *The Thorn Birds* to *Rivals* and inevitably *Fifty Shades of Grey*. This sparked a debate on spanking, leading one member to see a few boyfriends and husbands in a new light...

The Groups for Our Age

In all their different guises, reading groups are surely the adult education classes, Bible studies, political hustings, sewing bees, coffee mornings, Women's Institutes, and girls' nights out of our age. They have so many advantages. For a start, they get women away from domestic space at minimal cost to be part of a female community for a few hours, usually in the evening when family duties can oppress. They broaden women's reading choices and provide reading lists—in a world full of book choices that can bewilder and overwhelm us. This is especially important as university costs soar and prevent both young and mature women from taking degrees, while adult day and evening classes close, and libraries and librarians, once relied on for guidance, decline in number. Providing a literary rhythm to each year, they give women permission to have a monthly date with non-family members, to confer a seriousness and dignity on what can so easily be dismissed by male family members as a gaggle of gossips, and they confirm women's right to see themselves and be seen as thinking, reflecting beings rather than nurturers, workers, partners, mothers, and so on.

Since many women now work outside as well as inside the home (with grandparent duties occupying much of retired women's time), and often feel separated from other women and female concerns in male-dominated workspaces and atmospheres, the groups allow a space for feminine discourse and sharing of experiences. They give women the reason—or, within busy family lives, excuse—to carve out space for preparatory reading ('I have to finish this for my book club tomorrow night'). And they give women a focus for engagement with one another, debate and argument, the deepening of friendships over time as reading experience is shared. Group members are emboldened to trust their own responses to reading, to discuss ideas, and to put up their hands at bookshop readings, literary festivals, and more modest gatherings. And they offer great female pleasures. Margaretta J recalls:

> . . . one evening at my house where we discussed Alison Bechdel's comic graphic memoir *Fun Home* over some fruit salad covered in crème fraiche and burnt sugar. Also, notably, the evening under an apple tree in the feminist preacher's garden, where we were deep into whether the Virgin Mary could be an icon of liberation for women, and all of a sudden spied

a naked man peering out of her upstairs window…the conversation at that point changed direction.

It is impressive to see the proactive way groups develop, circumventing orthodox organizations to forge special links to suit particular individuals and communities. Sheila W joined an Essex adult education class in 1998, but fees became expensive with cuts to education budgets so the group re-established itself within a U3A branch. For some reason this was unsatisfactory, so they moved on to become the independent Stansted Literature Group. They pay modest fees to cover a rented hall, insurance, speakers' fees, and so on, and the professional tutor with whom they began gives her services without charge. Tutor Judith has provided materials under the title 'Writers in Context', with handouts, biographies, articles, recorded interviews, and so on. Carolyn F is a Royal National Institute of Blind People (RNIB) facilitator who runs a reading group of six or eight people every month via telephone conferencing, with members using Braille or audio books; for half the meetings, she organizes guest speakers. Cathy P is in a postal reading group because she couldn't find a group she could get to in her local area. Members send a book to another member on the list, together with a small notebook which describes why they've chosen that particular book; this means that each member receives a book and notebook from another. At the beginning of each month they send a different book, and in the final month of the year they receive back their notebook containing everyone's comments on their choice. The process is then repeated. For ten years, without ever meeting them, she's been in that group and kept all her notebooks containing everyone's comments.

Of course there are quarrels, tensions, and jealousies. Monthly discussion in a medium-sized group prevents profound emotional engagement with either the book itself or the issues it may throw up for readers, and can lead to members feeling frustrated or short-changed. Women who conscientiously read every book resent women who show up with a half-read novel and don't want the ending discussed. The woman who dominates conversation and displays her superior intellectual capital is a general problem. Patricia M told me she nearly ended an important friendship over a bitter disagreement about Philip Larkin. Journalist Tash Bell says that

Book Club is 'the only competitive sport to occur in the homes of participants', and she quotes Theresa of Ealing: 'I hate the way wealthier members flaunt their perfect lives and massive house with a Filipina maid laying out home-made nibbles to the rest of us living in a two-up, two-down with the kitchen cupboard doors falling off.'[14]

It is beyond the remit of this book, but I would love to see an analysis of the book choices these thousands of groups make, and how those have changed over the years. It would be good to know how many BAME or mixed-race groups exist (something I couldn't establish, though I know of at least one London-based Black Women's Group and a Bengali Women's English Reading and Writing Group). To what extent are book choices driven by the market, with heavy PR for book prize-winners, media figures, and accessible rather than challenging reads? Why do most read few novels in translation, by British black and Asian writers (African Americans are well represented), or from cultures other than the UK and USA? Is there a type of book and author that suits a white middle-class reading group, and are there writers who get overlooked because they don't fit into a certain pattern? I suspect groups are less independent than they think, with the publishing industry shaping taste, choice, and availability.

But that's not the whole story. It's easy to mock suburban or rural women ordering their Amazon copies and fitting book group into comfortable lives, but when you read lists that include (a random selection from my correspondents) Chimamanda Ngozi Adichie, Andrea Camilleri, Wilkie Collins, Roopa Farooki, Edmund Gosse, Ernest Hemingway, Jo Nesbo, Michael Ondaatje, Orhan Pamuk, Ahdaf Soueif, and Edith Wharton, you appreciate the intellectual ambition and willingness to experiment with lesser-known authors from a range of historical periods and cultures. Since some book club members are graduates (and being women, usually of arts or social science subjects), they have been introduced to international writing through courses in world literature, women's, cultural, gender, and queer studies, postcolonial writing, and more. Feminist criticism—supplemented by burgeoning feminist publication—has introduced women readers to lesser-known and little-celebrated fiction by women, which is reflected in their book selections.

'Reading Is My Window'

So far I have discussed groups in the community and especially domestic spaces. But there's one place in which reading groups are a treasured lifeline, facing particular challenges. Until 2016, the £5 note showed Victorian prison reformer Elizabeth Fry reading to prisoners in Newgate Prison. Literacy has long been recognized as a force for individual autonomy and power, as well as social progress. American slave narratives and novels such as *Uncle Tom's Cabin* describe the ways learning to read liberates and empowers enslaved, incarcerated, and impoverished people. In our time, apart from literacy classes, there's been a vigorous drive to encourage reading within prisons, where some of the nation's most disadvantaged people are thirsty for stimulation and further education.[15] Belinda Jack describes a women's prison group in Cornton Vale, Stirling, Scotland, where the chaplain offered a weekly contextual Bible study to try to help the inmates come to terms with their experiences.[16] This is by no means unusual.

In 1999, Prison Reading Groups (PRG) began to promote, fund, and support prison reading (mainly in men's prisons, because there are very few women's). Two decades later, PRG works with more than forty groups in thirty-five prisons nationwide, with no 'syllabus', targets or set texts; the informal groups, often facilitated by the prison librarian, are about the pleasure of reading together, and books are given to prisoners to keep or pass on (they sometimes get tea and biscuits, a very special treat). Prisoners are generally offered few individual choices, so facilitators encourage inmates to select their own books. Many prisoners are dyslexic, non-English speakers, and/ or poor readers, so PRG promotes reading aloud and sharing simple stories or poems. Often the discussions move into quasi-therapy sessions with everyone sharing experiences in a rare safe collective space. Large print and 'shorter reads' work well, while Family Days provide books and book bags for children visiting parents. PRG recruits and trains volunteers, providing suggested titles and materials.

For incarcerated women, who rarely have a reading habit, this can be a huge treat in a grim and monotonous daily life. 'Reading is my window,' said one American female inmate (giving academic Megan Sweeney the title of a book about women's prisons).[17] Sweeney suggests that reading in women's gaols counters isolation, abandonment, and dehumanization, encouraging prisoners to empathize with other people and engage with ideas in the outside world. At a deeper level, it provides them with contexts for their experiences, mediates their histories of victimization and violence, and offers something resembling therapy and consciousness raising: 'We read to deal with life.' And holding a book with its 'tactile and aesthetic properties' can offer prisoners the 'soothing touch, pleasing sensation, and beauty' that are lacking in their lives.[18]

UK publishers donate sets of books to prison libraries; Persephone Books contributed to one women's prison copies of the suffrage-themed *No Surrender*. The charity Give a Book[19] donates books, and works closely with PRG, while collecting all the royalties of a collection edited by Antonia Fraser, *The Pleasure of Reading* (forty-three contributions by well-known writers). One of their ventures has been in collaboration with publisher Child's Play, which supports five mother and baby units. With little stimulation for mothers with very young children, this initiative has been a considerable success: mothers at HMP Styal, for instance, commented: 'It's great to read with Charlie. He loves the rhymes and songs. Thank you for sending these books. It means a lot'; 'No, I'm not a reader. You could never get me in the library before but Ella adores books. It's great that we have these books to take away and keep.' As I discussed earlier, establishing a reading habit between mother and child has always been crucial to the creation of new readers.

My friend Susan invited me to observe the reading group she ran in a women's prison, so on a cold October morning I accompanied her. Susan had told me that the group, all older women, enjoyed the poems of Carol Ann Duffy and Wendy Cope, Sue Townsend's fiction, and Katie Piper's autobiography *Beautiful*. She said the women preferred writing by women, as well as true crime and celebrity biographies (Jade, for instance)—though they want to feel 'elevated'; Caitlin Moran's frequent swearing upset them. Because so many had experienced serious violence in their lives, Susan was careful not to provide sexually explicit material or writing about self-harm or sexual abuse as this can distress women who then flee from the group. Upbeat writing works best; a real hit was Benjamin Zephaniah's witty poem 'Talking Turkeys' about freeing the Christmas turkey (a metaphoric call to respect the exploited and ignored). While they read, the women knit and crochet with materials gathered from charity shops.

On one occasion, a male prison officer had to accompany one of the group. This woman became very impatient with her knitting, so—somewhat sheepishly—he gently untangled it and showed her how to purl. Some years ago, a Chinese prisoner who spoke no English and had never knitted or crocheted joined the group. She learned to speak and read English, always taking the reading material back to her cell. She also learned how to crochet, and her 'Coat of Flowering Hope' won the 2012 Kenneth Harper memorial Highly Commended Award for Needlecraft in the Koestler Exhibition, where it sat as the centrepiece in the South Bank Centre. These anecdotes alone remind us how creative juices and collegiality flow through the experience of collective reading, potentially transforming lives.

The Limitations of the Book Club

Now, not everyone is convinced, and Virginia Ironside's witty book about growing old disgracefully speaks for more than one woman: *No! I Don't Want to Join a Bookclub*. Seeing this activity as one of the clichéd hobbies of the over-sixties—learning Italian, taking an Open University degree, joining U3A—Ironside's narrator complains that 'Book-club people always seem to have to wade through *Captain Corelli's Mandolin*, or *The God of Small Things* or, groan, *The Bookseller of Kabul*. I think they feel that by reading and analysing books, they're keeping their brains lively. But either you've got a lively brain or you haven't.'[20] The tabloid press has always had fun at the expense of the book club, with one article claiming 'They're full of show-offs, drunks and fibbers', with membership requiring a woman to read a book a month 'not because it appealed to her, but because it had been selected by her sister-in-law's neighbour's aromatherapist who'd read about it in a magazine at the hairdresser's.'[21]

Helen Dunmore had a more nuanced critique:

My only reservation is that not all work is immediately very approachable. Some you need to give quite a lot of time to, or it's a solitary and incommunicable delight; others there's a lot to talk about other than how beautiful it is! In the end reading is a solitary rather than a communal process and people trust their own reading identity quite strongly.

I'm very aware as a writer that each reader is bringing forward the cargo of their life and their sensibilities and their responses and their whole very complicated—couldn't be more complicated!—everything to a book so each time the book is read it's transformed. Even in a reading group they're only partially communicating that to each other.[22]

Writer Ali Smith concurs. Arguing that books take more time than we are used to giving them, she says: 'Books need time to dawn on us, it takes time to understand what makes them, structurally, in thematic resonance, in afterthought, and always in correspondence with the books which came before them.' She goes on to say: 'Great books are adaptable; they alter with us as we alter in life, they renew themselves as we change and re-read them at different times in our lives.'[23]

It isn't surprising that fiction writers have reservations about one of their works being discussed during one evening by a heterogeneous group that won't revisit that particular book. And of course no monthly two-hour session can deal with the many formal and structural aspects of a book or the reading process involved; discussion tends to focus on the plot, characters, and appeal of the subject matter. Besides, by randomly selecting books, there's little chance for members to make meaningful connections between writers and works, and to understand the complexities of literary culture. A more serious objection, to my mind, is the fact that most book clubs are personal invitation-only, so will tend to select birds of a feather without reaching for very different people who might disrupt or challenge existing members. This is what school and college classes, open groups in libraries, and adult education have always done. Their decline threatens to undermine publishers' and writers' potential to reach wider and more diverse audiences, and stimulate healthy debate about the process of writing.

Among many others, Guy Pringle of *newbooks* claims that reading groups are a white female movement. He told me: 'Journalists had a pop at "white middle-class women swigging chianti" then realized these were their readers.' (Figure 7.2). I asked the mixed-race writer Kit de Waal whether she knew of BAME reading groups. Confirming Pringle's point, she suggested that this is where online community and

Figure 7.2 A reading group at Hay Festival, 2018
Photo by Helen Taylor

online reading groups come into their own: 'I think the web is so much more democratic in that people can find their tribe easier, if they are not living in a community that represents their interests or where they feel they have something in common with the majority.'[24] Guy Pringle acknowledges that women writers are generally under-represented in literary culture, but suggests that book groups helped secure Hilary Mantel's reputation for *Wolf Hall*. Her memoir *Giving Up the Ghost* and novel *Beyond Black* were already favourites with groups, so 'it became a rite of passage for groups to tackle it'.[25] Whatever their limitations, these clubs, circles, and groups that aspire to read a wide range of fiction, and are open to new writers and writing, have strongly supported literary fiction that has seen a sales decline in recent years.[26] They are a reliable market and debating chamber for contemporary writing in a world full of other distractions. If their book choices sometimes seem predictable, critic John Sutherland defends them: 'Reading groups have changed the way we talk about literature and have opened up new lines of communication between producers and consumers...Reading groups help to keep reading alive and pleasurable. And without that, literature itself would die.'[27] I find it astonishing that in the Arts Council England 2017 report, 'Literature in the 21st Century', there is hardly a word about readership, and no mention whatsoever of reading groups. In a downbeat report expressing gloom about the future of literary fiction, at no point does it acknowledge the enthusiastic support given by real and online book clubs, and the potential use that could be made of their members to boost writers' sales and profiles, and to extend to new, currently under-represented markets.

Women's reading groups support bookshops, libraries, publishers, book prize-winners, and new writers, as well as reinforcing the importance of literary culture. But what does *being in* a group do for female readers? Margaret Atwood shrewdly suggested: 'I suppose you could say that the real, hidden subject of a book group discussion is the book group members themselves.'[28] In so many ways, women have found their intellectual feet and self-identity in these groups, as well as consolidating through the rhythms of the reading year friendships and acquaintances that have seen them through years and sometimes decades of life. For Jenny Hartley, the reading group points to something that runs through the whole story of women's reading, the feminization of culture:

> a forum for the kind of talk associated with women: co-operation rather than competition, the model of "emotional literacy" which values teamwork, listening, and sharing over self-assertion and winning the argument.[29]

In all my discussions with reading groups, I've been impressed with their commitment to one another through reading together. Book clubs don't exist to help women pass exams, get better jobs, or win arguments with others (though they may have that effect!) They are there for the love of literature—especially fiction—and they satisfy a need all human beings have for collective activities that stimulate and inspire. Women are list-makers and social secretaries par excellence, and have always been good at forming groups, keeping alive and quietly running organizations, workplaces, places of religious worship, and political parties. In recent times, however, especially with social media, we are losing face-to-face contact with one another. Care of children and elderly parents is a heavy burden of time and cost that increasingly falls on women of many ages. Women's incomes have declined badly in recent years, and many are working on zero hours or short-term contracts. Meanwhile, technological innovations are making many women redundant and thus home-bound, and home working has isolated women from colleagues. High street meeting places are shrinking, and pubs and coffee bars are largely inhabited by men, the single, and childless. Political parties' membership is dropping. Prisons, hospitals, and other institutions offer few opportunities to stretch the mind.

The book group may not fulfil all the needs of other social groups, but at least it provides regular, structured human contact which gives its members a supportive constituency of the like-minded—a considerable bonus in fragmented and difficult daily lives and times. Many groups I've met keep detailed records of their reading, often over decades, with scores given to particular books and notes on discussions. As I've argued throughout this book, women can trace life stages and changes through reading, and often remark to one another on personal memories associated with a particular book choice. The book club is a significant place in which women can articulate the intertwined relationship between real and imagined lives.

At the end of Elizabeth Noble's saga novel, *The Reading Group*, the five members of a reading group find that all has been turned on its head, and all their lives are different. For many book clubs these words will ring true, a reminder of how reading apart and together can punctuate and define our life stories:

> Some of their lives had become simpler, some had gone through complications they could never have imagined. And through it all, there'd been this forum where they had come together, sometimes to share their secrets, sometimes to escape them, but always to listen to each other and talk about life, in the abstract or absolutely in the present. They had learnt so much more than they had expected to.[30]

And in a moving epilogue to her *Reading Lolita in Tehran*, Azar Nafisi quotes one of her group, writing five years after the formation of their secret reading group:

> Hardly anything has changed in the nonstop sameness of our everyday life. But somewhere else I have changed. Each morning with the rising

of the routine sun as I wake up and put on my veil before the mirror to go out and become a part of what is called reality, I also know of another "I" that has become naked on the pages of a book: in a fictional world, I have become fixed like a Rodin statue. And so I will remain as long as you keep me in your eyes, dear reader.[31]

What better tribute could there be to the power of literature, and the emancipating force of reading together?

8

Festivals, Literary Tourism, and Pilgrimage

[Hay Festival] is a bit like summer camp. It's warm, there's tons of cool stuff to do, it's all crammed onto one site and is slightly chaotic yet somehow comes together at the last minute.

Tracy Chevalier, Hay Festival brochure

A recent tweet caught my eye. @JenElleCair wrote: 'A man just called me a f****g b****h for reading my book [Barbara Comyns, *Our Spoons Came from Woolworths*] on a crowded bus. I said "I'm so sorry but I love this book so much I just can't wait to continue reading it. It's very wonderful, listen..." And what did I do? I read out loud for two whole stops until he got off. Yes I did.' Reading aloud on a bus—like reading together in a library, prison, or reading group—brings literature alive. In refreshing contrast to individual heads bent over mobile phones and laptops, sharing words in real time with real people can be a wonderfully gregarious experience. In earlier chapters, I've discussed the pleasures of reading with families and friends, membership of book groups, education classes, and browsing in libraries and bookshops. I've discussed the way we fold reading experiences into our memories (and vice versa), and value those writers and novels that enable us to tell our own stories. But I've also shown that these days women want more from their reading, be it prequels and sequels, TV or film adaptations, contact with writers about their tastes, relationships, and homes, and goodie bags from online companies. Reading is part of a wider 'edutainment' movement in which we expect our pleasures to be heightened by informative events and experiences.

And two kinds of festive and group literary pleasures are becoming increasingly popular with women. First, the literature festival which provides opportunities for cultural exchanges between writers and readers, mixed with refreshment, pleasure, and relaxation. And second, literary tourism, once referred to as 'a text for the glove compartment of the tourist's car', offering travellers site-specific associations with places where writers lived and wrote, or set their novels.

The Literature Festival

Festivals have a long pedigree in human societies, suggesting celebration, merry-making, musical or dramatic performance, and joyous or honorific celebration. Indeed, if you Google 'festival' you will find hundreds of entries from Raindance Film Festival, the Edinburgh International Television Festival, and Bangalore's peanut festival, to London's Coffee Festival and Scotland's Snowdrop Festival. Festivals are everywhere, celebrating almost anything you can think of. This is perhaps surprising given that our digital world allows us to access almost all knowledge, watch films and musical performances, analyse paintings or photos, or read online rare manuscripts and collections of poetry. Why would anyone who can sit at home or in a coffee shop consuming all those on their phone or tablet need to congregate to celebrate anything?

Yet live performance of all kinds continues to hold its own. Among the fastest-growing are literary festivals which—at their best—offer concentrated experiences in public intellectual life, outpacing those of the Church, political parties, and other community groups. As I've suggested about book clubs, they are becoming the modern world's cosmopolitan and internationalist debating societies, political hustings, Open University-style summer schools, adult education and Third Age classes, and gossip at the proverbial well. Their influence extends way beyond the festivals themselves, provoking debates and addressing urgent social and political questions. They can raise spirits, enhance community cultural engagement, and boost local economies. In Kevin Parker's words, they 'provide entertainment, escapism, intellectual muscle exercise, an excuse to visit an area and a joy for voyeurs . . . a cultural depth to daily lives saturated by digital overload'. Speakers now use them to make controversial statements or offer personal confessions that produce the next day's headlines. In Fiona Sampson's words, they allow readers to 'go backstage' after falling in love with a writer's work. Artemis Cooper says she loves Hay Festival audiences: 'exactly the right balance between the serious and the playful'.[1]

In the early 1990s, I was invited to speak at two literature festivals. One was in Cheltenham. Held in the grand Victorian Town Hall, sessions were (rather solemn and dry) talks or interviews with writers, with tea and sandwiches on hand for modest-sized audiences. The second was the Tennessee Williams Literary Festival, New Orleans, which was a very different experience. Yes, there were talks, debates, and some amateur dramatics. But in the Deep South, where the pleasures of eating and drinking come before everything, I was stuffed with po'boy sandwiches and pastries from local bakeries, tempted into cocktails by mid-morning, and by the end of the day reeling after oysters on the half shell were washed down by mint juleps and sazerac. There were concerts, comedy turns, literary exhibitions, and sales of festival tote bags, mugs, tapes, and books. Not to mention a 'Stanley and Stella shouting contest'—emulating a scene in Williams' play *A Streetcar Named Desire*. I didn't realize at the time that this carnivalesque style would be adopted by British and other nations' literary festivals.

Hay Festival was described by one of its most famous speakers, Bill Clinton, as 'the Woodstock of the mind'—a tag that has stuck because it seems to promise an intelligent consumer an irresistible mixture of visceral pleasures with intellectual stimulation. Writers describe India's Jaipur Literature Festival as 'part-circus, part-postgraduate seminar and part-revolutionary assembly' (Lawrence Norfolk), and 'the most fabulous literary love-fest on the planet' (Simon Schama).[2] This sounds like a whole lot of fun. In Britain, however, while literary festivals aim at a glamorous and buzzy atmosphere—'the pop concerts of literature' as John Sutherland put it[3]—most resemble an intellectual drinks party or polite middle-class political meeting, with elements of an adult education class or university seminar thrown in. While it's accepted that *music* festivals attract people of every class, age, gender, and (to a certain extent) race and ethnicity, literature festivals have a certain class cachet and thus bias—more garden party than rave. The food and drink from local independent suppliers are wholesome and rather expensive, and there are few raucous bands or stalls of cheap tat. Sponsors tend to be upmarket investment companies, estate agents, bookshops, universities, and charities. Festivals have, however, moved in the commercial direction I saw in New Orleans, and are now a significant part of the UK culture industries. You are served scholarship and debate with a light touch, interspersed with convivial gatherings around music, food, and drink—in earlier days rather meagre but now offering artisanal burgers, organic wines and beers, and vegan cakes. Alex Clark noted a workshop at one festival boasting 'gin tasting while playing a ukulele'[4] and another a £45 'Style' event with bestselling author Marian Keyes, plus an astrologer, romantic advice from dating experts, and Autumn fashion—all to be consumed during a two-course lunch with fizz and wine, with a goodie bag to take home.

In recent years, in this country and elsewhere, literary festivals have proliferated and thrived, with turnovers in the millions. In the UK, Cheltenham was the first (established in 1949), while the Edinburgh International Book Festival followed in 1983, Hay in 1988, and Oxford in 1998. Both Hay and Oxford have international spinoffs. Many others have followed, often on a smaller scale. The website literaryfestivals.co.uk claims there are between 350 and 400, and its publisher notes that the big four sell in excess of 600,000 tickets each (so his guesstimate is the UK has two million attendees annually, and rising).[5] Many small towns or villages have jumped on the bandwagon as a way of increasing tourist footfall, consolidating community culture, and supporting local businesses.

So why is this a growing movement? The British publishing industry is under considerable pressure, faced with many challenges: the takeover by large profit-oriented corporations of smaller publishers; shrinking book purchases and the rise of online and self-published writing; the closure or reduction of public libraries and local and independent bookshops; and the growing economic power of online sales, especially from Amazon. Profit margins are tighter than ever because a fixed sale price for books (the Net Book Agreement) was abolished some years ago, and thus supermarkets and Internet outlets can offer books for any price they choose. Books are in competition with many other consumer items. In a celebrity-obsessed culture, publishers must market aggressively, so the haughty or discreet distance writers used to keep between themselves and readers is no longer acceptable. Festivals—registered charities largely floating on the unpaid labour of enthusiastic board members and volunteers—bring writers and readers into contact to boost sales, raise profiles, and increase readerships. For all publishers, they provide vital showcases for new books and authors, while for small and independent presses (especially based in the regions) they are a welcome opportunity to gain visibility in a crowded market.

Popular author Amanda Craig decried the way festivals have become 'a bloated commercial enterprise in which authors are like farmers before Walmart. We are expected to hand-sell our books to customers instead of sharing what is loved, and to do so without fees or even travel expenses... It's the cold hand of capitalism meddling with what should be what is best in our culture.'[6] Some of my correspondents see festivals as road shows for new books by known faces, 'a circus, the discussions a new sort of performance art with mutual back-slapping' (Gail W), or—in Rosie J's words—'a closed circle of glitterati, mostly predictable names, rarely radical, mostly middle class, prohibitive to others because of the high costs of tickets'. All float on writers' most recent publications, their need for publicity, and thus the contribution of some expenses and PR by publishers. Even though the costs of attending are beyond many people's budgets, ironically readers like to think they're participating in a genteel cultural gathering; many told me they hated to see writers blatantly promoting their latest novel to 'celebrity-chasers'. They want to feel this is a meeting of minds, not a grubby marketplace. Crysse M (herself a writer) suggested: 'I think real-time contact makes us feel more of a community of writers, and makes books feel more like shared language and less like commercial products.'

Given the increasing festival promotion of celebrity chef cookbooks and TV personality ghosted autobiographies, festivals have had to counter accusations of dumbing-down by pointing to their challenging intellectual and political debates and (free or cheap) family events in conjunction with local schools and universities. These are designed to convince writers, sponsors, and Arts Council or local authority funders that they are providing educational events, keeping costs low, and helping to produce the readers of the future. In these days of tight funding, everyone recognizes the benefits of cultural collaboration and the revenue uplift to local economies.

But what about writers themselves? Festivals pay expenses and/or a fee of £150–200, and the most prestigious festivals claim to pay everyone the same (though one suspects Bill Clinton didn't go to Hay for £200). In 2016, novelist Philip Pullman, president of the Society of Authors, resigned as patron of the Oxford Literary Festival in protest at the non-payment of authors, 'expected to work for nothing'.[7] As I write, the average (pitiful) annual earnings of a professional writer in the UK are around £10,500, so £200 will barely swell the coffers. However, festivals give writers vital visibility and affirm their status, enabling them to meet readers and hang out with other writers, get a feel for literary tastes and trends, and take them temporarily out of the isolation of their writing huts or kitchen tables to a jamboree where they're bathed in a little luxury and flattery. If you have a new book out, you're expected to do the rounds of large and small festivals. For young or newly published writers, this can be exciting and may make them feel they've arrived; for more established authors it is either a welcome reminder they're not forgotten or a chunk of time out of a lucrative career. A few years before her death, Doris Lessing was chauffeured to the Bath Literature Festival, and sat gleefully enjoying everyone's awed attention while eating all the biscuits in the writers' room. When she left to take the car home, she whispered to me that she would welcome yet more biscuits in a napkin for the journey. But as novelist Patrick Gale said wearily: 'You arrive in Tresoddit Parva just in time to glimpse an author you've always admired before you're ushered before an audience to talk and sign books before catching a train to St Wallop.'[8] And this festival circus places demands on writers that can undermine their energy, self-confidence, and belief in their own work (especially if audiences and book sales are meagre). One first-time novelist told me she was doing forty festivals in a year and wondered if she'd ever write again. Ali Smith said she hated the 'performance' required of festival speaking and refused to play the part. Gale, himself a consummate performer, says most writers are at the 'shy end of the spectrum—sly watchers of life rather than noisy graspers of it' and he claims many have had to develop 'a performative persona behind which the sly watcher can continue to lurk'. He now advises all writing students 'to act, or at least get some training in handling an audience'.[9] Festivals are a new form of theatre, and—like it or not—writers are having to adapt to their audiences' high expectations.

Women and Literature Festivals

Festival directors are wary of answering questions about their audience demographic. In terms of gender, most will claim they don't keep statistics on gender or race; what they do know is that women's names are on most of the ticket bookings and post-festival questionnaires, so women's engagement with festivals is clearly stronger than men's. I spoke to Nick Barley, director of Edinburgh International Book Festival, and one of his press staff, who both claimed they didn't know the gender breakdown of audiences—though they are careful to try to balance gender within the programme. Another major festival (which wishes to remain anonymous) did some detailed demographic research in 2015. It, too, attempts to programme male/female speakers equally, but found that its main stage audience was 70 per cent female. The day and time of an event, and whether in school holidays, affect the nature of ticket-holders, though everyone seems to agree that men are drawn more to political discussion, historical talks, and panels on cycling, sport, and naval exploits, while women are drawn to novelists and memoirists of both genders. However, Sarah LeFanu, formerly director of Bath Literature Festival, claims that women are more eclectic in their choices, drawn to non-fiction as well as fiction, writers and subjects of political and historical interest, and male novelists such as William Boyd, David Mitchell, and Martin Amis. Men, on the other hand, rarely buy tickets for feminist discussions or feminist literary fiction writers such as Margaret Drabble, Rachel Cusk, or Michèle Roberts.[10] What surprised me, in my discussions with festival directors and PR people, was how strongly they resisted questions about gender—almost as if embarrassed or a little exasperated that women are their key audience.

Most interviewees, however, concede that festival audiences are predominantly women, often in book clubs, groups of female friends, mothers and daughters, and so on, sometimes dragging along a reluctant or indifferent husband. Women go to enjoy 'me-time', meet speakers, share experiences, be inspired, learn more about the subject matter, be with people of like minds, 'in an atmosphere of

ideas' as Pauline H puts it, and enjoy the surroundings that are
congenial for women alone or in groups. Jess H always goes alone,
giving her 'a nice opportunity for some time to myself'. She describes
the experience as 'a safe space and a nice night out . . . I get to be
myself and be surrounded by books.' Sally F compares festivals with
libraries, since they give her the chance 'to immerse myself in a literary
space and expand my imagination'. Many unpublished or wannabe
writers find their way to festivals to see how the literary world works,
make contact with their role models, and network with other writers
and readers. (At one crime festival, every woman I spoke to had a
novel in progress . . .)

However, feminist Bidisha takes a more jaundiced view of women
at festivals. She published two novels in the 1990s and became an
instant literary celebrity, but was suspicious of the adulation offered by
readers and eventually shunned their attentions, giving up fiction
writing for a long time, except for commissioned pieces:

> I think women read a lot of fiction because life is so crappy. When I was
> a novelist, it freaked me out. I looked in the audience [at literature
> festivals] and saw all these women sitting there submissively like sacks of
> cement, never asking questions. Their body language was so telling.
> When the author spoke they would look at him or her with such faith,
> belief, worship and trust. It's groupie behaviour: worshipping great
> men. I thought, oh my god I know who you are, you are that mouse
> who lives in books, the kid who wasn't cool so you stayed at home
> reading books. Do you not know you are the pawn in the entertainment
> wing of the patriarchal military industrial complex? The sheer amount
> of themselves that they put into it is some kind of 'trauma response'.
> Men don't read that much fiction as they are fully invested in the world
> and are worshipped. Women read books about heroines because
> they're not heroines and when we go out for adventures in the real
> world we're subject to harassment and male violence. This is why
> I became a journalist; I wanted to go out into the world. "I stayed at
> home and read all Saturday and laughed and cried." It depresses me
> the amount of faith they put into fictional narratives. It says something
> about the actual reality of women's lives.[11]

I was shocked to hear Bidisha speaking so negatively about female
festivalgoers and fiction readers, and wondered why she felt compelled
to see them as a homogeneous group of passive stargazers with no

autonomy. If a strong feminist can dismiss such women, I dread to think what male writers and presenters feel when they too look out at the sea of wrinkled women in the audience. As I've said, there is a certain amount of celebrity-chasing at festivals, and I've already described the ways women use fiction reading as an escape from difficult or intolerable lives and situations. But it's dangerous to condemn them as uncritical, home-centred pawns in a global society that reduces them merely to 'trauma response'. Her critique ignores the proactive and engaged way women respond to their reading (and writers at festivals) and its assumptions are dangerously ageist and sexist—this from my own experience of teaching mature women students and being closely involved in festivals (and being a woman of mature years myself!). I'm aware that women of thinning hair and fading looks can all too easily be dismissed as passive and dull. Yet these women are the mainstay of literary events and institutions such as churches, theatres, festivals, reading groups, and indeed the publishing industry. When I suggested to Bidisha that such intelligent, attentive reading is vital for the future of literary culture, she waved this aside as the kinds of quality women are taught to have, and argued instead for edginess, 'less over-investment . . . schoolgirl attention to the text'.

I quoted these words to Helen Dunmore, who hailed those 'mousy types': 'You should be glad that there are these wonderfully open-minded enthusiastic readers who are so bold. Particularly older women—they are so fearless, they'll read anything, they're not fazed, self-conscious or embarrassed, and they're beyond trying to seem cool or intellectual.'[12] Rosie J offered another generous perspective when she said that women 'have low self-esteem so look to others for vicarious success, perhaps as a substitute for them being creative themselves'.

Meeting the Writer—Star-Gazing?

I've already pointed out that seeing writers—touching the hem, as it were—is a large attraction for festival punters. If you've read a book it's interesting to see what the author looks like and how they speak—'putting flesh on the bones', as Deanna Walsh puts it. Sarah LeFanu suggests: 'When you read a book by someone you're in an intimate relationship with them, and if the book has moved or excited you, you

Figure 8.1 Jackie Kay signing books at Cheltenham Literature Festival, October 2017
Photo by Helen Taylor

do feel something emotional, beyond intellectual stimulation. "Who is that person who made me cry or laugh, what do they sound and look like?"' There's a scattering of stardust over writers appearing on stage, if only in a small marquee. Many women buy books, or take copies bought elsewhere more cheaply, to be signed for themselves, relatives, and friends (mothers and sisters often cited) or to mark a special occasion. The signing element of the event—even a brief chat with the author—means that for one precious moment you are a special reader sharing the limelight (Figure 8.1).

Many respondents expressed the view that women are more interested in engaging with people than men, and being more people-centred enjoy coming together with others to hear different perspectives. 'Women are hungrier', said Heather W, for 'the joy, the buzz, the learning, the sharing'. Short events (usually an hour or so) allow for convivial coffee and drinks breaks. They share a strong desire to *learn*. As I've argued about book clubs, since the earliest days of adult and further education, women who missed out on the highest levels of education have shared a thirst for knowledge and self-improvement, which festivals can provide. Sue T enjoys having her horizons broadened, 'both in terms of expanding my reading matter and my exposure to points of view at variance with my own—it's so easy to get comfortable in one's own "zone" and simply dismiss different points of view. A bit of challenging keeps the grey matter working.' Alexandra D admits: 'I have a sneaking feeling I like the idea of seeming rather intellectual by attending a literature festival.'

Zoe Steadman-Milne, formerly Literature Producer, Bath Festivals, said:

> I think a lot of it is to do with stimulation...women may feel understimulated intellectually. The day-to-day monotony of caring, looking-after, housework...so maybe it's the opportunity to be yourself and think as yourself not as a mother or a wife. Women may not see themselves as intellectual creatures, and feel they need permission to think, allocated time not to think about anything else but the subject in hand. An opportunity to do something with friends that doesn't involve going out. When you get to a certain age, in a relationship, there are few places you can go to have a nice time—you don't want to go in a pub or bar, but you want to do something in a short period of time and then discuss it afterwards. Done and dusted in two or three hours, reasonably priced, daytime not a late night. This works quite well in the framework of a lot of women's lives.[13]

Pauline H bears this out when she writes: 'The literature festivals take one away from normal life, the household chores, bring back a little of intellectual life. Pure pleasure walking through the streets of Cheltenham, knowing there is another talk to come, and a good meal in the evening cooked by someone else.'

For Hannah S, 'to be at a book-centred event is heaven' and she enjoys the rhythm of festival days—coffee before event, drink afterwards. Hazel H says going to a festival is 'affirming of reading as an activity' and she suggests that when you read a book, it's hard to imagine it being written:

> We buy the completed book and it is as though that is the only way it could have been completed and almost as though it arose fully formed. When an author talks about their thoughts and considerations when writing a book, it makes me think about why they made the choices they did, and appreciate their writing more.

When writers describe the way a book came about in their imagination (and give an insight into their own lives) readers find this illuminates a novel already read or gives them a way into the book they will later buy—sometimes with humorous results. When Colm Tóibín and Kamila Shamsie discussed at the 2018 Hay Festival their new novels based on classical themes, Shamsie told the audience that—when planning *Home Fire*—she took the bold decision to make her Home Secretary character a Muslim, thinking a woman prime minister was one imaginative leap too far. (In 2018, when the book came out, Sajid Javid and Theresa May were in those posts.)

As Steadman-Milne said, women of a certain age don't often go to pubs alone, or with friends. While more young women do so, middle-aged and older women (as well as some singletons) can feel isolated from casual communal group activities outside the family. Festivals are thus an arena in which female readers feel a part of live, contemporary cultural and social history, participants in national and international conversations. Besides, as family social secretaries, women invite friends and arrange the bookings. Often they go with an old friend or two, a partner, or their book club ('When Mary Beard is on, all our Latin group goes,' said Hazel H). A festival steward told me that keen women festivalgoers 'park' their husbands who then come up sadly and say they're 'looking for their wives'. Often groups of friends meet up annually at various festivals. I met three women who had many years ago bonded through their husbands who were water-polo players; now they are all widows and make a regular excursion to a festival mid-way between their homes. You don't see many men on their own or with male groups—though Hannah S suggested that the timing of festivals was more conducive to many women's flexible and part-time work. Alexandra D was adamant: pointing to the predominance of women in choirs, operatic societies, and painting courses, she said: 'Women are more "doers" than men when it comes to the arts.' She also pointed out that—unlike actors or singers—writers are relatively invisible, so there's always intense curiosity about their appearance, though Margaret Atwood wryly described the 'disappointments' of meeting writers who are 'always shorter and older and more ordinary than you expected'.[14]

Sarah LeFanu said that while women attended in groups, she couldn't imagine groups of men coming without their female partners:

'It goes very deep in the way women and men socialize in our culture. Women are more outgoing. Men will go out to sporty things but on the whole are happy to stay at home with computers or TV.' Both she and Steadman-Milne note that men tend to ask the first questions following talks (something Germaine Greer always points out, insisting a woman ask instead), and—when asking for a signature in the bookshop afterwards—will offer some kind of comment or question as intellectual challenge to the writer, while women will gush, 'you're great. I really love your writing and enjoyed this book.'

Why More Women than Men?

I was interested in the reasons my correspondents gave for women being the main festival attendees. Sue T suggested: 'Early social conditioning, perceptions of literary culture as a female preserve, with literature perceived as an individualistic pursuit that is more suited to female participation, whereas men (may) prefer group experiences, e.g. sport. But what do I know?!' Marion W claimed women retain their interests in life well into retirement while men fall by the wayside unless they're 'in charge' and recognized for being so. Sandra J suggested that men may feel reading books is an activity for recreational purposes only and thus they need to do something more active with their time, 'although the male obsession with angling rather defeats that argument!'

A perspective on this came from Lynn Goold, co-Chair of Cornwall's Fowey Festival. Beginning in 1997 as the Daphne du Maurier Festival, it remains a successful fixture in the county's calendar, attracting dozens of du Maurier aficionados. Although there's no official count, Goold believes two-thirds of attendees are women, and programming is organized accordingly. She suggests many women prefer to come alone or with other women. The reasons?

> It's simple. It's a safe venue; no one looks down on you; you don't stand out as a single woman and you meet nice people; there's a real camaraderie. The volunteers who steward and otherwise support the Festival tend to be mature and/or retired women so women audiences feel comfortable and at home.

As my correspondent Crysse M said, attending a festival is seen as 'an accepted bourgeois pastime for women'.

I've quoted from and discussed festivalgoers as mainly middle-aged and older women. Although this doesn't apply to all—such as the youthful Women of the World Festival on London's South Bank and some other large city festivals—it is true enough to alarm the Arts Council, some sponsors, and festival boards. There is a constant refrain: 'We need new audiences' for the 'replenisher effect'—which usually means diverse younger people of both genders, and non-reading boys. But, as I argued about book clubs in relation to the publishing industry, it's important not to forget the loyal audience which has made festivals the success they are. The 'older woman audience' can be seen negatively, as Bidisha does, yet it's surely that loyal audience which will get you the new punters because (in the most effective form of publicity—word of mouth) they enthuse to their children, neighbours, and friends. Steadman-Milne claims:[15]

> People make assumptions about their taste that are untrue—my mum is thirty years older than me and we share the same tastes. A marketing-led problem in that it's always the new that is deemed valuable, which isn't true because the things most festivals programme use history and existing ideas to reflect on now—so the audiences are those who know about these things and want to reflect, whereas a new audience hasn't got there yet.

In other words—as with BBC Radio 4, opera, and sensible shoes—people grow into festivals as they mature.

Empathy

Nevertheless, the whole festival business could do with a shakeup, and it's probably time to consider a post-festival cultural strategy. For the time being, however, most festival boards are desperate to broaden their demographic base, and offer free education programmes and multicultural panels and events in an attempt to attract mixed audiences. The middle-class composition of those audiences is a concern of festival organizers (I myself struggled with this in the two Liverpool Literary Festivals I directed). On a positive note, following children's writer Natasha Carthew's call for a working-class writers' festival to showcase neglected writers and attract working class audiences, publishing professionals and writers responded by proposing such a festival in 2020.

Figure 8.2 The bookstall at Bradford Literature Festival, July 2017
Photo by Helen Taylor

In terms of race, Danuta Kean's report, *Writing the Future*, focused on the Big Three festivals – Edinburgh, Hay, and Cheltenham—and found that among visitors only 4 per cent were BAME writers and other professionals (such as footballers), and a mere 2 per cent if non-authors were discounted. Then, in 2014, two British Pakistani women set up the Bradford Literature Festival (Figure 8.2) with multi-cultural programming that broke the mould by attracting 48 per cent of its audience from black and ethnic minorities, and 8,000 school children. Their mission is more overtly political than that of others:

> At a time when imagination and empathy are crucial tools for tackling the big issues of our time, there are many who would prefer a narrower vision of life, in which increasingly smaller boxes divide and define us. The festival seeks to break down these artificial barriers, by creating a space where ideas and stories can lead to mutual understanding, reminding us that it is our shared humanity that is the common denominator.[16]

In this thinly coded message, Bradford Festival is acting as cheerleader for liberal values of tolerance and mutual respect, especially in terms of race and religion. The notion of 'empathy' as a social and political healing force is one of the themes of this book, and it seems to be gathering steam. Festivals, like reading itself, are now seen as sites where this quality can be demonstrated to enlarge human understanding. When asked why people go to festivals, director of Hay, Peter Florence, uttered the word, 'Empathy'. He went on to say that writers deal in all human experience and the big questions—life, love, death, and so on. At his own festival—which quotes UK Children's Laureate Chris Riddell, 'a good book is an Empathy Engine'—Empathy Lab held a session for families.[17] While empathy is not confined to women, I believe this *vocabulary* of emotional response and therapeutic relationship to literature appeals strongly to them, and suggests a way of making cultural events exciting and relevant for new audiences.

Literary Tourism and Pilgrimage

Festivals are a magnet to some women, but there are millions who never set foot in one but who seek special experiences relating to writers and their work. In all my discussions with women about the pleasures of fiction reading, words that recur most often are 'escape' and 'a sense of place'. They are of course linked, since reading allows us imaginatively to leave our familiar spaces and go elsewhere, inspired by descriptions of different and sometimes exotic places. Immersing yourself in a story set within a Greek island, a Scottish castle, or a Louisiana bayou, or indeed in a place you know well and want reflected afresh through a creative eye, is one of the joys of reading fiction. And increasingly we want to visit those places, conjured by writers, to imagine ourselves within their narratives. Hence the rise of literary tourism.

Since 1863, when a North Devon village was named after Charles Kingsley's bestselling novel *Westward Ho!* (one of only two places in the world with an exclamation mark[18]), readers have taken journeys across the UK to immerse themselves in the atmosphere of writerly places. Wealthy travellers in the eighteenth and nineteenth centuries would embark on the Grand Tour to see Dante's tomb in Florence, or pay homage to homes of classical or Renaissance writers. From

Victorian times this pastime has become more commercially organized and undertaken by a broader social spectrum. In the UK alone, the tourism industry is worth £127 billion to the economy (projected to be worth 10 per cent of the UK's GDP by 2025, with 3.8 million jobs). In terms of *literary* tourism, VisitEngland claims that half of British holidaymakers intend to visit a literary attraction on holiday in England, and that in 2017 one in four visited such a site and had read literature relating to it. VisitEngland director, Patricia Yates, paid tribute to fiction's role in boosting her business:

> Books fire up our imagination, they conjure up people and places and they inspire us to explore locations and landscapes associated with our favourite stories. Our literary heroes have created a wealth of must-see literary attractions across the country, motivating generations of readers to explore and discover more of regional England.[19]

Most 'must-see' is London, its book and film associations with Charles Dickens, Sir Arthur Conan Doyle, and John Keats, but a close second is Yorkshire—notably for *Dracula*'s Whitby Abbey and *Wuthering Heights*' Haworth Parsonage and the Moors. VisitEngland named 2017 'The Year of Literary Heroes', noting milestone events including the 200th anniversary of Jane Austen's death, the twentieth anniversary of *Harry Potter*, and seventy-five years of Enid Blyton's *The Famous Five*. Birthplaces or houses of best-loved British authors such as Robert Burns, Shakespeare, and Virginia Woolf all attract huge crowds, while the National Trust makes capital out of its writers' homes (Coleridge's cottage in Nether Stowey, Thomas Hardy's birthplace near Dorchester) and film settings for *Alice in Wonderland* (Antony House), *Harry Potter and the Deathly Hallows 1 and 2* (Hardwick Hall), and *Pride and Prejudice* (Lyme Park, where Colin Firth emerged from the lake (Figure 8.3)).

The much-hailed sexual frisson caused by Firth's damp déshabillé has led many a female reader/TV viewer to Lyme, and the erotic possibilities suggested by such a visit were echoed in a critic's wry comment that tourists to the Brontës' Haworth were suffused 'less with the excitement of treading in the Brontës' footsteps, than with the thought that Heathcliff might appear'.[20] Wandering along the North Cornwall coast, star-struck viewers of the most recent BBC TV version of Winston Graham's *Poldark* have fantasized about catching

Figure 8.3 Lyme Park House, Disley, Cheshire (Mr Darcy's Pemberley in BBC *Pride and Prejudice*, 1995)
Andrew Turner / Alamy Stock Photo

a cliff-top glimpse of a bare-chested haymaking Ross Poldark (played by Aidan Turner). Indeed, in August 2018 Cornwall's tourism CEO warned tourists to stay away from two beaches on which filming had taken place, because of huge traffic jams and gridlock.

As I pointed out earlier when discussing *Fifty Shades of Grey*, if you're prepared to travel far, you can visit Seattle's Escala Apartments in which Christian Grey had his Red Room of Pain. The tourist industry hasn't been slow to appeal to female lust.

For most tourists, like literary festivalgoers, seeking out particular locations satisfies a desire for authentic experiences that can enrich our reading histories. I've already argued that readers want ever more from their writers so—along with the paraphernalia of a contemporary digital world—there's a yearning for real-life associations with them to make reading live away from the page. We want to feel 'in the presence' of a writer: the thrill of writing with a quill and ink at Wordsworth's Dove Cottage; seeing Jane Austen's creaking door at Chawton; spotting egrets and oystercatchers on Taf Estuary from the Dylan Thomas Boathouse. Mark Lawson claimed that literary fans have always venerated manuscripts and mansions, but in recent years 'the greatest excitement seems to be spreading from the pads they wrote on to the pads they lived in'.[21] Visitors feel they imbibe information about writers from the places that formed and inspired them, and such 'pads' are now designed to offer learning and hands-on experiences.

A Sense of Place

Readers' pleasure in literary associations with places emerged frequently from my correspondence and interviews. Of course, writers create those places in their imaginations (often from many sources) and transform them through language, so it's dangerous to be too literal in seeking them out. However, because readers enjoy fiction's specific atmospheres, landscapes, weathers, houses, and rooms, many want to tread in and absorb the ambience of places from which they believe writers drew that material. Local councils have jumped on this bandwagon. Whole areas and cities have been branded at different times by their celebrated writers—Shakespeare/Hardy/Catherine Cookson Country, Walter Scott's Edinburgh. Across the UK, tourist boards have found the literature enthusiast a splendid target for its hotels, cafés, National Trust properties, and bus and train excursions. Harry Potter fans make a beeline for Platform 9¾ at King's Cross station. Every summer, Cornwall information centres are inundated with German visitors looking for the fictional settings of their national favourite, Rosamunde Pilcher. Many a motorist leaves the West Country's A30 on a bleak stretch of Bodmin Moor for comfort breaks at Daphne du Maurier's Jamaica Inn (where a plaque announces that the fictional character Joss Merlyn 'died here') and tries unsuccessfully to glimpse the inaccessible Menabilly near Fowey (one setting for *Rebecca*'s Manderley). Guided walks may be followed: the Beatrix Beyond Hill Top Tour (Beatrix Potter's Lake District), Walking Tess's Journey (Dorset) and the Tarka Trail (Devon). At Agatha Christie's Devon summer house, Greenway, visitors can walk into the boathouse to enjoy the frisson of knowing that is where the fictional murder in *Dead Man's Folly* took place (Figure 8.4). And in strategically positioned cafés and gift shops, visitors enjoy themed afternoon teas and purchase illustrated pens, fridge magnets, tea

Figure 8.4 Greenway Boat House at Agatha Christie's South Devon home
John R Elliott / Alamy Stock Photo

towels, and postcards to take home as cultural memorabilia. I'm aware that mixed couples and families enjoy all these together, and no one keeps statistics on gender, but from all my conversations I'm fairly sure these pleasures—especially when focused on women writers—are suggested, organized, and relished by the female family tour guide.

In a secular age, some writers have become the high priests and moral and spiritual leaders of our age, sanctified in popular imagination. The tourist industry differentiates between 'tourists' and 'pilgrims', seeing the former as casual trippers who just want a good day out, while the latter are obsessives on a serious quest for literary shrines. Many international groups fall into the 'pilgrim' category, paying devout respect at sites around the country associated with our greatest writers from Wordsworth to Woolf. But they are not alone, for many British pilgrims travel long distances to capture authentic experiences associated with a revered author or (as with figures such as J. R. R. Tolkein or Roald Dahl) to evoke emotional memories of childhood reading that enhance home and family bonds. When in reality and metaphorically walking in writers' footsteps, pilgrims hope to see landscapes or particular spots as intensely and poetically as they did. Fictional settings intensify a reading memory, and readers can thus hope for a deeper emotional response to those words on the page.

Of course, pilgrims can feel let down. They may expect an epiphanic moment when entering a literary space, and be disappointed that it looks and feels like many another. A writer's home may be smaller and less picturesque than they hoped, or a pilgrim may feel there has been a commercial venture too far. Many a visitor to Bath's Jane Austen Centre has noted the complete absence of Austen artefacts in a house she never entered (described only as 'very similar to No. 25, where [she] lived for a few months following her father's death') and might be sceptical about the promise of 'taking tea with Mr Darcy'. Alan Bennett took his mother to Haworth Parsonage and her (very Bennettian) comment on the 'slovenly' décor was: '"Too busy writing their books to keep the place up to scratch"'.[22]

Throughout this book, I've argued that women draw on fiction reading to create and complete our life narratives, and tell stories about different phases of life in relation to that reading. Journeys to memorial plaques and places connected with writers and novels we love, treks to birthplaces and homes that enable us to imagine ourselves sitting in a chair where they composed, or in a kitchen where they cooked and ate, are increasingly attractive to bookish holiday-makers and day-trippers. Such journeys encourage us to travel through or alongside the lives and creations of particular writers (sharing their space at a festival or the domestic space they occupied while creating). Forays to Crickhowell, Dundee, or Ilkley Festivals, and trips to the Sherlock Holmes Museum or Chesil Beach, all facilitate imaginative leaps and creative narratives in ordinary lives, as well as memories to forge bonds between family members and friends. These journeys also give women the sense we are participating in and celebrating the nation's literary heritage (often accompanied by a damned fine cream tea).

Fiction in Lives, Lives in Fiction

I asked four women to describe one work of fiction that they had incorporated into their lives.

Jodi Picoult, *My Sister's Keeper* (by Val Jenkins)
A lot of my choices of books come from being introduced to 'new' authors through our local book club. Probably the one that had the most consequence was *My Sister's Keeper* by Jodi Picoult. First and foremost it rang many bells with me because, as a teenager with a seriously ill sister, I was put in a very similar situation with the same emotional dilemma. After this I chased up all of her books and was very impressed by the way she tackled various fictional, but very believable, conflicts. She does this without defining any right or wrong answers but showing the pros and cons in equal measure. This not only gets the reader very involved but also makes them realize that things are very rarely (if ever) black or white.

Zadie Smith, *On Beauty* (by Zoe Hope Bulaitis)
On Beauty is significant to me because it proves how novels can communicate values beyond the reach of literary criticism. *On Beauty* reminded me that the value of English literature is found in the practice of reading as well as the art of critique. *On Beauty* is a dense web of literary allusions: an homage to E. M. Forster's *Howards End*, part cliché campus novel, and the title is a reference to Elaine Scarry's academic treatise 'On Beauty and Being Just'. The central male protagonists are both academics (art historians) and most other characters also work or study within higher education. *On Beauty* was pivotal in my decision to teach and research. I first read it during the summer holidays—for fun—on the brink of starting a PhD which would explore the changing funding climate surrounding the

humanities in the UK. From the outset the project was bleak: funding cuts to arts and humanities courses, the marketization of higher education, the dominance of economic value as *sine qua non* for all value. *On Beauty* was a blast of hope when I needed it the most. The characters struggle but, throughout, the novel maintains the value of the pursuit of a liberal (non-economically oriented) education. Zora Belsey is a likely nominee for the most naïve character in the novel, but she is also a vision for change. She supports her friends and colleagues and does not compromise her belief that education is important. *On Beauty* does not just tell you why reading and studying literature is amazing, it shows you. Smith's realistic and compassionate portrait of the struggles of race, class, gender, and individual pride convinced me that although no one person—or indeed novel—is perfect, it is the process of trying regardless that counts.

Gail Honeyman, *Eleanor Oliphant is Completely Fine* (by Jane Manley Jackson)
I found *Eleanor Oliphant is Completely Fine* very moving, sad, and also incredibly uplifting.
It made me realize that I don't always appreciate the richness of my life with friends, family, neighbours, and colleagues around to talk to, but it also made me feel strongly for the main character, Eleanor, whom the reader really wants to have a happier and more interesting, fulfilling life. Reading the book coincided with me getting interested in Mindfulness which involves noticing and accepting aspects of our life and how we feel about them. The book also made me remember small kindnesses can go a long way and perhaps in our hectic day to day lives we don't always give those things the weight they deserve.

Stella Duffy, *London Lies Beneath* (by Catherine Filmer)
I first heard about this book when Stella Duffy was interviewed on the BBC. Her novel is a fictional retelling of a real-life tragedy, loosely based on the lives of some of my ancestors. It is set in a poor and diverse East End community around 1912, when a scout troop went on a sailing trip on the Thames. After a violent storm capsized the boat at Leysdown, Isle of Sheppey, eight of the twenty-four scouts onboard drowned. (David Beckham's great-great-uncle was among them). This novel portrays the day-to-day struggle of different

families' lives and the strength of the community through adversity. I was particularly interested in it because it tells the story of my great-grandfather's family. He was the oldest of ten children, and two of his brothers, aged 12 and 14, died. His parents' marriage ended not long after the accident and I think they never recovered from the trauma and the blame. As Stella Duffy incorporated real events into a novel, and developed the characters around them, I gained a different perspective on the tragedy, in comparison with the version of it that I grew up with. I feel that I now understand more about what that area was like at the time and the strength of people's bonds. The book really brought to life the impact that the tragedy had on such a close community and the cohesion this created. In turn, this helped me to better understand and empathize with some aspects of my family background.

PART IV

The Stories of our Lives

9

Conclusion

I began to write this book to answer questions I'd often put to myself. How important is fiction to me, and how have I incorporated it into my life story and journey? What do I have in common with other women readers I meet at festivals, in libraries, in the gym? Which books and writers have changed my life? I wanted to explore the reasons why women are the main readers of fiction, and to find out why we love to share books and thoughts about our reading. I wondered if there was a special bond between women writers and readers, and whether other women shared my tendency to see life in literary terms. The more I wrote, the more fascinating and complex these questions seemed.

I have been moved by the different ways the simple practice of reading resonates in daily and larger life narratives. Reading lives cross over with and complement our real lives, each giving substance and depth to the other. Women have described to me their lifelong passion for novels and short stories, their gratitude to those who taught them to read, and nostalgia for earliest childhood books. They've named writers and books that have comforted, challenged, and transformed them. Correspondents expressed guilt and anxiety about reading, hence the equation with self-indulgent eating, especially of sweet foods (or 'print tooth'), as they often felt this solitary pleasure took them away from their primary responsibility to care for others rather than themselves. Reading shared with mothers, daughters, friends, and in education classes, libraries, book clubs, festivals, and cultural days out, all strengthen confidence and bonds between women. Guy Pringle's description of reading groups as 'the female equivalent of freemasonry' seems apt for female readership in general. I believe women have long understood what scientists and experts are now claiming: reading fiction can improve empathy, brain function, and relationships with others; reduce depression symptoms and dementia risks; and increase well-being throughout life.[1]

It's a cliché of modern life that everyone has musical choices as 'the sound track to our lives', devising individual playlists that express who we are and what our place is in the world. Percussionist Dame Evelyn Glennie has said that people have a 'soundscape' of their listening lives, and I want to suggest many of us have a literary soundscape of books to which we return because of special associations and memories. We perhaps imagine we've had a unique reading life, one in which choices of special novels or writers were ours alone. But—as with music—there is a complex and gregarious network that helps us make those choices.

Like everything else in a consumer capitalist economy, reading is strongly influenced by education and the market. We don't choose in a bubble, and when people respond to opinion polls asking for a favourite book, many seize on the names of 'classics' or texts studied at school or college, however loathed at the time (*Emma*, *The Great Gatsby*, *To Kill a Mockingbird*, and so on). Furthermore, those books we and generations of our sisters felt we found all by ourselves (*Cold Comfort Farm*, *Things Fall Apart*, *The Essex Serpent*) turn out to have found their way onto women's shelves not only through personal recommendation, but also via bookshop, library and online placements and recommendations, marketing campaigns around prizewinning novels, enthusiastic broadsheet reviews, and media adaptations of various kinds. But perhaps most of all, the power of word-of-mouth influences us largely through women in our family and friendship and reading groups. It's not surprising that, after losing the 2016 US presidential election, Hillary Clinton spent her time reading Elena Ferrante's Neapolitan novels; I'm sure her women friends and supporters recommended those powerful studies of female friendship, betrayal, and loss for this distraught reader.

And these choices are to a certain extent generation-specific. I realize that some of the writers who mattered to me hardly feature in later generations' soundscapes—partly because the zeitgeist of the times in which they featured is long gone. In the light of fast-changing sexual, racial, and political mores and concerns, novels that were a crucial part of my personal development now seem far less powerful: (for instance) Richard Wright's *Native Son*, Marilyn French's *The*

Women's Room, and John Kennedy Toole's *A Confederacy of Dunces.* My correspondent Sara D says she can hardly believe she read the entire *Illuminatus* trilogy (by Robert Shea and Robert Anton Wilson, 1975): 'I remember I was at university, stoned a good deal of the time, and very influenced by a lot of hippie guff. That was definitely my weekend hippie phase.' While we can treasure reading memories of books that still resonate for us, some titles can bring back times we don't wish to recall, and from which we now feel estranged. But many women also share my distress at the way books fade from memory so that you can no longer recall characters' names, plotlines, or what made them speak to you. However, writer Kirsty Gunn offers some comfort here; she says people are too hung up on remembering stories, characters, and so on, since everything you read in some way affects and changes you.[2] That is a salutary and comforting thought.

Reading through my hundreds of questionnaires, and talking to friends and acquaintances about their reading, I'm struck by how many of us go to fiction not just for entertainment and escape but also to help us get through life's daily trials and major challenges. One woman said we 'use it like a fix'. So many recall books read at particular times of their lives, in joyous periods, on or by sickbeds, and at crisis points. (I'll always remember the Michèle Roberts novel I was finishing when a nurse rang me to say my mother had died.) There's a great pride in owning books and claiming a personal collection. Trudi L told me she used to arrange books on a bookcase and write numbers in them like a library, and many others keep their books long after they've given away favourite clothes to the charity shop. A large number of women have kept lifetime reading diaries, listing all books they've read (some with plot summaries and comments)—the proud tally of a bibliophilic life.

Earlier I quoted Hilary Mantel saying that what she had taken from reading *Jane Eyre* was a conviction that 'you have to go on a journey, you have to leave home and you have to make your way in the world'. That familiar notion of 'life's journey' is one I suspected women might see in terms of literary chapters, and so it proved. Shakespeare's Seven Ages of Man become the various ages of woman: childhood, adolescent love and sexuality, marriage or partnership, children, work, retirement, care, and then death of parents or partners, with appropriate reading choices along the way. Emylia H traced her own 'chapter' development:

> ...teenage yearning, with Emily Dickinson and J. D. Salinger; by evening disappearing into the utterly absorbing pages of [Donna Tartt's] *A Secret History* when working in a job that pulled me from pillar to post in London...my Las Vegas wedding and honeymoon reads of Alice Munro short stories and just before that, Anne Tyler's wonderful *The Amateur Marriage*...

Others echoed this shift of literary choice: one from loving Emile Zola 'as a morose teenager', then Angela Carter and Isabel Allende 'as a 30-year-old working full time in a job I didn't like', and finally reading crime fiction 'now I am older and recognize how finite life is'.

Jane L described reading as the thing that made her chemotherapy tolerable:

> When recovering in hospital from major surgery, the first thing I did as soon as I could sit up was to read. I cannot imagine how I would have survived this very challenging period in my life without reading. Perhaps because of illness and survival (following cancer) I do think of the present period as a sort of bonus chapter—hopefully it will become more of a sequel.

And in terms of hoping for a good sequel, Helen W wittily responded: 'Yeah, I've just passed through chapter 13, "Divorce Rehab", and onto chapter 14, "Autumn Fruits". I'm hoping for a chapter 15, "Enter the handsome stranger".'

The question of life chapters—usually seen in terms of women's reproductive life (marriage, children, post-children)—can unsettle women who don't share that. As a woman without children who married late in life, I valued Tania Herschmann's enthusiastic account of a novel that resisted that classic narrative:

> I read *The Woman Upstairs* by Clare Messud in 2013 and I then did something I have never done before, which was to read it again from the beginning almost immediately, I was so affected by it. Partly this was because the protagonist was the same age as I was then, 42, and a woman living on her own, as I was and am, but which was a fairly new state for me at the time, something I was just getting used to. I felt her anger, which is right there from the first page, and her frustration, her desire, as I saw it, for different kinds of love, to not have to fit into

cultural expectations involving couples and families. This book seemed to illustrate for me an intimacy that I hadn't found in other books, that which can occur between friends and which can be just as passionate and romantic as the so-called 'romantic' love that is the stuff of so much of what we are offered nowadays.[3]

And Marion G movingly summarized her own reading history that goes against the grain of many other women's lives:

> I am intermittently troubled that my life has no conventional narrative, especially no marriage or children. Reader, I did not marry him and there was no Galsworthian family saga either . . . But there are many other narratives and ultimately I am not a book character (or I am an author/character in my own experimental novel, perhaps). But I have to accept that I will not teach any child to read and my books will end up in charity shops when I die . . . How very *Middlemarch* (which ends with the thought that women like Dorothea make a real difference but rest in unvisited graves).

Nevertheless, a few readers suggested the idea of lives divided into chapters may be too neat. Sandra J: 'Our lives are not as flexible as a work of fiction—we can't go back and undo what has been done. We live in linear time, unlike fiction which can transcend time and move through different dimensions.' Margaretta J rejected the idea of chapters in favour of 'ages', arguing that 'these ages are soothed, supported, excited and pulled onwards by reading'. A few women describe a sadness from which they have 'escaped' into books, living vicariously rather than engaging with life, a way of 'blotting out' the world and keeping separate from people or situations. For others, that is the whole point of reading!

The idea of life chapters may seem a little programmatic or po-faced, whereas for many women readers the whole pleasure of reading lies in playing with imaginary lives and friends through fictional models. Susan C S posited: 'We all create our own scripts and live our lives according to them', while Judith S joked that her life was more like soap opera. Sally F said she thinks of her life as separate books, or poetry collections, and Shelley H that she feels life is 'arbitrary and badly-plotted'—something with which I think we'd all agree. Twenty-seven-year-old Louise A told me she strives to have 'a storybook life. Something with a bit of drama, passion, travel, romance, and of course a happy ending!' A reader aged 72 told me she read Margaret Drabble when she was young, 'to know how to behave in the world', but no longer needed fiction for that. For another older woman, poet Rosie B, reading is a kind of kinship: 'I see every book I've read as *part of who I am*. I feel the writers I've read are part of my world, almost part of my ancestry—more, even, perhaps, than my real ancestors. They are *kin*, in some inexplicably essential way.' This deeply felt expression of reader attachment is a more eloquent way of expressing that much-repeated view of books as 'friends'— reliable, responsive to your needs, and vital companions for life.

We live in an age of stories, in which narratives are more contested than ever—post-truth, fake news, alternative facts, and so on. Adam Phillips' suggestion (quoted in Chapter 1) that more important to us than our 'real' lives are the lives we live in fantasy, the 'wished-for lives', suggests why fiction has so much power over us. Gwenda M told me: 'I often make mental links between the fiction I'm reading and incidents that happen in real life...I find myself "fictionalizing" events and writing dialogue in my head as things happen', and Claire M told me that reactions of characters in some books have shaped her responses to life. She gives the example of Fanny Hackabout Jones (in Erica Jong's *Fanny*, 1980) of whom she says: 'If she can be that tough, then so can I, darn it.' But one woman—in what seems like an admission of low self-esteem or confidence—said that in her reading she could see herself as a minor, but never the main character.

Some readers suggest that one's own life can be lived or imagined in literary terms. Novelist Susan Hill jotted down in her notebook this anonymous quotation: 'Life is a Handful of Short Stories Pretending to be a Novel.'[4] Lisa S feels her whole perspective is coloured by her reading—for example everything becoming dream-like after she's reread *Mrs Dalloway*. My niece Megan describes spending an entire summer in Gormenghast Castle 'though I was actually on the Isle of Wight, when I was 14, on a window seat looking out to sea'. But Clare D suggests: 'Possibly my catholic and eclectic reading choices reflect my at-times chaotic life.' Jan B wrote: 'I relate my life to those of characters in novels, cross-referencing experiences, and that "cross-referencing" can also have political implications.' Anne K suggested: 'I sometimes compare my own Western identity and ideologies to books written about other cultures and the rights that we females in the West take for granted.'

So the relationship between our fiction reading and our lived lives is a complex one, and there are many factors to consider when looking at a woman's response to a novel or short story collection. As I've argued, female readers come from all class, race, ethnic, and educational backgrounds, so it's dangerous to generalize about such a heterogeneous community. From my own experience of teaching and meeting different kinds of people, boosted by my questionnaires and interviews, I'm struck by the way fiction—with all the imaginative demands it makes of readers—can empower and liberate women, often giving us greater self-knowledge and confidence to define and change our lives for the better. I'm reminded of the late nineteenth-century Cheltenham Ladies College girls reading (after dark in the dorm) Olive Schreiner's *The Story of an African Farm*. One of them wrote: 'The whole sky seemed aflame, and many of us became violent feminists.'[5] In more recent times, Sylvia Plath's *The Bell Jar* and Naomi Alderman's *Disobedience* have created more 'violent feminists'. I've known students who left husbands after studying Kate Chopin's *The Awakening*, and friends who felt able to come out as lesbian after reading Alice Walker or Sarah Waters. When one woman wrote, 'I believe reading has saved my sanity if not my life', she was speaking for many more who have found a strong personal identity (often through a blog, literature class, reading group, or online chat group) and read their way out of stifling and unsatisfactory families and relationships.

In 2018, *The Bookseller* magazine announced that female writers (including two BAME women) dominated the UK's top ten bestselling authors of literary fiction. Only one male writer joined the rollcall that included Margaret Atwood, Helen Dunmore, Sarah Perry, Arundhati Roy, Ali Smith, and Zadie Smith. Penguin plans to open more 'Like a Woman' pop-up bookshops to sell books by women only (Figure 9.1). The same year, Allison Devers, an American bookseller and publisher, opened in central London a bookshop The Second Shelf, selling rare and antiquarian books, manuscripts, and modern first editions, by women writers (Figure 9.2). Showing a photograph of herself at a book fair among an all-male group of collectors and sellers, she emphasized the value of books written by women and those early editions that can easily get lost in junkshops. She suggested women

Figure 9.1 'Like a Woman' pop-up bookshop, Shoreditch, London, March 2018

Photo by Helen Taylor

should collect women's books in order to validate their literary contribution, and asserted that—unlike male collectors, who go for volumes in pristine condition—women treasure a book with a personal inscription (from a mother to a daughter, an aunt to a niece). And as part of a research project called 'Ambient Literature', digital novelist Kate Pullinger published a high-tech short story, 'Breathe', designed to be read on your smartphone with you, the reader, at the centre of the plot.[6] With access to your camera and location, the story's narrative shifts with your place, environment, time of day, and year. This suggests a whole new direction in reader-centred fiction, something I suspect women will eagerly adopt as—smartphones at the ready—we squeeze personalized and creative reading into precious spaces of bedtime, workplace lunch hours, gaps between domestic chores, and school runs. Quite literally, we may be able to draw on fiction to mould our own narratives.

Figure 9.2 The Second Shelf bookshop, 14 Smiths Court, London
Photo by Helen Taylor

In his influential study, *Being Mortal*, surgeon Atul Gawande emphasizes the right of the sick and dying to tell their own stories, to
construct and complete the narrative of their lives. 'All we ask,' he
says, 'is to be allowed to remain the writers of our own story...the
chance to shape one's story [transforms] the possibilities for the last

chapters of everyone's lives.'[7] But this is true not only at the end of life, for—as Gawande suggests—we all live our lives inhabiting and developing stories that offer us dignity and autonomy. While visiting her birth family in Nigeria in the 1980s, Jackie Kay recalls reviewing the novel *Efuru* by Nigerian writer Flora Nwapa. 'How our lives are mapped by books,' she reflects.[8] For women who love fiction, this mapping is crucial to our intellectual and emotional development, as we imagine ourselves into, and draw sustenance from, those stories of our lives.

In my correspondent Caroline K's simple but resonant words: 'I am so glad I have had a reading life.'

Appendix
Questionnaire about Women's Fiction Reading

I am writing a book about women's reading lives and habits. This questionnaire asks you about your own reading history and daily practices. I'd be very grateful if you could complete it electronically or send back to me at the address below. Your second-class postage will be refunded.

Please write as much as you like, and add any material you wish.

1. When did you learn to read, who taught you, and what is your earliest memory of reading?

2. Do you recall the children's books you read, and which remain in your heart?

3. Were you encouraged or taught to read by parents, siblings, teachers, friends? Was your earliest reading teacher male or female?

4. Have your parents, partner(s), children, and friends encouraged and supported your reading habit? Has it sometimes been a secret or illicit pleasure?

5. Did/do you read religious/sacred texts, e.g. the Koran, the Bible? How important are these to you?

6. Do you read poetry, and if so which poets and poems are most special to you?

7. Have you read all your life, or have you had periods when you read little or nothing (perhaps in hard or challenging times)—or just newspapers, comics, magazines, etc.?

8. How has your education formed and influenced your reading—at school, further education college, evening class, university, etc.?

9. Did you read 'set books' at school and/or college and do you recall and cherish (or now hate) them? Please give examples.

10. Do you read every day, and if so at what time? Do you read at bedtime, and is that choice of reading matter different from other times of day?

11. Do you buy fiction regularly? At a bookshop or online?

12. Do you borrow books from a library or libraries? How often?

13. Would it matter to you if your local library and/or bookshop closed down? Why?

14. Do you read fast or slowly, and do you ever abandon books before finishing?

15. Do you read from the beginning of a book, or sneak a look at the ending first?

16. How do you choose what to read, and do you read more than one book at a time?

17. Have you chosen fiction because you saw their adaptation on TV or in the cinema?

18. Do you select your reading by genre, e.g. crime, science fiction, romance, memoir, graphic novel?

19. Do you read more fiction (novels and short stories) than non-fiction (biography, memoir, history, etc.)?

20. Do you read more female than male writers? If so, why?

21. Did the feminist movement influence your reading, and do you read books from feminist publishers such as Virago?

22. Which books, magazines, religious texts, etc. are currently on your bedside table or coffee table, or on your Kindle?

23. Do you re-read books and are there books you have read many times? Which are they?

24. How has your reading choice and enthusiasm changed over the years? e.g. do you read more poetry than when you were young? Do you read romantic fiction?

25. Do you read a daily and/or Sunday newspaper? Which one and why?

26. Do you read women's magazines? Which one and why?

27. Do you share your books/magazines/reading experiences with friends and family?

28. Are you in a book group and is it mixed or women only? What does this experience give you, and if you're not in a group, would you wish to be? Please briefly describe your group and the way it works.

29. Have you attended literary festival(s)? If so, which festivals, and what do you think you get from meeting writers and hearing books discussed? Do festival events influence your reading choices?

30. Do you read reviews of books and/or literary blogs?

31. How important is reading in your daily life, and at moments of joy, celebration, crisis, and stress?

32. Have you taken a creative writing course, and how has this changed the way you read?

33. Do you write a blog and/or post on Facebook, Mumsnet, or other social networks?

34. Do you own a Kindle or other form of electronic reader, and has this changed the way and what you read?

35. Would it matter if books disappeared and we all read on Kindles?

36. Do you have a favourite writer and book? Can you explain your choices?

37. Do you see your life in terms of books you've read? e.g. do you think about your relationships and life story in terms of stories you know, and do you ever think of your own biography in terms of 'chapters'?

38. Please add any other thoughts and memories you have about your reading life.

39. How would you describe the class and ethnic group you come from? Please indicate your parents' occupations, your own occupation, and how you describe your race/ethnic identity.

If you'd like to be named in my Acknowledgements, and if you'd be prepared to keep a reading diary and/or give me a personal or telephone interview, please give me your details:

Your name   Age
Address (email, home, or work)
Phone number(s)   Email address

Notes

Preface

1 P. Smith, *M Train* (London: Bloomsbury, 2015), 93.
2 J. Barnes, *A Life With Books* (London: Jonathan Cape, 2012), 4.
3 I do not distinguish between short and full-length fiction, because my correspondents rarely do. Short fiction in the UK has a far smaller market than novels, but does feature in book club selections. And, although the publishing industry retains an uneasy distinction between 'literary fiction' (non-formulaic character/theme/language-driven) and 'genre' fiction (formulaic plot/narrative-driven), these categories have been challenged and broken down in recent years. They do, however, still matter to women readers, as I discuss in Chapters 4 and 5.

Introduction

1 I. McEwan, https://www.theguardian.com/books/2005/sep/20/fiction. features11 (accessed 1 April 2015).
2 A. Pringle, 'Fiction has always been a woman's world, too', *i*, 12 April 2013, 16.
3 For a good overview of literary fiction and the current state of publishing, see Michael Bhaskar, 'Not going gently: How literary fiction survives in the UK', *The Author: Journal of the Society of Authors* (CXXIX, 1, Spring 2018), 4–5.
4 Nielsen Books and Consumers @ Nielsen Market Research: 'Fiction purchases bought for oneself in 2017 by genre, % of purchases bought by age, sex and ethnicity', 26 April 2018. Audiobook numbers tend to be more evenly distributed, though the pattern is similar to those of book readers.
5 This statistic is from Nielsen 2018, and the latest reliable statistic of the white population, 81.9%, comes from the 2011 census. I will drop the descriptor 'white' but in later chapters will discuss the ethnic and racial imbalance among writers and readers.
6 Bel Mooney, response to questionnaire from Helen Taylor, 2011.
7 M. Yousafzai, on https://www.roomtoread.org.
8 A. Nafisi, *Reading Lolita in Tehran: A Memoir in Books* (London and New York: Harper Perennial, 2003), 3.
9 B. Jack, *The Woman Reader* (New Haven and London: Yale University Press, 2012), 49.
10 O. Vuong, *The Echo Chamber*, BBC Radio 4, 16 December 2017.

11 J. Winterson, https://www.theguardian.com/books/2018/dec/07/jean ette-winterson-books-that-made-me (accessed 8 December 2018).

12 Kit de Waal, https://www.bbc.co.uk/sounds/play/b09fzmjt (accessed 28 February 2019).

13 K. de Waal and D. Shahwar Mughal, in Nathan Connolly, ed., *Know Your Place: Essays on the Working Class by the Working Class* (Liverpool: Dead Ink, 2017), 64 and 71.

14 D. Kean, *Writing the Future: Black and Asian Writers and Publishers in the UK Market Place* (London: Spread the Word (ALCS and Arts Council England), 2015); *The Bookseller*, 15 June 2018, 14.

15 'Locked in Literacy', *New Statesman*, 14–20 March 2014, 45.

16 J. Pearson, *Women's Reading in Britain 1750–1835: A Dangerous Recreation* (Cambridge: Cambridge University Press, 1999); K. Flint, *The Woman Reader 1837–1914* (Oxford: Clarendon Press, 1993); and Jack, *The Woman Reader*.

17 S. Williams, *Climbing the Bookshelves: The Autobiography of Shirley Williams* (London: Virago, 2009), 2.

18 See S. Bollman, *Reading Women* (New York and London: Merrell Publishers, 2006) and *Women Who Read Are Dangerous* (New York: Abbeville Press, 2016).

19 Jack, *The Woman Reader*, 6.

20 A. Smith, *Public Library and Other Stories* (London: Hamish Hamilton, 2015), 169.

21 Smith, *Public Library*, 48.

22 D. S. Opel, 'Self-representation in literary fandom: Women's leisure reader selfies as postfeminist performance', *Transformative Works and Cultures*, 18 (2015), accessed online, September 2017.

23 Catherine Kerrison, quoted in Jack, *The Woman Reader*, 261.

24 Quoted in Jack, *The Woman Reader*, 137.

25 Quoted in Pearson, *Women's Reading*, 42.

26 Jack, *The Woman Reader*, 231.

27 Flint, *Woman Reader*, 51.

28 Similar warnings have been given in recent years about the pernicious effect of romantic comedies on women viewers; see, for instance, Llewellyn Smith, 'Lights . . . Action . . . and Pure Treacle', latimes.com 2016, quoted in Alice Guilluy, ' "A Big Sugary Confection?" The Reception of Contemporary Hollywood Romantic Comedy in Britain, France and Germany', PhD thesis, King's College London, 2017, 19.

29 S. Hill, *Howards End is on the Landing: A Year of Reading from Home* (London: Profile, 2009), 173, 224.

30 Victoria Fox, interview with Helen Taylor, 26 July 2017.

31 L. Grant, *I Murdered My Library* (Kindle Single, 2014), 269.

32 Pearson, *Women's Reading*, 45.

33 Quoted in Jack, *The Woman Reader*, 246.

34 Jack, *The Woman Reader*, 166.

35 Jack, *The Woman Reader*, 196.
36 Flint, *Woman Reader*, 113.
37 Pearson, *Women's Reading*, 4–5, 132–3.
38 H. Lee, *Body Parts: Essays on Life-Writing* [2005] (London: Pimlico, 2008), 46.
39 Quoted in M. Grover, https://www.readingsheffield.co.uk/research/everyday-reading-in-sheffield-1920-1960/ (accessed 28 December 2017).
40 Statistic quoted at FutureBook Conference, London, 1 December 2017; http://news.kobo.com/news-releases/behind-the-digital-screens:-reading-habits-of-the-industrys-most-valuable-customers (accessed 16 August 2018; no longer available).
41 C. Tóibín, *A Guest at the Feast: A Memoir* (Penguin Special, kindle version, 2011), 176.

Chapter 1

1 G. Steinem, *My Life on the Road* (London: OneWorld, 2015), 8.
2 https://facebook.com/TheLiterary Heroes, posted 21 September 2013 (no longer available).
3 Pearson, *Women's Reading*, 17.
4 A. Fraser, ed., *The Pleasure of Reading* (London: Bloomsbury, 1992), 159.
5 M. Lipman in R. V. Bailey and J. Hall, eds, *The Book of Love and Loss: Poems for Today* (Bath: The Belgrave Press, 2014), 19–20.
6 M. Rosen, *Saturday Live*, BBC Radio 4, 31 August 2013.
7 S. Rushdie, *The Guardian*, 26 January 2018; https://www.theguardian.com/books/2018/jan/26/salman-rushdie-the-books-that-changed-me (accessed 5 April 2018).
8 https://www.thebookseller.com/news/rare-books-dealer-launches-journal-and-shop-dedicated-female-authors-845721 (accessed 16 August 2018).
9 http://www.persephonebooks.co.uk/faq/ (accessed 6 April 2018).
10 K. Mosse, 'Great speeches of the 20th century: Shakespeare's sister, Virginia Woolf October 20 and 26 1928', *The Guardian* News and Media, 2007, 5–6.
11 'Speaking out of the silence', *TLS*, 25 May 2018, 31.
12 J. Barnes, *A Life with Books* (London: Jonathan Cape, 2012), 25.
13 Harriet Gilbert, Interview by Helen Taylor, Bristol, 4 May 2014.
14 Goodreads, cited in 'Woolf is for women – and Mailer's for men? How readers favour authors of own gender', *The Guardian*, 26 November 2014, 3.
15 See Danuta Kean's report, 'Are You Serious? The Emelia Report into the Gender Gap for Authors', http://www.eilenedavidson.com/wp-content/uploads/2019/03/The-Emelia-Report.pdf (accessed 19 March 2019).
16 R. Cooke, 'Recognition at last for a domestic goddess', *The Observer New Review*, 13 March 2016, 39.

17 M. Wolitzer, 'The second shelf: On the rules of literary fiction for men and women', *The New York Times*, 30 March 2012, https://www.nytimes.com/ 2012/04/01/books/review/on-the-rules-of-literary-fiction-for-men-and-women.html (accessed 3 August 2017).

18 https://www.theguardian.com/books/2011/jun/02/vs-naipaul-jane-austen-women-writers and https://www.theguardian.com/books/2017/dec/ 12/double-x-factor-why-women-are-better-writers-than-men (accessed 15 December 2017).

19 L. Goodings, 'The Woman Writer', lecture notes, Cardiff, March 2014. I am grateful to Lennie Goodings for sharing this with me.

20 S. Ellis, *How to be a Heroine: Or, What I've Learned from Reading too Much* (London: Penguin Random House, 2014), e-book 75, 2236, 2945.

21 A. Bennett, *The Uncommon Reader* (London: Faber and Faber, 2007), 102.

22 https://www.theguardian.com/books/2017/dec/12/double-x-factor-why-women-are-better-writers-than-men (accessed 17 December 2017). Guy Pringle, former editor of *newbooks*, told me men are more self-obsessed and don't have curiosity about women.

23 S. Elderkin and E. Berthoud, *The Novel Cure* (London: Canongate, 2013). https://www.canongate.tv/the-novel-cure-1.html.

24 http://psycnet.apa.org/record/2016-37488-001 and https://www. theguardian.com/books/2010/jun/12/life-in-writing-barbara-kingsolver (accessed 7 July 2017).

25 E. L. James, *Fifty Shades of Grey* (London: Vintage, 2011), e-book 24.

26 Ellis, *How to be a Heroine*, 747.

27 M. Keyes, *The Guardian Review*, 3 March 2018, 2.

28 Lennie Goodings, Interview by Helen Taylor, 24 June 2014.

29 Judy Finnigan, email Interview by Helen Taylor, 17 October 2013.

30 Hilary Mantel, Interview by Helen Taylor, Budleigh Salterton, 18 December 2012.

31 Roxane Gay, quoted by Hadley Freeman, *The Guardian Weekend*, 9 September 2017.

32 A. Phillips, *Missing Out: In Praise of the Unlived Life* (London: Hamish Hamilton, 2012), xi, viii–xiv, xvii.

33 T. Thorn, 'Off the record', *New Statesman*, 12–18 January 2018, 57; P. Lively, *Ammonites and Leaping Fish: A Life in Time* (London: Fig Tree, 2013), 184–5.

Chapter 2

1 I am grateful to Pauline Trudell, early years specialist, for helping with my argument here and later in the chapter.

2 Grant, *I Murdered My Library*, 93.

3 A. Chekhov, *Plays* (Harmondsworth: Penguin, 1951), 392. Thanks to Liz Bird for this quotation.

4 D. Athill, *Somewhere Towards the End* (London: Granta, 2008), 48.

5 Molly Flatt, *The Bookseller*, 22 June 2018, https://www.thebookseller.com/futurebook/neuroscience-research-shows-audiobooks-are-more-emotionally-engaging-film-and-tv-816301 (accessed 23 September 2018).

6 Hill, *Howards End is on the Landing*, 26.

7 https://www.penguin.co.uk/articles/features/2017/mar/caitlin-moran-how-books-made-me-a-feminist/ (accessed 20 January 2018).

8 Conversation with Helen Taylor, Budleigh Salterton Literature Festival, 14 September 2017.

9 https://www.thebookseller.com/news/representation-childrens-literature-827841 (accessed 15 August 2018).

10 https://www.theguardian.com/books/2018/dec/14/readtheonepercent-brixton-bookshop-knights-of (accessed 3 January 2019).

11 Thanks to Professor Debra Myhill and Professor Kim Reynolds for their observations on children's literature, emails to HT, 20 and 21 December 2017.

12 e.g. B. Vincent, *Five Go On a Strategy Away Day* (London: Quercus, 2016).

13 P. Lively, *Ammonites and Leaping Fish: A Life in Time* (London: Fig Tree, 2013), 180.

14 Hill, *Howards End is on the Landing*, 24.

15 V. Chok, 'Yellow', in N. Shukla, ed., *The Good Immigrant* (London: Unbound, 2016), 36.

16 Quoted in *The Observer Review*, 25 November 2012, 10.

17 Hill, *Howards End is on the Landing*, 23.

18 https://www.readingsheffield.co.uk/research/everyday-reading-in-sheffield-1920-1960/ (accessed 10 December 2017), and conversation between Mary Grover and Helen Taylor, Sheffield, 15 December 2017.

19 Hilary Mantel, Interview with Helen Taylor, Budleigh Salterton, 18 December 2012.

20 *The Bookseller*, 15 June 2018, 10.

21 L. Mangan, *Bookworm: A Memoir of Childhood Reading* (London: Square Peg, 2018), 1, 81.

22 The groups held in June–July 2017 are 'Friends for Life', Southmead Library (coordinator Fiona Philipp Rigg); 'Love Reading Fiction Group', Henleaze Library (Jill Morgan) and Wick Road Library Parents Book Club, Brislington (Cheryl Warner)—all in Bristol; plus the Bramley Reading Group (Karen Weatherly).

23 L. M. Alcott, *Little Women* ([my ancient edition], London: Puffin Story Books 1953), 46.

24 Alison Waller, '"Girls Like it Most": Challenging Gendered Canons and Paracanons in the Case of *The Secret Garden*', in B. Kümmerling-Meinbauer and A. Müller, eds, *Canon Constitution and Canon Change in Children's Literature* (London: Routledge, 2017), 162.

25 M. Jefferson, *Negroland: A Memoir* (London: Granta, 2016), 211, 215–16.

26 Hilary Mantel, interview with Helen Taylor.

27 'A dream come true', *Radio Times*, 23 December 2017–15 January 2018, 10, 12.
28 Quoted in Waller, '"Girls Like it Most"', 167.
29 Mangan, *Bookworm*, 188–9.
30 Athill, *Somewhere Towards the End*, 49.
31 https://www.theguardian.com/books/2018/jan/06/katherine-rundell-only-time-kids-understand-world-when-they-read (accessed 8 January 2018).

Chapter 3

1 https://www.theguardian.com/books/2016/apr/16/charlotte-bronte-bicentenary-birth-jane-eyre-by-sarah-waters-margaret-drabble-jeanette-winterson (accessed 1 May 2016).
2 Opel, 'Self-representation in literary fandom', 2.
3 M. Kirkham, Letter to Helen Taylor, 22 October 2017. Also see M. Kirkham, *Jane Austen: Feminism and Fiction* (Sussex: Harvester Press, 1983).
4 H. Jones and M. Lane, *Celebrating Pride and Prejudice* (Bath: Lansdown Media, 2012), 10.
5 C. Tomalin, *A Life of My Own* (London: Viking, 2017), 306.
6 L. Lethbridge, 'Austenmania: Seven books about Jane Austen', *Literary Review*, July 2017, 16–17.
7 The banknote reproduces the engraving made for J. E. Austen Leigh's 1870 *Memoir*, an image softening and embellishing Cassandra Austen's sketch *c*.1810.
8 'Pride and Prejudice: Celebrating 200 years', *The Guardian Review*, 26 January 2013, 4. The two suggestions come from Janet Todd and Lucy Mangan.
9 H. Fielding, *Bridget Jones's Diary* (London: Picador, 1996), and *Bridget Jones: The Edge of Reason* (London: Picador, 1999). There are three film versions: *Bridget Jones's Diary* (2001), *Bridget Jones: The Edge of Reason* (2004), and *Bridget Jones's Baby* (2016).
10 Jones and Lane, *Celebrating Pride and Prejudice*, 27.
11 'Literature in Britain Today', The Royal Society of Literature, March 2017, 26.
12 A. E. Stallings, 'Symposium: What does Jane Austen mean to you?', *Times Literary Supplement, Jane Austen*, 2017, 18.
13 S. Ellis in Stallings, 'Symposium', 19.
14 'Pass Notes No 3,207: The Janeites', *The Guardian G2*, 28 October 2013, 3.
15 https://www.bbc.co.uk/news/uk-england-40093010 (accessed 17 July 2017).
16 A. Walmesley, 'Secrets behind the female passion for reading books', *Western Morning News*, 20 February 2013, 13.
17 *My Friend Jane*, BBC1, 17 July 2017, dir. Richard George.
18 *My Friend Jane*.

19 Sarah Moss, panel discussion, 'Jane Austen: Britain's most beloved author', Cheltenham Literature Festival, 15 October 2017.

20 https://www.bbc.co.uk/films/2004/09/16/bride_and_prejudice_2004_review.shtml (accessed 28 February 2018).

21 A. Goodman, '*Pemberley Previsited:* Pride and Prejudice, *by Jane Austen*,' in A. Fadiman, ed., *Rereadings* (New York: Farrar, Straus and Giroux, 2005), 160, 161, 164.

22 Bramley Reading Group, Surrey, July 2017, transcribed by Karen Weatherly.

23 Quoted in Lionel Trilling, 'Emma', *Encounter*, June 1957, Issue 14, 49 and 50.

24 C. L. Johnson, 'Austen Cults and Cultures', in E. Copeland and J. McMaster, eds, *The Cambridge Companion to Jane Austen* (Cambridge: Cambridge University Press, 1997), 211.

25 Johnson, 'Austen Cults', 220.

26 I. Sansom, 'We're All Janeites Now', in *Jane Austen* (London: TLS, 2017), 24.

27 Paula Marantz Cohen, 'What would Jane Austen do?', in Stallings, 'Symposium', 95.

28 Letter from Charlotte Brontë to George Lewes, 12 January 1848, quoted in Jones and Lane, *Celebrating Pride and Prejudice*, 42.

29 Trilling, 'Emma', 49.

30 Hill, *Howards End is on the Landing*, 96–7.

31 Joyce Carol Oates, in Stallings, 'Symposium', 18.

32 Deidre Lynch, 'Cult of Jane Austen', in J. Todd, *Jane Austen in Context* (Cambridge: Cambridge University Press, 2005), 117.

33 L. Grant, *The Dark Circle* (London: Virago, 2016), 115.

34 Moss, panel discussion, 'Jane Austen: Britain's most beloved author'.

35 Pearson, *Women's Reading*, 145.

36 J. Austen, *Northanger Abbey* [1818] (London: Penguin, 1985), 58.

37 L. Doughty, 'Inspired by the Brontës', panel discussion, Bradford Literature Festival, 8 July 2017.

38 https://www.theguardian.com/books/2018/feb/04/book-clinic-literary-page-turners-recommended-reads (accessed 1 March 2018).

39 Best known are Daphne du Maurier, *Rebecca*, 1938, and Jean Rhys, *Wide Sargasso Sea*, 1966. But there are many others, such as Mary Stewart's *Nine Coaches Waiting*, 1958 and *The Ivy Tree*, 1961; Hilary Bailey, *Mrs Rochester: A Sequel to Jane Eyre*, 1997; and Emma Tennant, *Thornfield Hall: Jane Eyre's Hidden Story*, 2007. Young contemporary interpretations include the Young Adult novel, Kay Woodward, *Jane Airhead*, 2009; the sci-fi vampire version, Sharon Shinn, *Jenna Starborn*, 2010; and the erotic mashups *Jane Eyre Laid Bare* and *Jane Eyrotica*, 2012. After her death in 1992, Angela Carter left a synopsis for a sequel about Jane's stepdaughter, Adèle Varens.

40 T. Chevalier, ed., *Reader, I Married Him: Stories Inspired by Jane Eyre* (London: The Borough Press, 2016), 2–3.

41 Quoted in Chevalier, *Reader, I Married Him*, 284 and 290.

42 G. Greer, 'Gender expectations in the lives of the Brontës', Bradford Literature Festival, 8 July 2017.

43 L. Coaklye, 'Why Jane Eyre is most definitely a YA novel', *The Guardian*, 19 April 2016, https://www.theguardian.com/childrens-books-site/2016/apr/19/why-jane-eyre-is-a-ya-novel-charlotte-bronte (accessed 27 September 2017).

44 Hilary Mantel, Interview with Helen Taylor, Budleigh Salterton, 18 December 2012.

45 Women's Reading Group, Southmead Library, transcribed by Fiona Philipp, July 2017; Love Reading Fiction Group, Henleaze Library, Bristol, transcribed by Jill Morgan, July 2017; Avonmouth/Shirehampton & Sea Mills Libraries Group, transcribed by Catherine Filmer, June/July 2017.

46 Kit de Waal, 'An Open Invitation', in N. Connolly, ed., *Know Your Place: Essays on the Working Class by the Working Class* (London: Dead Ink, 2017), 65.

47 S. M. Gilbert and S. Gubar, *The Madwoman in the Attic: The Woman Writer and the Nineteenth-Century Literary Imagination* (New Haven and London: Yale University Press, 1979).

48 See Alison Light, 'Hitchcock's *Rebecca*: A Woman's Film?', in H. Taylor, ed., *The Daphne du Maurier Companion* (London: Virago Press, 2007), 296.

49 H. Taylor, ed., 'The Lasting Reputation and Cultural Legacy of *Rebecca*', in *The Daphne du Maurier Companion*, 47–101.

50 I am indebted to Margaret Kirkham's insights into and examples about readers in the novels.

51 Quoted in Jones and Lane, *Celebrating Pride and Prejudice*, 36. There is a lucrative literary tourism industry, and it's easy to be cynical about bandwagon jumping. See my comments on The Jane Austen Centre in Bath, Chapter 8.

52 See Jones and Lane, *Celebrating Pride and Prejudice*, 62–3.

Chapter 4

1 Quoted in C. Dyhouse, *Heartthrobs: A History of Women and Desire* (Oxford: Oxford University Press, 2017), 176.

2 See G. Beer, *The Romance* (London: Methuen, 1970).

3 Quoted in Dyhouse, *Heartthrobs*, 149.

4 Quoted in S. Wendell and C. Tan, *Beyond Heaving Bosoms: The Smart Bitches' Guide to Romance Novels* (New York: Fireside, Simon & Schuster, 2009), 123.

5 Lesbian, Gay, Bisexual, Trans, Queer (and see note 20). For different kinds of romance, see https://www.goodreads.com.

6 Quoted in Wendell and Tan, *Beyond Heaving Bosoms*, 123; G. Greer, *The Female Eunuch* (London: Granada, 1970), 188; Boon quoted in Dyhouse, *Heartthrobs*, 177.

7 Wendell and Tan, *Beyond Heaving Bosoms*, 4.

8 See, for instance, T. Modleski, *Loving with a Vengeance: Mass-Produced Fantasies for Women* (Hamden, CT: Archon, 1982); J. A. Radway, *Reading the Romance: Women, Patriarchy, and Popular Literature* (Chapel Hill: University of North Carolina Press, 1984); J. Radford, ed., *The Progress of Romance: The Politics of Popular Fiction* (London: Routledge & Kegan Paul, 1986); H. Carr, ed., *From My Guy to Sci-Fi* (London: Pandora Press, 1989); H. Taylor, *Scarlett's Women: Gone With the Wind and its Female Fans* (London: Virago, 1989, repr. 2014).

9 Veronica Henry, email correspondence with Helen Taylor, 16 April 2018. Other quotations from Henry are from this correspondence.

10 V. Winspear, 1972, quoted in Dyhouse, *Heartthrobs*, 159.

11 K. Fforde, Interview with Helen Taylor, 30 July 2014.

12 https://www.quora.com/Why-do-women-love-reading-romance-novels (accessed 2 April 2018).

13 E. Murdoch, Interview with Helen Taylor, 10 April 2018, Bristol.

14 A. Light, 'Returning to Manderley – romantic fiction, female sexuality and class', *Feminist Review*, 16, Summer 1984, 23.

15 B. Nightingale, BBC Radio 4, 1971, quoted in Dyhouse, *Heartthrobs*, 177.

16 Jojo Moyes, *Me Before You* (London: Penguin, 2012).

17 https://www.millsandboon.co.uk/np/About-Us.

18 2017 figure from Nielsen Books and Consumers (Nielsen Market Research, 2018).

19 https://www.theguardian.com/books/2018/may/18/emma-healey-mills-boon-saved-my-life-you-need-happy-endings-when-youre-down- (accessed 2 June 2018).

20 Lesbian, Gay, Bisexual, Trans, Queer, Intersex, Asexuality, and all other sexualities, sexes and genders not included. https://romanticnovelistsassociation.org/news_article/announcing-the-rainbow-chapter/ (accessed 1 October 2018).

21 https://steamyromancebooks.com/heat-levels/. Thanks to Emily Murdoch for this.

22 https://www.millsandboon.co.uk/ch24/c1/series/blaze.htm.

23 Bryony Gordon, *The Daily Telegraph*, 2015, quoted in Dyhouse, *Heartthrob*, 187.

24 A. E. Quale, 'Pursuit of Empowerment: The Evolution of the Romance Novel and Its Readership in *Fifty Shades of Grey*', MA thesis, Minnesota State University, Mankato, 2014, 68.

25 Quoted in R. A. Deller and C. Smith, 'Reading the BDSM romance: Reader responses to *Fifty Shades*', *Sexualities* 16(8), 2013, 936.

26 A. O'Hagan, *London Review of Books*, 19 July 2012; C. Philipson and S. Brick, quoted in Deller and Smith, 'Reading the BDSM romance', 936.

27 Guilluy, '"A Big Sugary Confection?"'.

28 L. Appignanesi, 'Fifty Shades of my own', in L. Appignanesi, R. Holmes, and S. Orbach, eds, *Fifty Shades of Feminism* (London: Virago, 2013), 26.

29 Deller and Smith, 'Reading the BDSM romance', 942.

30 For an excellent and chilling summary of this in the UK, see H. Baxter and R. L. Cosslett, *The Vagenda* (London: Vintage, 2015), chapter 11.

31 Wendell and Tan, *Beyond Heaving Bosoms*, 143.

32 'Front Row', BBC Radio 4, 3 April 2018.

33 http://www.bbc.co.uk/news/world-44041947 (accessed 15 May 2018).

34 Baxter and Cosslett, *The Vagenda*, 185.

35 https://www.nytimes.com/2017/12/11/books/cat-person-new-yorker.html (accessed 3 January 2018).

36 Roupenian, *You Know You Want This*. Roupenian was speaking at Waterstones, Bristol, 6 February 2019.

37 2017 figures from Nielsen Books and Consumers (Nielsen Market Research, 2018).

38 Quoted in Sara Barnard, 'Fictions of girlhood: A gendered perspective on young adult literature', lecture at the Interdisciplinary Institute for the Humanities, University of East Anglia, 29 November 2017; telephone conversation between S. Barnard and Helen Taylor, 25 January 2018.

39 C. Flanagan, 'Love, actually', *The Atlantic Monthly*, 15 April 2009, quoted in A. H. Petersen, 'That teenage feeling', *Feminist Media Studies*, 12:1, 2011, 60.

40 'Gloria', in Petersen, 'That teenage feeling', 58.

Chapter 5

1 S. Gilbert, 'Why men pretend to be women to sell thrillers', *The Atlantic*, 3 August 2017.

2 Gilbert, 'Why men pretend to be women'.

3 All quotations and references from L. Brewster, 'Murder by the book: Using crime fiction as a bibliotherapeutic resource', *Medical Humanities*, 43:1, February 2017, 62–7.

4 D. Sayers, quoted in David Glover, 'The Thriller', in M. Priestman, ed., *The Cambridge Companion to Crime Fiction* (Cambridge: Cambridge University Press, 2003), 136.

5 L. Browder, 'Dystopian romance: True crime and the female reader', *The Journal of Popular Culture*, 39:6, 2006, 928.

6 M. McGrath, 'Women's appetite for explicit crime fiction is no mystery', https://www.theguardian.com/books/booksblog/2014/jun/30/women-crime-fiction-real-anxieties-metaphorical (accessed 30 June 2014).

7 https://www.karinslaughter.com/about-books/ (n.d.) (accessed March 2018).

8 A. Hill, 'Sexist violence sickens crime critic', *The Guardian*, 25 October 2009, https://www.theguardian.com/books/2009/oct/25/jessica-mann-crime-novels-anti-women.

9 Gilbert, 'Why men pretend to be women'.

10 Hill, 'Sexist violence sickens crime critic'.

11 J. Rose, 'Corkscrew in the neck', *London Review of Books*, 37:17, 10 September 2015, 25–6.

12 F. Cummins, conversation at Crimefest, Bristol, 2018.

13 https://www.theguardian.com/books/2018/jan/26/staunch-prize-launched-for-thrillers-that-avoid-sexual-violence-against-women (accessed 1 February 2018); https://www.thebookseller.com/news/crimefest-withdraws-offer-host-staunch-prize-winner-743101 (accessed 11 December 2018).

14 Val McDermid's short story, 'Homecoming', echoes this when protagonist Miranda, asked why she writes the crime thriller rather than the literary novel, says: 'The desire for revenge, Simon. There were people I wanted to murder but I knew I'd never get away with it. So I decided to kill them on the page instead' (*Insidious Intent* (London: Little Brown, 2017), end pages).

15 L. Mangan and K. Slaughter, blurbs for paperback edition, Lee Child, *A Wanted Man* (London: Bantam, 2013).

16 S. LeFanu, *In the Chinks of the World Machine: Feminism and Science Fiction* (London: The Women's Press, 1988), 2.

17 See, for example, M. Pugh, ' "You canna change the laws of fiction, Jim!": A personal account of reading science fiction', *Changing English*, 6:1, 1999, 19–30.

18 S. LeFanu, email to Helen Taylor, 14 November 2018.

19 https://www.theguardian.com/books/2017/jun/24/feminist-dystopian-sci-fi-naomi-alderman-handmaids-tale (accessed 3 February 2018).

20 https://theconversation.com/friday-essay-science-fictions-women-problem-58626, 15 September 2016 (accessed 3 February 2018).

21 https://www.theparisreview.org/blog/2018/01/18/wrinkle-time-science-fiction-fantasy-female-readers/ (accessed 3 February 2018).

22 Sarah R. Wakefield, ' "Your sister in St. Scully": An electronic community of female fans of the X-Files', *Journal of Popular Film and Television*, 29:3, April 2010, 130, 136.

23 Helen Merrick, , ' "Fantastic Dialogues": Critical Stories about Feminism and Science Fiction', in A. Sawyer and D. Seed, eds, *Speaking Science Fiction* (Liverpool: Liverpool University Press, 2000), 58.

24 https://www.theguardian.com/books/2017/jun/24/feminist-dystopian-sci-fi-naomi-alderman-handmaids-tale (accessed 3 February 2018).

Chapter 6

1 J. Myerson, 'Frenchman's Creek', in H. Taylor, ed., *The Daphne du Maurier Companion* (London: Virago, 2007), 156–7.

2 M. Mitchell and Clare Mackintosh, *Nudge-Book*, 92 (Spring 2017), 15.

3 Michèle Roberts, conversation with Helen Taylor, August 2012.

4 Exhibited in 'Agatha Christie and Collins: Rare Images and Documents from her life and Publishing Career', The Agatha Christie Archive and

HarperCollins Publishers, The Old Swan Hotel, Harrogate (part of Theakston Old Peculier Crime writing Festival, 20–23 July 2017).

5 M. Blackman, quoted in flyer for Appledore Book Festival Schools Programme, 2014.

6 J. Winterson, *Why Be Happy When You Could Be Normal?* (London: Jonathan Cape, 2011), 116 and 117.

7 Helen Dunmore, Interview by Helen Taylor, 4 July 2013.

8 https://publishingperspectives.com/2018/06/writers-income-alcs-uk-sur vey-2010-publishers-association/ (accessed 7 July 2018).

9 S. Beauman, Questionnaire, 6 October 2013. All subsequent quotations from the late Sally Beauman derive from this interview.

10 Bernardine Evaristo, email correspondence with Helen Taylor, 9 August 2018.

11 Alex Clark, 'The New Elizabethans', *TLS*, 6 April 2018.

12 M. Wolitzer, https://www.theguardian.com/books/2018/nov/25/meg-wolitzer-interview-im-a-feminist-so-i-write-like-a-feminist-the-female-persuasion-the-wife (accessed 5 December 2018).

13 Danuta Kean, 'Are you Serious? The Emelia report into the Gender Gap for Authors', http://www.eilenedavidson.com/wp-content/uploads/2019/03/The-Emelia-Report.pdf (accessed 19 March 2019).

14 J. Runcie, BBC Radio 4, *Open Book*, 26 December 2013; https://www.theguardian.com/books/2018/may/25/why-are-middle-aged-women-invisible-on-book-covers-anne-tyler-allison-pearson (accessed 7 June 2018).

15 E. Shafak, BBC Radio 4, *Bookclub*, 7 April 2013.

16 Alison Flood, 'Stop giving us soppy covers, say women writers', *The Guardian*, 10 May 2013, 5.

17 'Coverflip: author Maureen Johnson turns tables on gendered book covers', https://www.huffingtonpost.com/2013/05/07/coverflip-maureen-john son_n_3231935.html?guccounter=1 (accessed 18 August 2018).

18 C. Armitstead, https://www.theguardian.com/books/2019/jan/04/pat-barker-women-carry-the-can-long-term (accessed 10 January 2019).

19 Louise Doughty, email to Helen Taylor, 8 December 2014.

20 Hilary Mantel, Interview with Helen Taylor, Budleigh Salterton, 18 December 2012. All subsequent quotations come from this interview.

21 Sarah LeFanu, Interview with Helen Taylor, 14 February 2013. 'Quail' is published in C. Hope and P. Porter, eds, *New Writing 5* (London: Vintage, 1996), 454–69, repr. in S. Hayward, *Why2K?* (London: Booth-Clibborn, 2000), 206–11.

22 P. Lockwood, https://www.lrb.co.uk/v40/n09/patricia-lockwood/why-do-i-have-to-know-what-mcdonalds-is (accessed 12 December 2018).

23 Helen Dunmore, quoted in her obituary, *The Telegraph*, 6 June 2017.

24 https://www.the-tls.co.uk/articles/public/mary-mccarthy-charmed-life/ (accessed 1 December 2017).

25 Sarah Dunant, Interview with Helen Taylor, 13 March 2013.

26 Katie Fforde, Interview with Helen Taylor, 30 July 2014.
27 https://www.theguardian.com/books/2013/dec/13/rare-black-british-woman-literary-influence (accessed 18 April 2015).
28 B. Evaristo, email to Helen Taylor, 9 August 2018.
29 https://www.spreadtheword.org.uk/wp-content/uploads/2016/11/Writing-the-Future-Black-and-Asian-Authors-and-Publishers-in-the-UK-Marketplace-May-2015.pdf (accessed 15 April 2018).
30 Arts Council England, 'Literature in the 21st Century: Understanding Models of Support for Literary Fiction', 2017.
31 'Writing the Future', 14.
32 https://www.theguardian.com/books/2018/jan/06/jon-mcgregor-my-writing-day (accessed 6 February 2018).
33 Charlotte Higgins, 'Is this the Great American Novel for the 21st century?', *The Guardian*, 24 August 2013, 20.
34 L. McInerney, https://www.theguardian.com/books/2017/apr/16/lisa-mcinerney-i-have-known-people-who-have-done-appalling-things-meet-the-author-interview (accessed 3 May 2017).
35 K. de Waal, email to Helen Taylor, 28 May 2018.
36 https://www.theguardian.com/books/2015/feb/13/aminatta-forna-dont-judge-book-by-cover (accessed 20 February 2013).
37 https://www.theguardian.com/books/2018/jan/21/zadie-smith-you-ask-the-questions-self-doubt (accessed 29 January 2018).
38 S. Dunant, Interview with Helen Taylor, 13 March 2013.
39 Alex Clark talks to Naomi Alderman, *The Guardian Review*, 10 June 2017, 5.
40 Liz Bury, 'My inner bloke: Rowling spells out her alter ego', *The Guardian*, 25 July 2013, 5.
41 Elaine Showalter, telephone Interview with Helen Taylor, 10 July 2013.

Chapter 7

1 T. Bell, https://www.telegraph.co.uk/wellbeing/mood-and-mind/the-truth-about-book-clubs-thackeray-pass-the-chardonnay/, 6 February 2016 (accessed 1 March 2016).
2 G. Pringle, *Nudge-book*, 92 (Spring 2017), 8.
3 J.C., NB, *Times Literary Supplement*, 9, 16, 23, 30 March 2018, 44, 6, 36, 59, and 6 April, 40.
4 Nafisi, *Reading Lolita in Tehran*.
5 https://press.uchicago.edu/Misc/Chicago/492621.html (accessed 10 July 2018).
6 After issue 83, *newbooks* merged with the website nudge-book.com. Pringle retired after issue 94, but wrote a history of the magazine for the one hundredth issue, May 2019.
7 J. Hartley, *Reading Groups* (Oxford: Oxford University Press, 2001), 22. This remains the excellent standard work on the subject, even if some of its material is dated.

8 Roehampton University has undertaken many studies of reading, and as I write has an AHRC-funded project on 'Memories of Fiction'. See https://memoriesoffiction.org/about (accessed 6 May 2017).

9 See E. Noble, *The Reading Group* (London: Hodder and Stoughton, 2003); K. J. Fowler, *The Jane Austen Book Club* (London: Viking, 2004); M. A. Shaffer and A. Barrows, *The Guernsey Literary and Potato Peel Pie Society* (London: Bloomsbury, 2010); and F. Weldon, *The Reading Group* (London: Samuel French, 1999). There is also an anthology produced to support Breast Cancer Care, edited by Meera Syal, *The Best Little Book Club in Town* (London: Orion, 2011).

10 Interview with Egidia Bonomini and Sarah Chopes, The Bookclub, 15 February 2013.

11 Email from Eila Huxford to Helen Taylor, 9 August 2012.

12 https://www.spectator.co.uk/2014/07/why-im-now-scared-of-book-clubs/, 12 July 2014 (accessed 17 August 2018).

13 Clare Balding, *Ramblings,* BBC Radio 4, 9 February 2013.

14 Bell, as note 1.

15 In 2014, the high court overturned a punitive measure by Conservative justice secretary Chris Grayling that banned the sending of books into prisons. This was challenged by many of the UK's leading writers, including the Poet Laureate.

16 Jack, *The Woman Reader,* 284–5.

17 Sweeney, M., *Reading Is My Window: Books and the Art of Reading in Women's Prisons* (Chapel Hill: University of North Carolina Press, 2010).

18 Sweeney, *Reading Is My Window,* 3, 6, 7–8.

19 http://giveabook.org.uk/project/mother-baby-units/, updated March 2019 (accessed 20 November 2018).

20 V. Ironside, *No! I Don't Want to Join a Bookclub* (London: Fig Tree, 2006), 44–5.

21 Julia Llewellyn Smith, https://www.dailymail.co.uk/femail/article-2145613/Book-clubs-offs-drunks-fibbers.html (accessed 1 October 2018).

22 Helen Dunmore, Interview with Helen Taylor, 4 July 2013.

23 A. Smith, *Artful* (London: Hamish Hamilton, 2012), 30–1.

24 Kit de Waal, email to Helen Taylor, 28 May 2018.

25 G. Pringle, Interview with Helen Taylor, Winchester Newbooks Readers Conference, 27 June 2014.

26 https://www.theguardian.com/books/2017/dec/15/literary-fiction-in-crisis-as-sale-drop-dramatically-arts-council-england-reports (accessed 4 January 2018).

27 J. Sutherland, *A Little History of Literature* (New Haven: Yale University Press, 2013), 259.

28 M. Atwood, quoted in Hartley, *Reading Groups,* 113–14.

29 Hartley, *Reading Groups,* 137.

30 Noble, *The Reading Group,* 546–7.

31 Nafisi, *Reading Lolita in Tehran,* 343.

Chapter 8

1 Kevin Parker, http://www.literaryfestivals.co.uk/announcements/the-rise-and-rise-of-literary-festivals (accessed 31 July 2018); Artemis Cooper, Hay Festival brochure, 2018.
2 https://jaipurliteraturefestival.org/ (accessed 5 August 2018).
3 Sutherland, *A Little History of Literature*, 259.
4 Alex Clark, https://www.theguardian.com/books/2016/may/28/can-literary-festivals-pay-their-way (accessed 6 June 2016).
5 K. Parker, email correspondence with Helen Taylor, 7 August 2018.
6 A. Clark, 28 May 2016.
7 https://www.theguardian.com/books/2016/jan/14/philip-pullman-resigns-oxford-literary-festival-patron-pay-authors (accessed 20 January 2016).
8 https://www.theguardian.com/books/booksblog/2016/oct/20/patrick-gale-why-started-north-cornwall-book-festival (accessed 5 August 2018).
9 https://www.theguardian.com/books/booksblog/2016/oct/20/patrick-gale-why-started-north-cornwall-book-festival (accessed 5 August 2018).
10 Sarah LeFanu, Interview with Helen Taylor, 14 February 2013. Other quotations from LeFanu in this chapter are from the same conversation.
11 Bidisha, Interview with Helen Taylor, 29 August 2013.
12 Helen Dunmore, Interview with Helen Taylor, 4 July 2013.
13 Zoe Steadman-Milne, Interview with Helen Taylor, 4 April 2013.
14 http://www.literaryfestivals.co.uk/announcements/the-rise-and-rise-of-literary-festivals (accessed 30 July 2018).
15 Steadman-Milne, Interview.
16 https://www.bradfordunisu.co.uk/articles/bradford-literature-festival-2018-programme-announcement.
17 P. Florence, BBC Radio 3, *Private Passions*, 27 May 2018; Chris Riddell, https://bookaid.org/blog/2017/03/02/engines-for-empathy/ (accessed 15 December 2018).
18 The other is Saint Louis-du-Ha-Ha! in Quebec.
19 https://www.visitbritain.org/literary-attractions-holiday-draw-more-half-brits (accessed 20 August 2017).
20 Quoted in D. Herbert, 'Literary Places, Tourism and the Heritage Experience', *Annals of Tourism Research*, 28:2 (2001), 314.
21 M. Lawson, 'A shrine for Saint Roald', *The Guardian*, 14 September 2011, 28.
22 Quoted in Blake Morrison, 'Birthday boy', *The Guardian*, G2, 7 May 2009, 5.

Chapter 9

1 J. Chiaet, 'Novel ending: Reading literary fiction improves empathy', 4 October 2013, https://www.scientificamerican.com/article/novel-finding-reading-literary-fiction-improves-empathy/ and https://readingagency.org.uk/news/media/reading-for-pleasure-builds-empathy-and-improves-wellbeing-research-from-the-reading-agency-finds.html (both accessed 16 July 2018).

2 K. Gunn, panel on short fiction, Budleigh Salterton Literary Festival, September 2018.

3 T. Herschmann, email to Helen Taylor, December 2018.

4 S. Hill, 'Life is a Handful of Short Stories Pretending to be a Novel', *Howards End is on the Landing: A Year of Reading from Home* (London: Profile Books, 2009), 98–105.

5 A. H. Jackson, *A Victorian Childhood*, 1932, quoted in C. Dyhouse, *Girls Growing Up in Late Victorian and Edwardian England* [1981] (London: Routledge, 2012), 173.

6 https://ambientlit.com/index.php/2018/01/17/session-promise/ (accessed 16 July 2018).

7 A. Gawande, *Being Mortal: Illness, Medicine, and What Matters in the End* (London: Profile Books, 2014), 243.

8 J. Kay, *Red Dust Road* [2010] (London: Picador Classic, 2017), 217.

Select Bibliography

Athill, D., *Somewhere Towards the End* (London: Granta, 2008).

Bailey, R. V. and Hall, J., eds, *The Book of Love and Loss: Poems for Today* (Bath: The Belgrave Press, 2014).

Barnes, J., *A Life with Books* (London: Jonathan Cape, 2012).

Baxter, H. and Cosslett, R. L., *The Vagenda* (London: Vintage, 2014).

Beer, G., *The Romance* (London: Methuen, 1970).

Bennett, A., *The Uncommon Reader* (London: Faber and Faber, 2007).

Brewster, L., 'Murder by the book: Using crime fiction as a bibliotherapeutic resource', *Medical Humanities*, 43:1, 2017, 62–7.

Carr, H., ed., *From My Guy to Sci-Fi* (London: Pandora Press, 1989).

Chevalier, T., ed., *Reader, I Married Him: Stories Inspired by Jane Eyre* (London: The Borough Press, 2016).

Clark, A., 'Fair play: Can literary festivals pay their way?', *The Guardian*, 28 May 2016. https://www.theguardian.com/books/2016/may/28/can-liter ary-festivals-pay-their-way.

Connolly, N., ed., *Know Your Place: Essays on the Working Class by the Working Class* (Liverpool: Dead Ink, 2017).

Copeland, E. and McMaster, J., eds, *The Cambridge Companion to Jane Austen* (Cambridge: Cambridge University Press, 1997).

Davis, P., *Reading and the Reader* (Oxford: Oxford University Press, 2013).

Deller, R. A. and Smith, C., 'Reading the BDSM romance: Reader responses to *Fifty Shades*', *Sexualities*, 16:8, 2013, 932–50.

dovegreyreader, https://dovegreyreader.typepad.com/.

Dyhouse, C., *Heartthrobs: A History of Women and Desire* (Oxford: Oxford University Press, 2017).

Elderkin, S. and Berthoud, E., *The Novel Cure* (London: Canongate, 2013).

Ellis, S., *How to be a Heroine; or, What I've Learned from Reading too Much* (London: Penguin Random House, 2014).

Fadiman, A., ed., *Rereadings* (New York: Farrar, Straus and Giroux, 2005).

Fadiman, A., *Ex Libris: Confessions of a Common Reader* (London: Penguin Books, 1998).

Flint, K., *The Woman Reader 1837–1914* (Oxford: Clarendon Press, 1993).

Fowler, K. J., *The Jane Austen Book Club* (London: Viking, 2004).

Fraser, A., ed., *The Pleasure of Reading* (London: Bloomsbury, 1992).

Freeman, L., *The Reading Cure: How Books Restored my Appetite* (London: Weidenfeld & Nicolson, 2018).

Gilbert, S. M. and Gubar, S., *The Madwoman in the Attic: The Woman Writer and the Nineteenth-Century Literary Imagination* (New Haven and London: Yale University Press, 1979).

Grant, L., *I Murdered My Library* (Kindle Single, 2014).

Grover, M. https://www.readingsheffield.co.uk/research/everyday-reading-in-sheffield-1920-1960/ (accessed 28 December 2017).

Hartley, J., *Reading Groups* (Oxford: Oxford University Press, 2001).

Hill, S., *Howards End is on the Landing: A Year of Reading from Home* (London: Profile Books, 2009).

Ironside, V., *No! I Don't Want to Join a Bookclub* (London: Fig Tree, 2006).

Jack, B., *The Woman Reader* (New Haven and London: Yale University Press, 2012).

Jefferson, M., *Negroland: A Memoir* (London: Granta, 2016).

Jones, H. and Lane, M., *Celebrating Pride and Prejudice* (Bath: Lansdown Media, 2012).

Lively, P., *Ammonites and Leaping Fish: A Life in Time* (London: Fig Tree, 2013).

Kean, D., *Writing the Future: Black and Asian Writers and Publishers in the UK Market Place* (London: Spread the Word, 2015).

Kirkham, M., *Jane Austen: Feminism and Fiction* (Brighton: Harvester Press, 1983).

Kümmerling-Meinbauer, B. and Müller, A., eds, *Canon Constitution and Canon Change in Children's Literature* (London: Routledge, 2017).

Lee, H., 'Reading in Bed', in *Body Parts: Essays on Life-Writing* (London: Pimlico, Chatto and Windus, 2005), 45–63.

LeFanu, S., *In the Chinks of the World Machine: Feminism and Science Fiction* (London: The Women's Press, 1988).

Lively, P., *Ammonites and Leaping Fish: A Life in Time* (London: Fig Tree, 2013).

Mangan, L., *Bookworm: A Memoir of Childhood Reading* (London: Square Peg, 2018).

Manguel, A., *A History of Reading* (London: Harper and Collins, 1996; Flamingo, 1997).

Mead, R., *The Road to Middlemarch* (London: Granta, 2014).

Miller, A., *The Year of Reading Dangerously: How Fifty Great Books Saved My Life* (London: Fourth Estate, 2014).

Modleski, T., *Loving with a Vengeance: Mass-Produced Fantasies for Women* (Hamden, CT: Archon, 1982).

Nafisi, A., *Reading Lolita in Tehran: A Memoir in Books* (London: Harper Perennial, 2003).

Noble, E., *The Reading Group* (London: Hodder and Stoughton, 2003).

Opel, D. S., 'Self-representation in literary fandom: Women's leisure reader selfies as postfeminist performance', *Transformative Works and Cultures*, 18, 2015, https://journal.transformativeworks.org/index.php/twc/article/view/607 (accessed September 2017).

Pearson, J., *Women's Reading in Britain 1750–1835: A Dangerous Recreation* (Cambridge: Cambridge University Press, 1999).

Petersen, A. H., 'That teenage feeling', *Feminist Media Studies*, 12:1, 2012, 51–67.

Priestman, M., *The Cambridge Companion to Crime Fiction* (Cambridge: Cambridge University Press, 2003).

Pugh, M., '"You canna change the laws of fiction, Jim!": A personal account of reading science fiction', *Changing English*, 6:1, 1999, 19–30.

Quale, A. E., 'Pursuit of Empowerment: The Evolution of the Romance Novel and Its Readership in *Fifty Shades of Grey*', MA thesis, Minnesota State University, Mankato, April 2014.

Radford, J., ed., *The Progress of Romance: The Politics of Popular Fiction* (London: Routledge & Kegan Paul, 1986).

Radway, J. A., *Reading the Romance: Women, Patriarchy, and Popular Literature* (Chapel Hill: University of North Carolina Press, 1984).

Rose, P., *The Shelf, from LEQ to LES: Adventures in Extreme Reading* (New York: Farrar, Straus & Giroux, 2014).

Rowlatt, B. and Witwit, M., *Talking About Jane Austen in Baghdad: The True Story of an Unlikely Friendship* (London: Penguin, 2010).

The Royal Society of Literature, 'Literature in Britain Today', March 2017, https://rsliterature.org/wp-content/uploads/2017/02/RSL-Literature-in-Britain-Today_01.03.17.pdf.

Shukla, N., ed., *The Good Immigrant* (London: Unbound, 2016).

Smith, A., *Public Library and Other Stories* (London: Hamish Hamilton, 2015).

Smith, P., *M Train* (London: Bloomsbury, 2015).

Sutherland, J., *A Little History of Literature* (New Haven: Yale University Press, 2013).

Sweeney, M., *Reading Is My Window: Books and the Art of Reading in Women's Prisons* (Chapel Hill: University of North Carolina Press, 2010).

Syal, M., *The Best Little Book Club in Town* (London: Orion, 2011).

Taylor, H., ed., *The Daphne du Maurier Companion* (London: Virago, 2007).

Taylor, H., 'Romantic Readers', in Helen Carr, ed., *From My Guy to Sci-fi: Genre and Women's Writing in the Postmodern World* (London: Pandora Press, 1989), 58–77.

Taylor, H., *Scarlett's Women: Gone With the Wind and its Female Fans* (London: Virago, 1989, rev. edn 2014).

Times Literary Supplement, Jane Austen (London: TLS, 2017).

Tóibín, C., *A Guest at the Feast: A Memoir* (Penguin Special, Kindle version, 2011).

Tomalin, C., *A Life of My Own* (London: Viking, 2017).

Weldon, F., *The Reading Group* (London: Samuel French, 1999).

Wendell, A. and Tan, C., *Beyond Heaving Bosoms: The Smart Bitches' Guide to Romance Novels* (New York: Fireside, Simon & Schuster, 2009).

Winterson, J., *Why Be Happy When You Could Be Normal?* (London: Jonathan Cape, 2011).

Index

Note: Figures are indicated by an italic "*f*" following the page number.

For the benefit of digital users, table entries that span two pages (e.g., 52–53) may, on occasion, appear on only one of those pages.

abandoned books 37, 183
AbeBooks 34
Abulhawa, Susan, *Mornings in Jenin* 31–2
Achebe, Chinua, *Things Fall Apart* 226
Adams, Douglas, *The Hitchhiker's Guide to the Galaxy* 140–1
Adams, Richard, *Watership Down* 66–7
adaptations *see* film and television adaptations
Adichie, Chimamanda Ngozi 32, 62, 188
   Half of a Yellow Sun 31–2
   The Women's Prize 156–7
age factors
   childhood reading 58–9
   choice of fiction 29, 226–7
   festival audiences 204–5, 209–10
Aidoo, Ama Ata 46–7
Alcott, Louisa M. 42–3, 125, 171
   Good Wives 68–9
   Jo's Boys 68–9
   Little Men 68–9
   Little Women 57–9, 68, 69*f*, 71–2
Alderman, Naomi 142–3
   Disobedience 231
   The Power 141–2, 142*f*, 170–1
Ali, Monica 9, 81
Allende, Isabel 138, 228
Amazon
   Best Books List 141–2
   bias towards male fiction 41–2
   book clubs 188
   choice of fiction 30
   Goodreads 4–5, 177
   literature festivals 200–1
   purchases from 33–4
ambiguous names 171–3
   crime writers 128
   science-fiction writers 141–2
Amis, Kingsley 92
Amis, Martin 37, 92, 203
Amnesty bookshops 34–5

Anderson, Gillian 141
Anderson, Paul Thomas 99–100
And Other Stories 167–8
Andrews, Sophie 85–6
Ankara Press 106–7
annotating books 34
anonymity 171
anti-sociality 20–1
Appignanesi, Lisa 118–19
Arabian Nights, The 101
Armitage, Simon 102
Arts Council England 166–7, 192–4, 201, 210
Asimov, Isaac 138, 140–1
Athill, Diana 57, 74–5, 98
Atkinson, Kate 40
Atlantic Monthly 164–5
Atwood, Margaret
   and Austen 90
   bestseller lists 231–2
   book clubs 194
   fears of women and of men 122, 134
   The Handmaid's Tale 141–2, 182
   Lady Oracle 108–9, 172
   literature festivals 208
   MaddAddam books 158
   mentoring of Alderman 170–1
   reader response 152–3
   'soft' sci-fi 141–3, 145
   The Testaments 141–2
audiobooks 23
   book clubs 187
   childhood reading 57
   gender differences 4, 239 n.4
Austen, Cassandra 244 n.7
Austen, Jane 81–2
   200th anniversary of death of 213
   bibliotherapy 44–5
   Emma 226
   as favourite writer 42–3, 45–6, 84–5
   marriage theme 94, 97

Austen, Jane (*cont.*)
  Northanger Abbey 45–6, 91–2, 94, 101–2
  Persuasion 101–2
  Pride and Prejudice
    childhood reading 58–9
    as favourite book 45–6, 79–94
    film and TV adaptations 80, 82–3,
      85–6, 88–9, 101–2, 213–14
    'gentle-Janeism' and 'Janeitism' 88
    legacy for women 101
    non-Janeites 89
    reading habits 27–8
    re-reading 87
    romance 105
    spin-offs 82, 85–6, 101
    tourism 79–80, 101–2, 213–14,
      214*f*, 217
    woman reader 91
  Real Reads 80
  romance 105, 122–3
  spin-offs 46, 101
  tourism 184, 213–15, 217
  warnings 118
  and Young Adult fiction 125
Austenland 82
Austen Leigh, J. E. 244 n.7
Austen Project, The 82

Bailey, Hilary, *Mrs Rochester* 245 n.39
Baileys Prize (earlier Orange Prize; later
    Women's Prize) 141–2, 142*f*,
    156, 168–71
Baker, Jo, *Longbourn* 82
BAME (black, Asian, minority ethnic)
  book clubs 188, 192–4
  childhood reading 59
  festival audiences 211–12
  writers 9, 155–7, 166, 169
    festivals 211–12
  see also ethnicity and race
Bannerman, Helen, *The Story of Little Black
    Sambo* 59–60, 66–7
Barclay, Florence, *The Rosary* 106
Barker, Pat 160–1
  The Ghost Road 160–1
  Regeneration books 160–1
Barley, Nick 203
Barnard, Sara 124–6
  Beautiful Broken Things 124–5
Barnes, Julian xvi, 30, 38–9

Barrow, Annie, *The Guernsey Literary and
    Potato Peel Society* (with Mary Ann
    Shaffer) 178–9
Bath Literature Festival 202–3, 207
Baudoin, Pierre-Antoine, 'The
    Reader' 18, 19*f*, 116
Bauer, Belinda, *Snap* 129
Baxter, Holly 121, 248 n.30
Bayliss, Nick, *A Rough Guide to
    Happiness* 20–1
BBC
  BDSM relationships 121
  Doctor Who 141–2
  'Listen With Mother' 56–7
  My Friend Jane 85–6
  Pride and Prejudice 81, 83, 88, 214*f*
  Radio 2 Book Club 177
  Radio 4
    Book Club 177
    Desert Island Discs 151
    Open Book 157
    'Where Are All the Working Class
      Writers?' 9
    Woman's Hour 81–2
  Roupenian's 'Cat Person' 121–2
Beard, Mary 208
Beaton, M. C. 171
Beatty, Laura, *Pollard* 183
Beauman, Nicola 35
Beauman, Sally 99–100, 155, 160–1,
    169–70
  Destiny 161
Bechdel, Alison, *Fun Home* 186–7
Bedford Bookworms 184–5
bedtime reading 25–6
Beecher Stowe, Harriet, *Uncle Tom's
    Cabin* 189
Beer, G. 246 n.2
Bell, Gertrude 185
Bell, Tash 187–8, 251 n.1
Bell, Vanessa, 'Amaryllis and
    Henrietta' 40*f*
Bennett, Alan 217
  The Uncommon Reader 43
bereavement, reading during periods
    of 28–9, 39–40, 227
  Pride and Prejudice 87–8
Berg, Leila 60
Bergen, Candice 116–17
Berthoud, Ella 44–5

Berwick-upon-Tweed Community
    Reading Group 175–6
Beswick's *Books of Birds* 101
Bhaskar, Michael 239 n.3
Bible 23, 30–1, 57, 101
    study groups 176–7, 186, 189
bibliotherapy 44–5, 129–30, 179–80
Bidisha 158, 204–5, 210
Binchy, Maeve 39–40
Birtwistle, Sue 83
Black Lives Matter 11
Blackman, Malorie 124–5, 153
Blackmore, R. D., *Lorna Doone* 77–8
Blair, Jessica 172
Block, Francesca Lia 141
Bloomsbury Publishing 3
Blume, Judy 58–9, 123
Blyton, Enid 22–3, 39–40, 59–62
    Famous Five books 58–9, 62, 66–7, 213
    The Magic Faraway Tree 72
    Malory Towers books 62
    Secret Seven books 62
    spoof *Ladybird* books 61
Boleyn, Anne 164–5
Bollman, S. 240 n.18
bond between women readers and
        women writers 46
    Austen 85–6
    writers' responses to readers 151,
        154–5
Bonomini, Egidia 252 n.10
BookBub 4–5, 29–30
Book Club 116–17, 178–9
book clubs 175
    choice of books 30, 178, 180–2, 188,
        192–4
        in prisons 189–91
    festivals 182–3, 193f, 208
    history 176
    informal styles 184
    limitations 191
    longevity 175–6, 178, 185
    prisons 189
    Reading in Heels 14–15
book covers *see* cover design
Booker Prize *see* Man Booker Prize
Book of the Month Club 176–7
Book People, The 29–30
book prizes *see* prizes
Bookseller, The 231–2

bookshops, disappearance of 33–5
Books of the Year 30
Book Talk 177–8
Booktube 29–30, 124, 177–8
Boon, Alan 107
Boon, Charles 112
Boots subscription libraries 64
Borges, Jorge Luis 63–4
Bourne, Holly, 'spinster club' books
        124–5
Boyd, William 203
Boyne, John 41–4
Bradford Literature Festival 211–12,
        211f
Bragg, Melvyn 69–70
Brewster, Liz 129–30, 248 n.3
Brick, S. 247 n.26
Bride and Prejudice 85–6
Brisley, Joyce Lankester, Milly-Molly-
        Mandy books 66–7
Bristol
    Book Circle 175–6
    'City Read' scheme 179–80
Brite, Poppy Z. 138
British Library 79–80
British Museum Reading Room 18–20
Brittain, Vera 12
Brontë, Anne 92, 102
Brontë, Branwell 92–3, 99–100, 102
Brontë, Charlotte 42–3, 90, 92, 102, 125
    on Austen 89–90, 102–3
    Gaskell's biography 92–3
    Jane Eyre
        appeal of 32–3
        childhood reading 58–9, 71
        as favourite book 79–80, 92, 94–5
        film and TV adaptations 97–8
        legacy for women 101
        reading habits 27–8
        re-reading 94–5
        romance 105
        spin-offs 93–4, 98, 101
        tourism 79–80, 101–2
    Shirley 12
Brontë, Emily
    comparisons 92, 102–3
    as favourite writer 42–3
    influence on du Maurier 99–100
    poetic language 32
    reading habits 26

Brontë, Emily (*cont.*)
　tourism 102
　Wuthering Heights 39–40, 43, 80, 93,
　　102, 213
Brontë, Patrick 92–3
Brontë Film and TV 171–2
Brontë Parsonage Museum 102, 103*f*
Brontë sisters
　bibliotherapy 44–5
　childhood reading 64–5
　as favourite writers 92–5
　influence on du Maurier 99–100
　legacy for women 101
　pseudonyms 171
　tourism 102–3, 103*f*, 213–14, 217
Brontë Society 101–2
Brookner, Anita, *Family and*
　　Friends 181–2
Browder, Laura 130–1
Browning, Elizabeth Barrett, *Aurora*
　　Leigh 98–9
Buchan, Elizabeth 157
Buckeridge, Anthony, Jennings books
　　58, 67
Buffy the Vampire Slayer 123, 177–8
Bulaitis, Zoe Hope 219–20
Bulgakov, Mikhail, *The Master and*
　　Margarita 184
Burnett, Frances Hodgson, *The Secret*
　　Garden 58–9, 61, 71
Burney, Fanny 20, 118
　Cecilia 91–2
Burns, Robert 213
Bush, Anna, *Milkman* 45–6
Bush, Kate 93
Butler, Octavia E., *Kindred* 141–2
Byatt, A. S. 92
　Possession 37, 182

Camilleri, Andrea 188
Carlyle, Jane 18–20
Carr, H. 247 n.8
Carroll, Lewis, *Alice in Wonderland* 28–9,
　　56, 213
Carter, Angela 93, 98–9, 141–2, 228,
　　245 n.39
Carthew, Natasha 210
Cartland, Barbara 106–8, 108*f*
Carver, Tania, *The Surrogate* 128
Cassatt, Mary Stevenson 14

Castano, Emanuele 44–5
Catton, Eleanor 160–1
censorship 23, 42–3
　see also forbidden books
Centre for Literacy in Primary Education
　　(CLPE) 59
Chadha, Gurinder 85–6
Chakraborty, S. A. 141–2
Chandler, Raymond, Marlowe
　　books 130
chapters of women's lives 227–31
charity shops 34–5
Charles, Prince 107–8
Charnas, Suzy McKee, *The Holdfast*
　　Chronicles 142–3
Chaucer, Geoffrey, *Troilus and*
　　Criseyde 105–6
Chekhov, Anton, *The Cherry Orchard* 57
Cheltenham Literature Festival 199–200,
　　206*f*, 207, 211–12
Chevalier, Tracy 93–4, 197
　Girl with a Pearl Earring 29–30
Chiaet, J. 253 n.1
Child, Lee xx, 128, 136–7
childhood reading 55
　favourite books 66
　　Danny the Champion of the World 73
　　Little Women 68
　　The Magic Faraway Tree 72
　　The Secret Garden 71
　libraries 63
Children's Laureate 153, 212
Child's Play 190
choice of books 29, 226–7
　book clubs 30, 178, 180–2, 188,
　　192–4
　in prisons 189–91
Chok, Vera 62
Chopes, Sarah 252 n.10
Chopin, Kate 42–3
　The Awakening 231
Christie, Agatha
　cozy crime 128, 133–4
　Dead Man's Folly 215–16
　film and TV adaptations 127–8
　photograph 152
　Poirot books 130, 133–4
　re-reading 39–40
　tourism 215–16, 216*f*
Churchill, Winston 83–4

Clark, Alex 199–200, 250 n.11
class factors 8
  childhood reading 60, 67, 74
  class mobility 22–3
  festival audiences 199–200, 210
  solitary reading 18
Clinton, Bill 199–200, 202–3
Clinton, Hillary 226
Coakley, Lena 94–5
Coe, Jonathan 161
Cohen, Paula Marantz 89
Cole, Martina 129
Coleridge, Samuel Taylor 105–6, 213
Collins, Jackie 108–9
Collins, Suzanne, *The Hunger Games*
    books 123, 138, 141
Collins, Wilkie 129, 188
Collins, William 152
Compton-Burnett, Ivy 162–3
Comyns, Barbara, *Our Spoons Came from*
    Woolworths 197
Conrad, Joseph 182
Conran, Shirley 108–9
  Lace 43
Cooke, Rachel 41–2
Cookson, Catherine 106, 215–16
Cookson, Sally 101
Coolidge, Susan 42–3, 58
  What Katy Did 58–9, 61, 66–7
Cooper, Artemis 198–9
Cooper, Jilly 23–4, 42–3, 106
  Riders 116
Cooper, Natasha 132–3
Cope, Wendy 190–1
Cornwell, Patricia, Scarpetta books 130
corruption, fiction as 16–17, 20
Cosslett, Rhiannon L. 121, 248 n.30
Costa Book Awards 75, 156–7, 168
cost of books 34–5
cover design 157–60, 159*f*
  choice of fiction 30
  Christie 133–4
  Mills & Boon 112–14
Cowley, Jason 161
Cox, Victoria 172–3
Craig, Amanda 201
crime 127–36
  appeal 129
  cozy 128, 133–4
  Trojan Horse feminism 134

Crompton, Richmal, *Just William*
    books 58–60
Crouch, Julia 134
Cummins, Fiona 135
Cusk, Rachel 163–4, 203
  Aftermath 163
  Kudos 163–4
  Outline 163–4
  Transit 163–4

Dahl, Roald 58–9, 73, 216–17
  Charlie and the Chocolate Factory 60
  Danny the Champion of the World 73
  James and the Giant Peach 60
  Matilda 58–9
Daily Mail Book Club 177
Dante Alighieri 212–13
Daphne du Maurier Festival 209
Daunt Books 185
Davidson, Max 82–3
Davies, Andrew 83, 101
Dawson, Juno 169
Day, Felicia 177–8
Day-Lewis, C., *The Otterbury Incident* 57
de Bernières, Louis, *Captain Corelli's*
    Mandolin 30, 182, 191
de Brunhoff, Jean, *Babar the Elephant*
    books 66–7
Deeping, Warwick 64–5
Defoe, Daniel, *Roxana* 183
Degas, Edgar 14
Delafield, E. M., *Diary of a Provincial*
    Lady 35
Delaney, J. P. 128
DeLillo, Don 168–9
Dell, Ethel M., *The Way of an Eagle* 106
Deller, Ruth A. 118–19
depression, reading during periods
    of 28–9, 129–30
Dessen, Meg 123
Devers, Allison 231–2
de Waal, Edmund 146
de Waal, Kit 9–11, 97, 169, 192–4
Diana, Princess 107–8
Dickens, Charles
  book clubs 182
  childhood reading 64–5
  as favourite writer 92
  food descriptions 17–18
  Great Expectations 46, 59–60

Dickens, Charles (*cont.*)
  re-reading 39–40
  tourism 213
Dickinson, Emily 6–7, 228
diversity 8
Donaldson, Julia 60
  The Gruffalo 66–7
Donoghue, Emma 94
Doughty, Louise 92–3, 102–3, 157, 161
  Apple Tree Yard 134–5, 161
  Crazy Paving 161
  Dance With Me 161
  Fires in the Dark 161
  Honey-Dew 161
dovegreyreader 145, 146*f*
Doyle, Sir Arthur Conan 129, 133–4,
  213, 217
Drabble, Margaret xvii, 92, 229–30
  literature festivals 203
  on McCarthy's *The Group* 164
  re-reading 39–40
  The Waterfall 98–9
Duffy, Carol Ann 32, 56, 190–1
Duffy, Stella 133–4
  London Lies Beneath 220–1
  Money in the Morgue 133–4
du Maurier, Angela 92
du Maurier, Daphne 92
  bibliotherapy 44–5
  correspondence with Myerson 151,
    154–5
  crime 133–4
  as favourite writer 42–3
  The House on the Strand 151
  Jamaica Inn 39–40, 59, 215–16
  literature festivals 209
  The Loving Spirit 99–100
  My Cousin Rachel 133–4
  Rebecca
    childhood reading 62–3
    crime 133–4
    as favourite book 99
    film and TV adaptations 80, 99,
      100*f*
    and *Jane Eyre* 93–4, 99–100,
      245 n.39
    spin-offs 46
    tourism 99–100, 215–16
  The Scapegoat 133–4
  tourism 215–16

Dunant, Sarah 43–4, 165, 170
Dunmore, Helen
  bestseller lists 231–2
  book clubs 30, 191–2
  gender differences in readers 155
  The Lie 164
  literature festivals 205
  photograph 154*f*
  as reader 153–5
  The Siege 155
Durrell, Lawrence, *Alexandria Quartet* 26

eating equated with reading 16–18, 20,
  225–6
  romance 110
e-books
  book clubs 181–2
  erotica 116
  freedom 23
  gender differences 3–4
  physical books versus 38–9
  Pullinger's 'Breathe' 231–2
Edgeworth, Maria 91–2
Edinburgh International Book
  Festival 200, 203, 211–12
Elderkin, Susan 44–5
Eliot, George
  book clubs 182–3
  Daniel Deronda 183
  as favourite writer 42–3
  importance of reading for women
    45–6
  Middlemarch 32–3, 229
  The Mill on the Floss 61–2, 98–9
  pseudonym 171
Elizabeth I 16–17
Elliott, Zetta 71–2
Ellis, Samantha 12, 43, 45–6, 84
Emerson, Ralph 105–6
Empathy Lab 212
endings, sneak peeks at 37–8
Epsom, Surrey book club 175–6
Erdrich, Louise 46–7
erotica 111, 115, 126
  Mills & Boon 112–16
ethnicity and race 8
  childhood reading 59–60, 62, 70
  romance 113–14
  sales of books 4
  see also BAME

Eugenides, Jeffrey, *The Marriage Plot*
  158–60
Evaristo, Bernardine 155, 166–7, 167*f*

Facebook 30, 79–80, 115, 152
Fairbairns, Zoe 108–9
  Benefits 142–3
fantasy 138–40
Fanthorpe, U. A., 77
Farooki, Roopa 188
feminism 169–70, 188
Feminist Book Fortnight 182
feminist presses 46–7
Ferrante, Elena 152, 157
  My Brilliant Friend 146–7
  Neapolitan books 42–3, 226
festivals 197, 210
  book clubs 182–3, 193*f*, 208
  empathy 210
  meeting the writer 205
Fforde, Katie 110–11, 114, 160, 165–6
  A Secret Garden 159*f*
Fielding, Helen, Bridget Jones books 82,
  155, 161
Fiennes, William 146
Fifty Shades of Black 117
Fifty Shades of Grey see under James, E. L.
film and television adaptations
  Brontë books 102
  choice of fiction 29–30
  crime 127–8, 134–5
  Fifty Shades of Grey books 116–19
  Jane Eyre 97–8
  Little Women 70–1
  Pride and Prejudice 80, 82–3, 85–6, 88–9,
    101–2, 213–14
  Rebecca 80, 99, 100*f*
  romance 106
  The Secret Garden 71–2
  tourism 213
  Wuthering Heights 80
Filmer, Catherine 220–1
Finn, A. J. 128
Finnigan, Judy 47–8
  Eloise 47
Firth, Colin 82–3, 88–9, 213–14
Fitzgerald, F. Scott, *The Great Gatsby*
  39–40, 226
Fitzgerald, Penelope 175–6
  The Bookshop 34–5

Flanagan, Caitlin 124
Flatt, Molly 243 n.5
Flaubert, Gustave, *Madame Bovary* 45–6
Flint, Kate 12, 240 n.27, 241 n.36
Flood, Alison 157, 250 n.16
Florence, Peter 212
Flynn, Gillian, *Gone Girl* 42–3, 134–5
Fonda, Jane 116–17
Fontaine, Joan 100*f*
food
  descriptions 17–18
  eating equated with reading 16–18,
    20, 225–6
  romance 110
forbidden books
  book clubs 176–7
  childhood 61–2
  see also censorship
Forbidden Planet 140
For Books' Sake 29–30, 42
Fordyce's *Sermons* 45–6, 101
Forna, Aminatta 169
  The Hired Man 169
Forster, E. M.
  Howards End 219–20
  A Passage to India 27–8
Forster, Margaret 21–2, 64–5, 151, 184
Fowey Festival 209
Fowler, Karen Joy, *The Jane Austen Book
  Club* 139–40, 177, 252 n.9
Fox, Victoria 17
Fraser, Antonia, *The Pleasure of
  Reading* 190, 241 n.4
Freely, Maureen 99–100
Freeman, Hadley 242 n.31
Freeman, Laura 17–18
French, Marilyn
  The Bleeding Heart 108–9
  The Women's Room 226–7
Friday, Nancy 61
  My Secret Garden 117–18
friendship between women readers and
  women writers 46
  Austen 85–6
Fry, Elizabeth 189

Galbraith, Robert 171–2
  The Cuckoo's Calling 171–2
Gale, Patrick 202–3
Gambon, Michael 89

García Márquez, Gabriel 138
Gardner, Sally 156–7
Garrod, H. W. 88–9
Gaskell, Elizabeth 92–3, 184
Gawande, Atul 233–4
Gay, Roxane 48
gender differences
  audiobooks 4, 239 n.4
  Austen, attitudes to 83–5, 88–9
  bond between readers and writers 46
  book clubs 178, 180–2
  book collectors 231–2
  childhood reading 58
  choice of author 32, 40, 43–4, 47–8
  cover design 157–8
  crime readers 128, 130, 136–7
  crime writers 132
  festival audiences 203–4, 208–9
  illiteracy/literacy 7–8
  impact of writing 43–4
  library use 65–6
  mindsets 7
  pay gap 155
  prizes 156–7
  readers by genre 3–4
  reviews 41–2, 155
  romance genre 106, 113
  sales of books 3–4
  science fiction readers 139, 142–3
  science fiction writers 140, 142–3
  tourism 215–16
  Young Adult readers 123
generational factors *see* age factors
George, Nina, *The Little Paris
    Bookshop* 34–5, 44–5
Gerritsen, Tess 128
Gibbons, Stella, *Cold Comfort Farm* 226
Gilbert, Elizabeth, *Eat, Pray, Love* 16,
    179–80
Gilbert, S. 248 nn.1–2, 9
Gilbert, Sandra M. 98–9
Give a Book 190
Glennie, Dame Evelyn 226
Godden, Rumer xvii, 39–40
  The Greengage Summer 39–40
Good Immigrant, The 9
Goodings, Lennie 41, 43–4, 46–7,
    242 n.19
Good Literary Agency, The 9
Goodman, Allegra 87–8
Goodreads 4–5, 177

Goold, Lynn 209
Gordon, Bryony 247 n.23
Gosse, Edmund 188
Goudge, Elizabeth 39–40
Graham, Winston, Poldark books 29–30,
    213–14
Grahame, Kenneth, *The Wind in the
    Willows* 39–40, 77
Grant, Hugh 89
Grant, Linda 17–18, 56–7
  The Dark Circle 90–1
Grayling, Chris 252 n.15
Green, John 125–6
  The Fault in Our Stars 123
Greene, Graham, *The Burnt-Out Case* 23
Green Metropolis 34
Greer, Germaine 25–6, 94, 107, 208–9
Gregory, Philippa 31–2
Grossmith, George and Weedon, *Diary of
    a Nobody* 39–40
Grover, M. 241 n.39
Guardian 140
Gubar, Susan 98–9
Guilluy, Alice 118, 240 n.28
guilt 18, 61–2, 225–6
Guilty Pleasures 185
Gunn, Kirsty 226–7

habits of reading 37
Hachette 9
Hadley, Tessa 41–2, 79
Haley, Alex xvii
Hall, Radclyffe 23–4
  The Well of Loneliness 116
Hall, Sarah 140, 142–3
  The Carhullan Army 140
Hamilton, Charles, Billy Bunter
    books 58
Hamlyn Children's Bible 22–3
Hanff, Helene, *84, Charing Cross Road* 34–5
Hannah, Sophie 133–6
happiness, reading during periods of
    28–9
Happy Reader, The 29–30
Haraway, Donna 142–3
Hardy, Thomas 39–40, 184, 213, 215–16
  Tess of the d'Urbervilles 17–18, 45–6,
    215–16
Harlequin 112–13
  see also Mills & Boon
Hartley, Jenny 178, 194

Hathaway, Anne 89
Hatwell, Lynne 59
Hawke, Maya 70–1
Hawkins, Paula, *The Girl on the Train* 134–5
Hawthorne, Nathaniel 105–6
  The House of Seven Gables 105–6
Hayder, Mo 132
Hay on Wye 33–4
  Festival 197, 200
    audiences 198–9
    BAME writers 211–12
    book clubs 193*f*
    Clinton, Bill 199–200, 202–3
    empathy 212
    Shamsie, Kamila 208
H. D. 171
Healey, Emma 113
  Elizabeth is Missing 113
Hemingway, Ernest 188
Henry, Veronica 107–8, 110–11, 118–19
Hepburn, Katharine 70–1
Herbert, D. 253 n.20
Herbooks 46–7
Herschmann, Tania 228–9
Heyer, Georgette
  childhood reading 59–60
  as favourite writer 42–3
  reader response 84
  reading habits 27–8
  re-reading 39–40
  secrecy 23–4
Higgins, Charlotte 251 n.33
Hill, A. 248 nn.8,10
Hill, Susan 230–1
  and Austen 90–1
  childhood reading 62–4
  eating equated with reading 17
  family's reading 58
  female reading culture 16
  reinterpretation of *Rebecca* 99–100
Hills, Laura Coombs 14
Hislop, Victoria 30
History Magazine, The 26–7
Hitchcock, Alfred 99, 127–8
Hitchens, Christopher 164–5
Hocking, Amanda 158–60
holidays
  book exchanges 30
  e-books 38
  reading habits 25–6

Holland, Agnieszka 71–2
Homer, *The Iliad* 20
Honeyman, Gail, *Eleanor Oliphant is Completely Fine* 41, 220
Horn, Dara 140–1
hospitalization, reading during periods of 27–8, 38, 228
Howatch, Susan 108–9, 145
Howe, Sarah 152
Hughes, Langston 59–60
Hull, E. M., *The Sheik* 106
Hurston, Zora Neale 46–7
Huxford, Eila 184
Hyland 113–14

illiteracy 7–8
illness, reading during periods of 27–8, 39–40, 228
  crime 129–30
  romance 113
Imagination Library 177
impact of writing 42
Indiana, Rita 167–8
initials *see* ambiguous names
inspiration, sources of 29
International Women's Day 173
iPads *see* e-books
Irish Censorship Board 23
Ironside, Virginia, *No! I Don't Want to Join a Bookclub* 191

Jacaranda 9
Jack, Belinda 26, 240 nn.23–4, 240–1nn.33–5
  women readers 8, 12, 15
  women's prison group 189
jacket design *see* cover design
Jackson, A. H. 254 n.5
Jackson, Jane Manley 220
Jackson, Rosie 52*f*
  The Light Box 51
Jacobs, Susan 175–6
Jade 190–1
Jaipur Literature Festival 199–200
James, E. L. 173
  Fifty Shades of Grey books 116–19, 134–5, 137
    abuse 118, 120*f*, 121
    book clubs 185
    importance of reading for women 45–6

James, E. L. (*cont.*)
  spin-offs 117–18
  tourism 117, 214
  Snowqueens Icedragon 116–17
James, Eloisa 114–15
James, Henry 87–8, 184–5
James, M. R. 39–40
James, P. D. 82, 171
Jamie, Kathleen 156–7
Jane Austen Centre, Bath 84–5, 85*f*, 217
Jane Austen Fan Fictions (JAFs) 85–6
Jane Austen House Museum 82
Jane Austen Society 84–5, 86*f*, 89, 101–2
Jansson, Tove, Moomins books 39–40
Javid, Sajid 208
Jefferson, Margo 70
Jemisin, N. K. 141–2
Jenkins, Val 219
Jhabvala, Ruth Prawer xvii
John, Gwen 14
  'The Convalescent' 27*f*
Johns, W. E., Biggles books 58, 67
Johnson, Claudia 88–9
Johnson, Maureen 158–60
Johnson, Samuel 16–17
Jones, Hazel 82–3, 244 n.4, 246 nn.51–2
Jong, Erica
  Fanny 230
  Fear of Flying 116–17
Jordan, Penny, *A Reason for Being* 113
Joyce, James, *Ulysses* vii*f*
Joyce, Rachel, *The Unlikely Pilgrimage of Harold Fry* 16
Juma, Zainab 173

Kaplan, Cora 109
Kay, Jackie 206*f*, 233–4
  Trumpet 30
Kean, Danuta 10–11, 41–2, 157, 166–7, 211–12
Keaton, Diane 116–17
Keats, John 105–6, 213
  Endymion 105–6
Kennedy, A. L. 171
Kerrison, Catherine 16–17, 240 n.23
Keyes, Marian 46–7, 199–200
  This Charming Man 158
Kidd, David Comer 44–5
Killer Women Crime Writing Collective, The 29–30, 132–3, 165–6

Kindle *see* e-books
King, Stephen 25
  Carrie 158–60
Kingsley, Charles, *Westward Ho!* 212–13
Kingsolver, Barbara 44–5
  The Poisonwood Bible 40, 182
Kingston, Maxine Hong 46–7
Kinsella, Sophie 109–10
Kipling, Rudyard 60
  'The Janeites' 88–9
Kirkby, Michelle 133–4
Kirkham, Margaret 80
Kitchen Table: Women of Color 46–7
Knights Of 59
Kobo 156–7
Krantz, Judith
  Princess Daisy 23
  Scruples 23
Kureishi, Hanif 9
Kushner, Rachel, *The Flamethrowers* 168–9

Lafferty, Judith 175–6
Laing, Olivia, *To the River* 184–5
Lamb, J. P. 64
Lane, Maggie 82–3, 244 n.4, 246 nn.51–2
Lange, Norah 167–8
Larkin, Philip 187–8
Lawless, Bridget 135–6
Lawrence, D. H. 32
  Lady Chatterley's Lover 23–4, 116–17
Lawson, Mark 214–15
learning to read 56–7
Lee, Harper 171
  To Kill a Mockingbird 58–9, 226
Lee, Hermione 20
LeFanu, Sarah
  literature festivals 203, 205–6, 208–9
  'Quail' 163
  science fiction 139–40
  'woman writer' term 163
Le Guin, Ursula K. 69–70, 139–41
L'Engle, Madeleine, *A Wrinkle in Time* 140–1
Lesser, Wendy 11–12
Lessing, Doris 42–3, 141–2, 171, 184, 202–3
  The Golden Notebook 42–3

Lethbridge, Lucy 81
Levy, Andrea 156–7
Lewes, George Henry 83–4
Lewis, C. S. 66–7
  The Otterbury Incident 57
Lewis, Matthew, *The Monk* 18
Lewis, Susan 109–10
LGBTQ
  coming out 231
  romance 108–9, 113–15
libraries
  book clubs 179–80
  childhood reading 63
  disappearance 35–7
  and festivals, parallels between 203–4
  nunnery 8
  virtual 48–9
  writers as readers 153
Library Campaign, The 63–4
Light, Alison 108–9, 111, 246 n.48
Like a Woman Bookshop 173, 231–2, 232*f*
Lindgren, Astrid, *Pippi Longstocking*
  books 66–7
Lipman, Maureen 28–9
literacy 8
  prisoners 189
literary prizes *see* prizes
literary tourism *see* tourism and
  pilgrimage
literature festivals *see* festivals
litlovers.com 177–8
Lively, Penelope 12, 48–9, 61–2
Liverpool Literary Festival 210
Llewellyn Smith, Julia 240 n.28,
  252 n.21
Lockwood, P. 250 n.22
Lofting, Hugh, *Doctor Doolittle* 64
Logan, Harriett 173
Loganberry Books 173
London Review of Books 29–30
Lorde, Audre 166–7
Lynch, Deirdre 90–1
Lynd, Robert 112

Maberly, Kate 71–2
Macfadyen, Matthew 82–3
Mackintosh, Clare 249 n.2
Macmillan, Harold 83–4
magical realism 138
Man Booker Prize 152–3, 156

Barker 160–1
Bauer 129
book clubs 184
Bush 45–6
Catton 160
dovegreyreader 145
Mangan, Lucy 12, 66–7, 72, 136–7
Mann, Jessica 132–3
Mantel, Hilary 173
  and Austen 90
  Beyond Black 192–4
  bond with readers 48
  Bring Up the Bodies 48, 164–5
  childhood reading 66, 70
  Costa Book Awards 156–7
  Cromwell books 164–5
  gender differences in readers 155
  Giving Up the Ghost 48, 192–4
  jacket design 157–8
  on *Jane Eyre* 95–6, 227–8
  photograph 162*f*
  reading inspired by 31–2
  TLS best novelists list 156–7
  Tudor books 155
  Wolf Hall 48, 192–4
  'woman writer' term 161–5
Marsh, Ngaio 133–4
  Money in the Morgue 133–4
Martin, George R. R., *Game of Thrones*
  books 138, 141–2
Martin, Jean 175–6
Mason, Charlotte 16–17
Maud, Constance, *No Surrender* 190
May, Theresa 208
Mayhew, Julie 124–5
Mayne, Michael 17
Mayo, Simon 177
McCarthy, Mary, *The Group* 164
McCullough, Colleen, *The Thorn
  Birds* 185
McDermid, Val 130–2, 131*f*, 135–6
  Austen Project 82
  'Homecoming' 249 n.14
  Insidious Intent 249 n.14
McEwan, Ian 3, 30, 46–7, 90, 184
  On Chesil Beach 217
McGahern, John, *The Dark* 23
McGrath, Melanie 128, 131–3
  White Heat 131–2
McGregor, Jon 168

McInerney, Lisa, *The Glorious Heresies* 168–9
McManus, Karen M., *One of Us is Lying* 125
Mead, Rebecca 11–12
men *see* gender differences
Merrick, Helen 249 n.23
Messud, Clare, *The Woman Upstairs* 228–9
Methley, Violet M., *Fourteen Fourteens* 75
MeToo movement 120–2
Meyer, Stephanie, *Twilight* books 116–17, 123–4, 138, 141
Michener, James xvii
middle class *see* class factors
Midsomer Murders 127–8
Miller, Andrew 11–12, 182–3
Mills, Gerald 112
Mills & Boon 107, 112–14
  e-books 38
  erotica 112–16
  escapism 109–10, 113
  Jane Eyre themes 98–9
  secrecy 23–4
  Spence, Bill/Blair, Jessica 172
Milne, A. A., Winnie the Pooh books 27–8, 66–7
Mina, Denise 130–2
Mischief Books 116
Mitchell, David 203
  Cloud Atlas 37
Mitchell, Margaret, *Gone With the Wind*
  childhood reading 58–9
  readers' relationship with xviii, 111–12
  responding to readers 154–5
  romance 109
  Scarlett O'Hara as inspiration xvii, 115
  spin-offs 46
Mitchell, Mel 151–2
Mitford, Nancy 17–18
MIT Technology Review 140
Modleski, Tania 108–9, 247 n.8
Monroe, Marilyn vii*f*
Montgomery, Lucy Maud, *Anne of Green Gables* 43, 58–9
Mooney, Bel 7
Moore, Lorrie 165
Moran, Caitlin 58–9, 190–1

More, Hannah 41, 91–2, 118
Morpurgo, Michael, *Listen to the Moon* 157
Morrison, Toni 155, 166–7
  Beloved 42–3
Moss, Sarah 85–6, 91, 155–6, 164–5
Mosse, Kate 36–7, 156–7
Motion, Andrew 32
Moyes, Jojo 40, 106
  Me Before You 111–12
Mslexia 29–30, 42, 177–8
Mudrick, Marvin 88
Mumsnet 30, 177–8
Munro, Alice 156–7, 184, 228
Murdoch, Emily 94, 110–11
Murdoch, Iris xvii, 160–1
Myerson, Julie 151, 154–5, 163

Nafisi, Azar 7–8, 12
  Reading Lolita in Tehran 176–7, 195–6
Naipaul, V. S. 41–2
Namjoshi, Suniti 46–7
National Literacy Trust 75–6
National Trust 213, 215–16
Naylor, Gloria 166–7
Nesbit, Edith 58
  The Railway Children 58–9, 61
  The Treasure Seekers 61
Nesbo, Jo 188
newbooks 175, 177–8, 192–4
New Yorker, The 121–3
Nielsen Book Research 3–4
Niffenegger, Audrey, *The Time Traveler's Wife* 179–80
Nightingale, Benedict 111
Nobel Prize for Literature 156–7, 184
Noble, Elizabeth, *The Reading Group* 178–9, 195
Norfolk, Lawrence 199–200
Norris, Sian 9–11
note making in books 34
Nudge Books 29–30, 251 n.6
Nwapa, Flora, *Efuru* 233–4

Oates, Joyce Carol 41–2, 90–1
Obama, Barack 183
O'Brien, Edna, *The Country Girls* 23
O'Brien, Patrick 28–9
O'Donnell, Mabel, Janet and John books 56–7, 153–4
Ofsted 66

O'Hagan, Andrew 118
Olivier, Laurence 80, 82–3, 100*f*
Ondaatje, Michael 32, 188
Onlywomen Press 46–7
Opel, D. S. 240 n.22, 244 n.2
Oprah Winfrey Book Club 30, 176–7
Orange Prize (later Baileys Prize,
        Women's Prize) 42, 156, 165
Orlean, Susan, *The Library Book* 34–5
Orwell, George 132–3
Our Shared Self 42, 177–8
Oxenford, Daphne 56–7
Oxfam 155–6
Oxford Literary Festival 200, 202–3

Palmer, Ada 142–3
Pamuk, Orhan 188
Pandora 46–7
Paretsky, Sara 165–6
Parker, Kevin 198–9, 253 n.5
Parks, Adele 160
Parr, Martin 146
Parton, Dolly 177
Pascal, Francine, *Sweet Valley High* 28–9
Patterson, James 136–7
Peacock, Ralph, 'The Sisters' 5*f*
Peake, Mervyn, *Gormenghast* books 230–1
Pearson, Allison 105, 157
Pearson, Jacqueline 240 nn.25,32,
        241 n.37, 241 n.3
  on Austen 91–2
  women readers 12
Penarth 33–4
Penguin Books/Penguin Random
        House 10–11, 167–8, 173, 231–2
Penn, Joanna/J. F. 171
  Pentecost 171
  Prophecy 171
Perkins Gilman, Charlotte 140
  Herland 142–3
Perry, Sarah 231–2
  The Essex Serpent 226
Persephone 35, 36*f*, 46–7, 177, 190
Peter, Ellis, Cadfael books 39–40
Phantom Thread 99–100
Philipson, C. 247 n.26
Phillips, Adam 48–9, 230
Picardie, Justine 99–100
Picoult, Jodi 158–60, 175
  My Sister's Keeper 219

Pierce, Tamora 141
Piercy, Marge 140
Pilcher, Rosamunde 215–16
pilgrimage *see* tourism and pilgrimage
Piper, Katie, *Beautiful* 190–1
Plaidy, Jean xvii
Plath, Sylvia, *The Bell Jar* 231
Poe, Edgar Allen 129
Poet Laureates 32, 252 n.15
poetry 32
Pomegranate 'Reading Woman'
        calendars 14
Port Eliot Festival 146*f*, 146
Potter, Beatrix 59–60, 215–16
Pratchett, Terry 138–9
Pringle, Alexandra 3
Pringle, Guy 175, 177–8, 192–4, 225–6,
        242 n.22
Prison Reading Groups (PRG)
        189–90
prisons
  book clubs 189
  crime fiction 129
  recording of bedtime stories for
        prisoners' children 75–6
Private Eye 30–1, 152
prizes 156–7, 160–1
  book clubs 178
  choice of fiction 30
pseudonyms 152, 171–3
  crime writers 128
  romance writers 110–11
Pugh, M. 249 n.17
Pullan, Matilda 16–17
Pullinger, Kate, 'Breathe' 231–2
Pullman, Philip 58–60, 139, 202–3
  His Dark Materials 66–7, 138, 141
  La Belle Sauvage 138
Pynchon, Thomas 37

Quale, A. E. 247 n.24
questionnaire 235–8

race *see* BAME; ethnicity and race
Radcliffe, Ann 45–6, 91–2, 94
Radford, Jean 108–9, 247 n.8
Radway, Janice A. 108–9, 247 n.8
Rafferty, Terrence 132
Random House 123
Rankin, Ian 90, 129

Ransome, Arthur, *Swallows and Amazons* 59–60
rape 113–14, 117–20
Raper, Mavis Maureen 175–6
Reader, The 44, 75–6
Reader's Digest 22–3
Reading Agency, The 44, 75–6, 129–30
reading aloud 57
reading diaries 48–9, 227
reading groups *see* book clubs
Reading in Heels 14–15, 35
ReaditSwapit 34
Real Reads 80
Red Circle libraries 64
Reekles, Beth, *The Kissing Booth* 123
Rego, Paula 98–9
Renoir, Pierre-Auguste 14
re-reading books 39–40
childhood reading 57, 67, 71–3, 75
Jane Eyre 94–5
Pride and Prejudice 87
reviews 41–2, 155
Rhodes, Emily 185
Rhys, Jean, *Wide Sargasso Sea* 96–9, 245 n.39
Rice, Anne, *Vampire Chronicles* 138
Richard III 130
Richard and Judy Book Club 4–5, 30, 47–8, 177
Riddell, Chris 212
Ripped Bodice, The 120–1
Robb, J. D. 171
see also Roberts, Nora
Roberts, Michèle 93, 152, 203, 227
Roberts, Nora 106–7, 171
Robson, Leon 11–12
Rodale, Maya 105
Roehampton University 252 n.8
romance 105
big business 114
and crime, parallels between 129–30, 134, 136–7
Mills & Boon 112
rape scenario 120
Roupenian's 'Cat Person' 121
taking it seriously 107
Young Adult fiction 123
see also erotica
Romance Writers of America 114

Romantic Novelists' Association (RNA) 106–7, 114–15, 165–6
Rooney, Sally 9–10
Conversations With Friends 9–10
Normal People 9–10
Roosevelt, Theodore 69–70
Rose, Jacqueline 134–5
Rose, Phyllis 12
Rosen, Michael 32
Rosenthal, Jack 28–9
Roth, Veronica, *Divergent* 141–2
Roupenian, Kristen
'Cat Person' 121–3
You Know You Want This 122–3
Roussel, Théodore, 'The Reading Girl' 18
Rowlatt, Bee 12
Rowling, J. K. 69–70, 73, 171–3
Harry Potter books 58, 60, 138, 171–2, 215–16
tourism 213, 215–16
Roy, Anuradha 36–7
Roy, Arundhati 231–2
The God of Small Things 191
Royal Society of Literature 83–4, 88–90, 92, 127–8
Runcie, James 157
Grantchester books 129
Rundell, Katherine 75
Rushdie, Salman 32–3
Russ, Joanna 140
The Female Man 139
Ryder, Winona 70–1

sadness *see* sorrow, reading during periods of
Saintsbury, George 88–9
Salinger, J. D. 228
Sampson, Fiona 198–9
Sand, George 171
Sansom, C. J. 182
Sansom, Ian 89
Sartre, Jean-Paul, *Nausea* 22–3
Sassoon, Siegfried 17–18
Saunders, Kate 61
Sayers, Dorothy L. 128, 130
Scarry, Elaine 219–20
Schama, Simon 199–200
school libraries 66

Schreiner, Olive, *The Story of an African Farm* 231
Schwab, V. E. 141–2
science fiction 138–40
Scott, Walter 215–16
  Marmion 101
screen adaptations *see* film and television adaptations
Second Shelf, The 65*f*, 231–2
Segal, Francesca 156–7
Seierstand, Asne, *The Bookseller of Kabul* 34–5, 191
self-publishing 46, 167–8
Selznick, David O. 99
Serong, Jock, *On the Java Ridge* 135–6
Serpell, Namwali 94
Sewell, Anna, *Black Beauty* 22–3, 57–9
sexuality
  erotica 115
  rape scenario 120
  romance 111
  Roupenian's 'Cat Person' 121
  solitary reading 18, 20, 23–4
  Young Adult fiction 124–5
  see also LGBTQ
Shafak, Elif, *The Forty Rules of Love* 158
Shaffer, Mary Ann, *The Guernsey Literary and Potato Peel Society* (with Annie Barrow) 178–9
Shahwar, Durre 9–11
Shakespeare, William 92, 97, 213, 215–16, 227–8
Shameless Hussy 46–7
Shamsie, Kamila 156–7, 167–8
  Home Fire 208
Shannon Trust 75–6
shared reading 44
Shea, Robert, *Illuminatus* books (with Robert Anton Wilson) 226–7
Sheba 46–7
Sheffield Group 175–6
'Sheffield Reading' project 64
Shelley, David 171–2
Shelley, Mary, *Frankenstein* 140, 142–3
Shepard, Sara, *Pretty Little Liars* 125
Sheridan, Frances 16–17
Sheridan, Richard Brinsley, *The Rivals* 18–20
Sherlock Holmes Museum 217
Shields, Carol 175–6

Shinn, Sharon, *Jenna Starborn* 245 n.39
short fiction 239 n.3
Showalter, Elaine 172–3
Shriver, Lionel 10–11
Shukla, Nikesh 9–11
signed books 205–6, 206*f*, 208–9
Silent Witness 130
Silver Moon 35
Sisters in Crime 165–6
Sittenfeld, Curtis 82
Sjöwall, Maj 155–6
  Beck books 130
Slaughter, Karin 128, 131–2, 136–7
smartphones *see* e-books
Smith, Alexander McCall 39–40, 82
Smith, Ali
  bestseller lists 231–2
  book clubs 192
  festivals 202–3
  labelling 163
  Public Library and Other Stories 15
  TLS best novelists list 156–7
Smith, Clarissa 118–19
Smith, Dodie, *I Capture the Castle* 58–60
Smith, Maggie 71–2
Smith, Mary M. 175–6, 184
Smith, Patti xv–xvi
Smith, Zadie
  bestseller lists 231–2
  book clubs 30
  labelling 169
  On Beauty 219–20
  TLS best novelists list 156–7
  Women's Prize 156–7
  working class and BAME experience 9
social media 30
solitary reading 18
Somers, Jane 171
Sorosis 176–7
sorrow, reading during periods of 26–7, 39–40
  Pride and Prejudice 87–8
  romance 113
  see also bereavement, reading during periods of
Soueif, Ahdaf 188
Spacey, Kevin 121–2
Spark, Muriel, *A Far Cry from Kensington* 185
Spence, Bill 172

Spenser, Edmund, *The Faerie Queen* 105–6
Spyri, Johanna, *Heidi* 58–9, 66–7
Stainton, Keris 124–5
Stallings, A. E. 84
Stansted Literature Group 187
Starnes, Joanna 85–6
Staunch book prize 135–6
Steadman, Alison 89
Steadman-Milne, Zoe 207–10
Steel, Danielle 106
Steenburgen, Mary 116–17
Steinem, Gloria 25
Stevens, E. S., *The Veil* 112
Stevenson, Robert Louis 60
    Kidnapped 95
    Treasure Island 22–3
Stewart, Mary 93
    The Ivy Tree 245 n.39
    Nine Coaches Waiting 245 n.39
Stockett, Kathryn, *The Help* 179–80
Stoker, Bram, *Dracula* 213
Stowe, Harriet Beecher 60
Streatfeild, Noel, *Ballet Shoes* 58–9
stress, reading during periods of 26–9,
    39–40, 227
Sullivan, Tricia 142–3
Susann, Jacqueline, *Valley of the Dolls* 185
Sutherland, John 192–4, 199–200
Sweeney, Megan 189–90
Swift, Jonathan, *Gulliver's Travels* 101
Syal, Meera, *The Best Little Book Club in
    Town* 252 n.9

tablets *see* e-books
Talbot, Mary 156–7
Tan, Candy 107, 248 n.31
Tanner, Elizabeth 175–6
Tartt, Donna, *A Secret History* 228
Taylor, Elizabeth 70–1
Taylor, Helen 114–15, 247 n.8
Tayport Book Circle 175–6
Teddington book club 175–6
television *see* film and television
    adaptations
Tennant, Emma, *Thornfield Hall* 82, 93,
    245 n.39
Tennessee Williams Literary Festival,
    New Orleans 199–200
Thackeray, William 16–17
    The Newcomes 16–17

Thatcher, Margaret 107–8
Theakston Old Peculier Crime Writing
    Festival 127–8
theliteraryaddict 29–30
Thomas, Dylan 214–15
Thomas, Heidi 70–1
Thompson, Emma 89
Thomson, Ian 184
    The Dead Yard 184
Thorn, Tracey 48–9
Thorpe, Vanessa 142–3
Times Education Supplement 124
Times Literary Supplement 26–7, 29–30,
    156–7, 175–6, 184
Time's Up movement 120–1
timing of reading 20–2
Tinniswood, Adrian 182–3
Tóibín, Colm 23, 168–9, 208
Tolkien, J. R. R. 66–7, 138, 216–17
    Lord of the Rings 66–7, 81
Tolstoy, Leo, *War and Peace* 155
Tomalin, Claire 81
Toole, John Kennedy, *A Confederacy of
    Dunces* 226–7
tourism and pilgrimage 197–8, 212–15
    book clubs 184–5
    festivals 200
    Fifty Shades of Grey books 117, 214
    Jane Eyre 79–80, 101–2
    Pride and Prejudice 79–80, 101–2,
    213–14, 214f, 217
    Rebecca 99–100, 215–16
To Walk Invisible 102
Townsend, Sue 190–1
Townswomen's Guild 178–9
Trabucco, Alia 167–8
Tressell, Robert 184–5
Triesman, Deborah 122–3
Trilling, Lionel 89–90
Trojan Horse feminism 134
Trollope, Joanna 82, 84–5, 160
Truffaut, François 99
Trump, Donald 121–2, 141–2
T. S. Eliot Prize 152
Turner, Aidan 213–14
Twain, Mark 60
Twitter
    choice of fiction 30
    'Coverflip' 158–60
    Fifty Shades of Grey books 118–19

Howe, Sarah 152
'Men React to Cat Person' 121–2
romance 115
Roupenian's 'Cat Person' 121–2
women readers 15
writers' accounts 151–2
Young Adult writers 124
Twomey, Clare 102
Tyler, Anne 157
The Amateur Marriage 228

Uncle Remus, *Brer Rabbit* 61–2
understanding, fiction as means of 43–5
University of Leeds Ladies Club 175–6
Updike, John 164
Couples 23

vacations *see* holidays
Vaginal Fantasy Romance Book
Club 177–8
Vaughan, Sarah, *Anatomy of a
Scandal* 134
Vermeer, Johannes 14
Vincent, B. 243 n.12
Virago 35, 41, 46–7, 61, 160–1
book club 177
VisitEngland 212–13
Vonnegut, Kurt 140–1
Vuong, Ocean 8

Wahlöö, Per, Beck books 130
Wainwright, Sally 102
Waites, Martyn 128
Wakefield, Sarah R. 249 n.22
Walker, Alice 166–7, 231
The Color Purple 40
Walking Book Club 185
Wallach, Janet, *Desert Queen* 185
Walliams, David 60
Walmesley, A. 244 n.16
Walpole, Hugh 112
Walsh, Deanna 205–6
Walters, Minette 128
Warner, Susan 45–6
'Wash Brook' Book Club 184
Waters, Sarah 23–4, 90, 231
Fingersmith 27–8
Waterstones 33–4
Watson, Emma 42, 177–8
Watson, S. J. 128

Watson, Winifred, *Miss Pettigrew Lives
for a Day* 35
Wattpad 123
Waugh, Evelyn, *Brideshead Revisited* 22–3
Webb, Mary, *Precious Bane* xvii
Wedmore Book Circle 180–3, 181*f*
'weepies' 111–12
Weinstein, Harvey 120–1
Weir, Andy, *The Martian* 138
Weldon, Fay, *The Reading Group* 178–9
Wells, H. G., *Invisible Man* 61–2
Wells Literature Festival 182–3
Wendell, Sarah 107, 248 n.31
Wesley, Mary 145
West, Jessamine, *The Massacre at Fall
Creek* xvii
Wharton, Edith 188
Whipple, Dorothy 39–40
Someone at a Distance 35
White, E. B., *Charlotte's Web* 59–60
Whitman, Walt 105–6
Whittaker, Jodie 141–2
W. H. Smith 4–5, 33–4, 99
Wiggin, Kate Douglas, *Rebecca of
Sunnybrook Farm* 66–7
Wigtown 33–4
Wikipedia 155–6
Wilder, Laura Ingalls, *Little House on the
Prairie* books 66–7
Williams, Shirley 12
Williams, Tennessee 199
A Streetcar Named Desire 199
Williamson, Henry, *Tarka the Otter* 215–16
Willmore, Ann and David 33–4
Wilson, Jacqueline 58, 60–1
Wilson, Robert Anton, *Illuminatus* books
(with Robert Shea) 226–7
Winfrey, Oprah 30, 176–7
Wings, Mary 99–100
Winsor, Kathleen, *Forever Amber* 61–2
Winspear, Violet 109–10, 112
Winterson, Jeanette 8–9, 153
Oranges Are Not the Only Fruit 42–3
Passion Fruit 108–9
wished-for lives 48, 230
Witherspoon, Reese 177
Witwit, May 12
Wodehouse, P. G. 112
The Code of the Woosters 27–8
Wolitzer, Meg 41–2, 157

Woman's Weekly 112
'woman writer' term 41–2, 155, 160, 168
Women Crime Writers 127
Women of the World Festival 210
Women's History Month 173
Women's Institute 178–9
Women's Liberation Movement 176–7
Women's Press, The 46–7
Women's Prize, The (earlier Baileys Prize,
    Orange Prize) 42, 156–7, 182
women's studies 46–7
Woodiwiss, Kathleen E., *The Flame and the
    Flower* 116
Woodward, Kay, *Jane Airhead* 245 n.39
Woolf, Virginia 36–7, 42–3, 213, 216–17
    Mrs Dalloway 230–1
    A Room of One's Own 36–7, 42
    To the Lighthouse 182
Wordsworth, Dorothy 20, 81
Wordsworth, William 105–6, 214–17
working class *see* class factors
World Book Day 75–6, 117
World Book Night 44
Wright, Heather 29–30
Wright, Richard, *Native Son* 226–7
writers
    accessibility 151–2
    anonymous 171
    appearance 152, 208
    BAME 9, 155–7, 166, 169
        festivals 211–12

book club talks 182–4
festivals 202–3, 205
gendered relationships and
        genres 155–6
names 171
    see also ambiguous names;
        pseudonyms
prizes 156–7
as readers 152
responding to readers 151, 154–5
restrictions of gender 168
support for other writers 165–6
'woman writer' term 41–2, 155,
        160, 168
Wyndham, John 138

X Files, The 141

Yates, Patricia 212–13
Yonge, Charlotte M., *The Heir of
        Radcliffe* 106
Young, Meg 65*f*
Young Adult (YA) fiction 75, 123
Yousafzai, Malala 7–8

Zemach, Harve, *The Little Speckled
        Hen* 66
Zephaniah, Benjamin, 'Talking
        Turkeys' 190–1
Zoe Ball Book Club 4–5, 177
Zola, Emile 228